The Last of the
Dinosaurs

The Last of the Dinosaurs

AN AUTOBIOGRAPHY

William L. Otto

GANGSTERS, GODFATHERS & GOOD GUYS

THE LAST OF THE DINOSAURS
AN AUTOBIOGRAPHY

iUniverse books may be ordered through booksellers or by contacting:

iUniverse
1663 Liberty Drive
Bloomington, IN 47403
www.iuniverse.com
1-800-Authors (1-800-288-4677)

ISBN: 978-1-4917-5266-1 (sc)
ISBN: 978-1-4917-5268-5 (hc)
ISBN: 978-1-4917-5267-8 (e)

Library of Congress Control Number: 2014920102

Printed in the United States of America.

iUniverse rev. date: 12/03/2014

<u>The Last of the Dinosaurs</u> is not only the story of a man, but also the story of a family, and age and a city. The book tells the story of Bill Otto, businessman, veteran, father, son, player, operator and friend. Otto grew up on the Depression-Era streets of the Bronx. His story begins with the hard scrabble life of a poor family doing whatever was necessary to get by, even as Otto's father took whatever meager amount they could pull together to spend on drinking and gambling. Like many boys of that time, Otto did whatever he could to earn money for his family, regardless of the risks. Through hard work and hustle, Otto moved up from job to job, parlaying his work ethic and natural people skills to get by. Otto eventually found himself in the office cleaning business, an industry that was populated with union bosses, power brokers and the kind of mob-connected characters infamous around New York City.

Contents

Preface

My daughter Tina said to me, "Dad, why don't you write down all these stories you've been telling us all these years, all these things you've been through. This way we'll have a background of you, we'll have something to remember you by. I'd like to see it Dad." "Sweetheart, you've got a good idea."

I started dictating about three years ago, to some of the girls in the office. One girl, Dorothy, was in the other office typing up it up. I walked in and she was crying.

"Dorothy, what are you crying for?" She looked at me, "Is this the way you grew up?"

"Yeah, that's the way I grew up. That's the way life is. Some people float through life, with never a care, a worry, or a problem, and other people have to break their ass to get through. Unfortunately, I went through a lot of headaches and a lot of problems, but that's a part of life."

You know, behind every face there's a story. Some of the stories will come out completely, and some won't. A lot of parts will be hidden. We all keep secrets.

Our recent trip to China left me with a lovely package: Asthmatic Bronchitis. You just can't breathe over there. The doctor who was examining me for my lungs left and the nurse said to me, "Mr. Otto, you are in very good shape for a man of 80 years of age. What do you attribute your good health to?" I said, "First of all, I played Judo for 14 years. I must have played 3,000 times. That was good for my heart. But the three basic rules you must listen to in order to keep your health are one: Exercise two or three times a week."

William L. Otto

"What's the second one?"

"Drink. You drink to kill the germs"

"Anything in particular?"

"Scotch, Gin, Bourbon, Vodka, Wine – all the good stuff."

"Well that's two. What's the third one?" I looked into her eyes and I said, "Get laid whenever you can."

Chapter One

"In the Beginning"

I just left my job at the florist at 63rd and Madison Avenue. I got laid off after all the Christmas deliveries were made. Two other fellas were let go. I walked the streets. I had about $9.00 in my pocket so I was feeling pretty good. I started to walk, heading south, towards Rockefeller Center. I wanted to see what the tree looked like all lit up. I walked down and it was snowing, a beautiful night. A little cold, but at that age, who cared? I got down to about 50th Street and realized that here I am still carrying this plant. What am I going to do with it? So I walked into St. Patrick's Cathedral. I figured, let's look around and see where I am going to put it. Nobody stopped me. On the left side by Veronica's Veil, there were very little plants so I gave her the poinsettia. It was so beautiful and quiet in St. Pat's, I said a couple of prayers, and started to reflect on my life.

I started to think way back, how far back could I go? I was born and raised on 152nd Street and Brook Avenue in the Bronx. That's the first place I remember living. My father was the superintendent there. We lived in the basement. There was a problem going downstairs at night because there were always rats running around the place. We had a little apartment, it was behind the meatpacking houses. There was a guy in Joe's butcher shop, I went up there when it snowed to shovel. He always gave me four pieces of bologna. I loved bologna. To this day I still like bologna. Things were different in those days. I must have been six years old but I liked to work. I liked to keep myself busy, I was always like that. So, for me to shovel snow was no big problem, gave me something to do and kept me out of the basement.

There was a young girl who jumped off the roof and landed on the picket fence in front of the house. It was in the papers. They had to come and take her off. She was dead. How she got off the roof of the house and on to the picket fence, I don't know, but I'll always remember her body hanging there, and the look in her eyes.

I used to have a cowboy suit and a little bicycle. I would ride on my bicycle wearing my cowboy suit. I was happy. I didn't know anything better. That was going back a long time.

We moved up to 165th Street and Park Avenue. It was the fifth floor of a walk-up.

I went to school up the "big hill" past the elevated train lines (I think they were called the Third Avenue L) up the hill to St. Augustine's Catholic School. This school was run by the Jesuit Brothers, and boy, were they tough. Nobody made noise in class, no one talked back to the teachers or they would get a crack in the mouth. Drugs, we never knew they existed. On this hill a young boy went sledding, lost control of his sleigh, went under the garbage truck, and was crushed.

In the summer, there was no air conditioning. On a hot night, everyone sat out on the fire escape. It's a wonder they never collapsed.

We played *"Kick the Can," "Johnny on the Pony," "Ring-A-Levio."* We would stay out till late at night, sometimes ten, eleven o'clock at night. We were young kids but it was safe then, even though we were in the Bronx. Those were the good old days. All the kids had a good time, and we laughed, we had a lot of good memories.

I remember my grandfather, God rest his soul. I called him Nana. I slept with Nana. He did snore like all hell, but he was a great man. He loved to play the drums. He would put the marches on an old time record player, he'd have to crank it up to get it to work. Then, he'd take his drumsticks out and play the drums, and I'd sit there and watch him.

Nana was always drunk. He worked for Con Edison. He was in the drafting department. He drew up the plans for the mechanical engineering equipment. His name was William L. Walsh, and his name is listed on the wall over at Sheffield Farms for doing some of the architectural work. He was a great old guy, and he'd come home all the time half loaded. Usually he had some candies in his pocket. We would meet him downstairs and he would give us the candies. If other kids were there, he would pass the candies down to them. If he felt flush on payday, he would buy the kids ice cream. He was a wonderful man. I remember the doctor told him that if he did not stop drinking, he was going to die. Well, he stopped drinking and two weeks later, he died.

We had a big funeral. Nana left $15,000, which was a lot of money in those days. My mother gave $7,500 to her brother John, and we had $7,500. Momma was handling the money, she kept it upstairs. She went out and bought a farm, figuring, "Let's invest it something." She bought 50 acres on the east side of the Hicksville Station on Long Island and she only paid $3,700 for it. It was a potato farm. Nobody wanted it, and now it's worth a fortune.

My mom also bought Dad a car. My father was a habitual gambler. There was a laundry next door, and there were always dice games. He would get involved in the game. One time he said to me, "Hey Willie, come here. Run upstairs and ask mom for $200." I asked Mom for $200. She said, "Tell Dad that's all he's going to get." I took the $200 and ran downstairs. "Kid, go back upstairs and get another $200." "Momma said that's the last." "I don't give a shit what Momma says. I said go back upstairs and get another $200." I went upstairs and got another $200. Momma knew there was going to be trouble. He went through $1,500 that weekend, and that was a lot of money. There were fights, screaming and hollering. It was a terrible time.

I think back about my grandfather and me. Every morning we had breakfast in a little tiny kitchen cubbyhole. We always had six pieces of buttered bread and a cup of coffee. We would cut the bread in half, and dunk it in the coffee. That was our breakfast, we didn't know any better. Everybody was poor, so it was just accepted by all of us as natural.

My father would send me around to the neighbors to borrow thirty-five cents. Thirty-five cents was a lot of money then. He'd take the thirty-five cents and buy a pitcher of beer. He and my mother would sit there and drink the pitcher of beer and argue all night. We'd just sit there and listen to it.

In the back yard, we had these Italian singers who would come in and sing. People would throw pennies at them. Sometimes people would throw a piece of bologna or a little piece of bread out in a plastic bag, or tin foil if we had it. We'd throw them what we could because things were tough. I would go out there thinking maybe I'd pick up a penny or two that they missed.

I was about seven years old when I met the local boys. They pretty much straightened me out telling me that this was their territory and to stay the hell out if I knew what was good for me. I sounded off to them a little bit and they figured they would teach me a lesson, which they did. Two guys grabbed by arms, and another guy grabbed my legs and this guy smacked the shit out of me. I found out later what his name was – Charlie Columbo. I never found him, never ran into him again and to this day I often wonder if he was a member of the Columbo family. He was a tough piece of work.

I started to learn my lessons at an early age. I can remember sometimes on a Saturday night my father and I would go to the steps that were over the railroad tracks at 165th street. The Park Avenue trains ran underneath, and we would sit on the other side facing the big Sheffield Farm plant. On Saturday nights there would be regular fist fights. They were nice, clean-cut fights. The guys used to strip down and they'd duke it out right under the big light. There was always about 20 or 30 people there. We'd all watch and cheer somebody on. Sometimes the guys would bet a little bit. It was an interesting thing to do on a Saturday night, because, we didn't have TV or anything else in those days. So what the hell are you going to do?

We lived there a while and my father either drove a cab or hung out in the pool hall making money there. He was a very good pool player. So good that the manager of the world famous pool player, Willie Hoppe, wanted to manage him. It didn't work out.

With my father's continual gambling, we lost the Hicksville farm and his car. With my grandfather dead, things got worse and we had to move to cheaper quarters. Because we ran out of money we wound up going to 177th Street off Tremont Avenue. We had the first floor, a railroad apartment. My father became the superintendent there.

We were on welfare, home relief they called it.

They used to give us a sack of meal. Now that was pretty good, my mother would mix it with some water and make biscuits. It was nice.

My father trying to make some beer, and it didn't work. He was mixing in the tub and blew out the wall in the bathroom. The fire department came, but they were all regular guys and they all knew that everybody was having a tough time trying to make a living.

I was working at eight years old, simonizing cars. The guy at the gas station would say to me, "Do a good job, Bill." Then, he'd say, "Kid, here's another customer." I used to wash the car down and spend the whole day Saturday polishing it all up. The car looked beautiful when I got finished. That gave me my first indication about the cleaning business, I guess. I got anywhere from thirty-five cents to fifty cents for the car. I would bring it home and my father would buy beer a pitcher of beer. He and my mother would sit there, drink the beer and argue. It was an existence that we just accepted, we knew nothing better.

I think about life at 177th and Tremont and I can remember saving money, and saving money. I don't know how long I saved for. I had to get seven cents, which was a lot of money to me. if I had seven cents, I could buy this toy in the Woolworth 5 & 10 Cent Store. There was a little airplane with another little airplane that sat on top of it. Oh boy, I wanted that so bad. I finally saved up and got the money for it.

I can remember my sister Alice, and I, going around to the bakeries, and we'd ask for, "Thirty-five cents worth of yesterday's buns." The baker would put it into a nice, big bag, and then say, "That will be 35 cents." "Alice, give him the 35 cents," "I don't have the 35 cents. You have the 35 cents." "Alice, Daddy gave *you* the money," "No, Daddy gave *you* the money." We would go back and forth like this a couple times. Meanwhile, there were customers in the store. They were kind of embarrassed; they didn't know what to do. Then someone would say, "Listen kids, go take the buns and get out of here. If you find the money, bring it back." So we would go outside say, "Boy, that's another bakery. Now, we've got to look for some more." We did that all over the Bronx, and that is how we got our buns.

Things were so bad in those days. We were constantly hungry. I can remember going into the breadbox and wetting my finger tips just to get the crumbs.

I can remember four things from the 177th Street house:

My father selling the big Lionel electric trains that my grandfather had bought me. I think he got $22 for them. Today they would be worth a fortune.

The kids from the neighborhood would go behind this garage. It had a really big, steep hill. We would open big cardboard boxes and lay them flat out on the top of the hill. Then we would run and dive onto the cardboard box and slide all the way down the hill. This one time I went over a broken milk bottle. It came up through the cardboard and cut my right hand pretty bad. I pushed the skin back together and ran home to Mom. She was a little under the weather. Without looking at it she said, "Go wash it with soap and water, put some iodine on it and a band aide." I needed three band aides to push the skin back. I still have a scar and think of it every time I look at it.

One night I had a terrible toothache. It must have been about eleven when my mother got dressed and went out in the cold, rainy night. She looked for two hours for an open drugstore to get some pain medication. She finally found one and came home with something to put on my gums. I thought my mother was the greatest that night.

On the corner was a big garage. Three or four of us would sneak in. One of the older boys would go into the key cabinet take the keys for whatever cars we wanted to use. We would drive it all around the garage. The last time we did this, suddenly the main door opened. A police car was blocking the entranceway with two policemen. Somebody had complained to the cops. All hell broke loose. They came in with their guns drawn and we took off. At that age you could run like a deer, and we did. They couldn't catch us, and they were really pissed. So, one of the cops let a bullet go to scare us. That bullet ricocheted all throughout the garage and somehow hit me on the inside of my right knee. We all ran like hell to get out of the garage. I was bleeding but I couldn't go straight home – the police would know where I lived. We went through the back alleyways and other building. When I finally got home, my mother said "Wash it with soap and water, put iodine and a band aide on it." When I look at the scar on my knee, I think about that garage.

We lived there for about two years, and then, somehow, my father made contact with the welfare department and we got an apartment in Long Island City, Queens. We had a fifth floor apartment. It was called the Long Island City Projects.

That was like a step up for us. This was a big three bedroom apartment, nice toilet, nice kitchen with an eating area, and a living room. It also had elevators, steel doors, and security. It was beautiful. And, we had trees around there and it was really nice.

My sister, Alice, and I went to Public School #83, about twelve blocks up, on Vernon Blvd. I recently went past the school, and it is now a condominium building. We would get free lunches at school, and we looked forward to it because that was the best meal we had for the day.

While attending Public School #83, I had a good friend, Donald Dunn. We missed a free lunch. He invited me back to his house, and back at his house his mother opened up Campbell's Alphabet Soup. I can't tell you how amazed I was to see the noodles in the shape of letters of the alphabet. It was an experience I'll never forget. That memory has stayed with me for so long.

I remember I needed a winter coat. So, my father took me to the pawn shop and bought me a long, black leather coat. It was in good shape, but needed cleaning up. So, I took black shoe polish and polished up the coat. It looked real good. But, when I went to school and stood on line to get in, some of the kids said, "Hey, do you smell shoe polish?" So, my coat became a joke. I washed it, cleaned it up, and it was okay.

We had a lot of problems in that apartment, mainly from my father. He was having a tough time making a living; he couldn't get adjusted and was doing a lot of drinking. He was a tough piece of work. I can remember my father and I would walk up to Queens Plaza, over the railroad bridge and out to Woodside to the Thomas' Bakery and Warehouse. They had a bread line and all the men would line up. My father stayed four or five guys behind me. When I came up to the platform and put my hands out for a loaf of bread, the guy in the platform said, "Kid, I can't give you any bread. Go home and send your father here." I looked up him and began to cry and said, "I don't have a father and my family needs the bread." My father yelled out, "Give the kid a loaf of bread," and pushed the guy in front of him and the guy behind him and told them all to yell out. Everybody was hollering, "Give the kid a loaf of bread!" Now, the guy on the platform was embarrassed. He said, "Okay, kid, but take it and get away from here." I took it and went around the corner to wait for my father. That's the only time he ever complimented me. He said, "We did good son. Now we have two loaves of bread." We did this in as many places as we could. Right near there was Cushman's Bakery. A few blocks away. We would see the drivers when they pulled in with their trucks. They would give us what they had left over from some of their deliveries. We would take the bread or the buns home, too. This was the only good time I can remember being with my father, other than sitting on 165th Street and Park Avenue and watching the guys fight.

But, we always had problems with my dad. As I said, he was a tough piece of work. He was so strong that he used to reach down and grab the couch and lift the couch up to the ceiling. At that time it didn't dawn on me that this was a hell of a feat to do. But he did it. And we accepted it.

Sometimes we'd have fights and we would lock him out of the house and he would dig up bricks that were in the walkway outside and he would throw the bricks through the windows on the fifth floor where we lived. And as I got older I had taken a brick myself and I tried to throw it that far and I couldn't do it. I don't know how the hell he did. And he was accurate – he got it through the windows. Finally, a guard came over one night and said, "Get out of here or I'll give you a bullet." He understood what the guard meant, and he left.

I can remember my older sister, Jeanette, breaking glass bottles and going after my father with the jagged edge. I can remember my mother being on the floor when my father hit her. I can remember sitting and reading at night with a knife under my pillow. I don't know really how everybody lived, but I remember going over the 59th Street Bridge to Kips Bay Boys Club by myself. The Kips Bay Boys Club was something like about 36th Street. There was a fellow there from the Coast Guard. He used to take care of the boys – kind of like a drill sergeant. I told him about my father and he got me started on judo and other techniques that were similar. He tried to teach me some different types of self-defense and so forth, and it was very interesting. He was very helpful and understanding because he knew my father was a bully.

I was doing my best to try to make a living. I worked in a fruit store that was on 40th Avenue and 21st Street called Sam's. I think I was eleven years old at the time. I used to go down there and load the potatoes from off the truck. They were 100 lb. potatoes, and believe it or not, I used to put them on my shoulders and carry them down to the basement. To this day I don't think I could pick up a 100 lb. bag of potatoes. But you did it in them days, and who the hell knew why? Because it was a job.

I went from there and got another job with a candy company called Lofts. I had a hell of a time there because they put me on an assembly line where the candies would come through on a conveyer belt and my job was to take a piece of wax paper and put it on top of the candies and put the cover on. But, somehow, I would fall behind and I would be pushing the candies back and I couldn't catch up with putting the wax paper on top and putting the cover on. So sometimes they would pile up and they would be falling over the side and the boss would come over and stop the conveyer belt and Holy Christ he would give me hell. He said, "This is not for you," and he gave me the job of taking what they called the "skid mover" and moving boxes and heavy equipment and stuff around the plant. It was a good job; I was making some money. That was the key thing: it didn't matter what you did, as long as you made some money because you needed money in the house to live. And that's what we all went through in them days. A good day was when you had something to eat and a good pair of sneakers without holes in them. At that time sneakers cost 69 cents, but who had 69 cents?

When I was thirteen and fourteen I worked in a shop on 10th Avenue between 39th and 40th Street. In the morning I used to pack cars that were being shipped to South America and in the afternoon I used to make cabinets for radios. It was interesting work. I liked working with the wood and working with finishes. I skipped school many times so I could work and make some money.

I can remember my father telling me, "I want you to come with me. We're going to a meeting." And I was very impressed with the idea of going to a meeting. We took the train to 13th Street off 5th Avenue and went to a building. We went down the steps and inside were pictures of Hitler and swastikas. It was a German Bund meeting. My father initially went there to see if they could get him work; he was looking for a job, but they couldn't help him. All they did was drink beer and sing German songs. We left and my father never went back, nor did I.

It was always a tough time getting money from my father. He thought he was Jimmy Durante. I remember one time, I must have been about nine, and my mother said to me, "Willie, go around the corner and get your father – he's over at Tony's. Tell him I need some money for groceries." I said, "Okay, Mom." Well, I went around the corner to Tony's Bar. Tony's Bar was the place when they made that picture *On the Waterfront*. Some of the actors played in the movie as union strong arm guys; some of those guys came from that bar. One of them was a heavy, short guy. I think they called him Two-Ton Galento. Anyway I walked into to Tony's Bar, there were a lot of people sitting at the bar, and they were all drinking. My father was in the back and he was "butting" a man. Now, I don't know if you have ever seen that. It scared the hell out of me. He had his arms wrapped around this man and he was butting him with his chin. The guy's face was all bloody, but nobody paid any attention. In fact, nobody ever bothered my father. I don't know if they were scared of him, or thought he was crazy, or what. He started singing "Umbriago" like Jimmy Durante, and the guys laughed and kidded with him and bought him a drink and he kept going. He was happy there in the bar. I guess that was about the only place he was happy. He didn't know anything else about education, or books or trying to improve himself. He just tried to get by, day by day, and it was tearing his guts out. He gave me some money and I ran home. Soon he came home and fought with his family, and beat up his wife – my mother.

One time he was sitting there eating steak and I didn't have any steak. I stood there and I watched him, and he just kept on eating. I was hungry, but that's the way he was.

Now I was getting bigger, I was growing up. The Projects moved us out of 40-07 and into 41-18. My sister left – she joined the WACS – and when one person left they moved you into a smaller apartment. We had two bedrooms there. I got home one night from the factory, went up the stairs and my father was pounding on the door trying to get in. I was sixteen then, about 6'3". I weighed about 165 lbs. – working my ass off. I saw my father and whatever happened, I don't know, but I reached my arms around him, and I grabbed him from behind. He was drunk, but I was taller than him. I picked him up and I swung him around two or three times in the hallway and I let go and I smashed him into the wall. He hit the wall with a hell of a shot and fell down. He was out almost like cold. He was numb, but he was drunk. He turned around and looked at me and he said to me, "Son, you got strong, Son, you got strong." And those were the last words I ever heard from my father. He went down the stairs, and I never saw him again. That was right before Thanksgiving. He left.

I found out, many years later, that he had died. I don't know from what. I always figured it was from a broken heart. I found out where he was buried and put a headstone on his grave.

Yesterday is
Gone forever
And
Tomorrow may
Never come

Chapter Two

"Life Goes On"

So now, here I was at St. Pat's Cathedral. It's after Christmas. I was going to leave. In fact, it was about 8:30 at night and this guy was asking me to leave – I guess they had to close the place up. I went over to see the Christmas tree and watch the skaters. I crossed over Fifth Avenue and headed towards Rockefeller Center. It was snowing fairly hard. I walked around to where the big tree was and stood on the left side of it. I just watched. The people were skating. I listened to the music. It was a beautiful sight. And then I stood there and said to myself, "Well, what do you do Bill? You don't have a father. You don't have an education. You don't have any real future. What do you do from here?" There were two things I knew: I knew that I didn't want to be hungry and I knew that I wanted to make some money. The rest is up to me to figure a way out.

For some reason or another I started to cry. It was a sad moment in my life. But sometimes, you get a feeling of being lost, and you don't know which way to turn. But a man is not supposed to get sad or cry – he's supposed to fight. So you weather the storm, you wipe your eyes, and you walk home.

I saved a nickel on the trolley and I walked over on the 59th Street Bridge. I got to the elevator, took that down, and I walked Vernon Boulevard back to the house. That was in 4118 Vernon Boulevard – The Projects. I went upstairs and said hello to Mom. I had a cup of coffee, we talked a little bit, and then I went to sleep because I had to go to work at 7:30 the next morning making radio cabinets in the factory.

So, I went to work – did that for a while. Meanwhile, I was saving money, anyway I could. I wound up with $375, which was a lot of money then, and I had a choice of two things I wanted to do: one, I wanted a car, and the other was to play the piano. So I said, "Flip a quarter, Bill. If it's heads, you get the car. If it's tails, you buy a piano." Now, I flipped a quarter, and it came out heads. I was getting closer to seventeen, I had to get a car, but I needed some kind of a sponsor because they wouldn't give it you at seventeen. You had to have somebody to say that they would be watching over you, co-sponsor you to get the license, which I did. I finally got the license. I shopped around and I bought a 1933 Pontiac. Boy, did I love that car. I cleaned it and polished it and babied it and looked out for it. I'd take Mom and my brother out for a ride, and we'd go out for a ride on Sunday and enjoy it. It was a great feeling having a car.

And now, I was working in the factory, and I had the car, so I was thinking, "Why don't I use the car for something – for sales?" I was close to eighteen, and I decided what I'd become was a Fuller Brush Man, and I went to the Fuller Brush people and got a job with them. I worked an area over in Woodhaven and had a hell of a time. In them days it was tough to make money. I was averaging $55-$58 a week and I was enjoying every bit of it.

At this point I was bringing some money into the house and we were doing a little bit better. I figured it was about time I started to move up the ladder, so I heard about a job in Cross & Blackwell, which is an English firm over in Long Island City. I went over there (I was always dressed very nice) and walked inside and I met the general manager, Mr. Mahar, who was a classy Englishman. He and I started talking, and I told him what I'd like to do: "I'd like to become one of the sales people," and he said, "Well, you're only twenty years old. You're a little bit young to be out in the field doing that. I don't know if you can make it." I said, "Well, why don't we try? Give me a shot at it."

So, he said, "Okay Bill, I'm going to give you a shot at it. But first, I want you to spend a month hanging around the warehouse to see what's going on. I want you to learn the products, see how the stuff is packed, what it is, and then I want you to come out to some of the local supermarkets. I'm going to set up a soup kitchen. I want you to display the soup. Let the housewives come in, give them a sample of the soup – tell them how good it is and get the product on the market. Do that for a month, then you'll be ready, and we'll put you out on the road." I said, "Well, that sounds great."

So I went to about six local supermarkets and got permission from the managers to set up a small soup kitchen. I had a great time. The housewives would come over and I would give them a small sample of the different soups. Most of them would buy. Some said they would buy it later. The program was a success because we wound up selling a lot of soup. Now I was ready to get my own territory. I was excited. I had my own car, I was dressed nice, and now, with Cross & Blackwell as my company, I was ready to take on the world.

They gave me a territory up by the Grand Concourse – a completely Jewish neighborhood. They had yamacas on and curls on the sides. Well, when you walked in and spoke to some of the people – they weren't looking to buy any Cross & Blackwell products. I had 55 accounts, but these accounts were dead, and there was nothing happening with them. But I guess they wanted to see what I could do. Well, at one of the stores I saw a man standing there with his Yamaka on, and I walked over to him and stuck my hand out, and I said, "Hello, I'm Bill Otto from Cross & Blackwell. I'd like to introduce our product to you."

He said, "Boy, look at this Goya. Such a handsome kid. He dresses nice, talks nice, what a gentleman. And look at this schmuck, my son," and he pointed to his son next to him. He said, "He can't count – can't do nothing. What can I do for you, kid?" And I said, "Well, it would be nice if you tried some of my products." He said, "Come, let me talk to you. Let's have a cup of tea. You know, the Jewish people don't use your products. This is your territory up here? Well, you're going to have a tough time unless you break the ice." I said, "What do you mean by breaking the ice? How do I do that?" He said, "I'm going to tell you what to do. Pick out the toughest store you got where you'd like to put the product in. Now with the Jewish Holidays, I'll tell you when they are, you're going to walk into the store, walk over to the boss, and you're going to say to him, *L'Shanah Tovah Tikatevu* and see what happens." I said, 'Well what does *L'Shanah Tovah Tikatevu* mean?" He said, "Well, in Hebrew it means you wish him a healthy, happy New Year. But, he's going to think to himself, 'This Goya comes into my store and takes the time to learn a Hebrew saying – I've got to do something for him.'"

Well, I picked one of my toughest stores up on the grand concourse, and I got prepared for the Jewish Holidays. It was right before the Jewish New Years, and I walked into the store. It was a little bit busy. I waited until the boss was a little bit free. He saw me standing there, and I walked over to him and I said, "I just want to say to you, *L'Shanah Tovah Tikatevu.*" And he backed off, and he looked at me, and he said, "Where did you learn that saying? Where did you learn how to talk like that?" And I said, "Well, it's your Jewish holiday." He said, "Yes it's my holiday; but where did you learn how to say that?" I said, "Well, an old friend of mine told me that it was a good saying, and it meant a lot to the Jewish people." He said, "It means an awful lot to me that you should say that, being that you're Goya and you come into my store and you talk like that." He said, "Come, we go in the back and have a cup of tea. You tell me what you got that we all could use."

Well, that was my first big account. From there I went from 55 dead accounts to 132 live accounts and the business was doing well. I was making money. Mr. Mahar was happy. Everybody was happy. I made friends in all the stores and when I walked in, they'd say, "Hey, how are you Bill? How about you come by and we'll have a cup of tea?" And I got to be friendly with everybody up there, and it turned out very well. This job lasted for about three years.

Well, that was an interesting part of my life. But unfortunately, for some reason or another, Cross & Blackwell was having problems over in England, and they weren't supporting the American store over here. Whatever reason, we got word that the place was closing up. Even to this day, when you go shopping around, you very seldom see a Cross & Blackwell product. Maybe you'll see the Cross & Blackwell marmalades or the Cross & Blackwell mint jelly, but that's about all I ever see anymore. I never see anything else from them, and their products were good. It was handled well, done well. I don't really know what happened in England. But because of that I found myself out of a job. What do you do?

I got a job with the Tyler Roofing Company out in Jamaica selling roofing. Tyler Roofing – what a joke that was. We used to walk down the neighborhood, look for what roofs had to be repaired, what needed work, knock on the door, and try to sell them on the product. We told them that heat was going out from the bad roof, and that you could see it very easily because if you looked at a roof after a snowstorm, and you saw that the snow melted off the roof, that meant their house had poor insulation because the heat was coming through the roof. If you passed a house, and the snow was still packed up on the roof that meant that the insulation was still good, and the roof was still good. So, this was our selling point. We went through a whole sales pitch in the morning, got ourselves all fired up and got out there.

Well, I did this for quite a while and was making some money. One problem came up, and quite frankly, I got out of the business because of this problem. I went to a house one time and I was talking to the husband and wife and two kids and I was telling them about the Tyler Roofing and that they should put a new roof on their house and so forth. Well, we discussed it. We sat down, and I could see that they were very poor, and for some reason or another, the kid asked for milk, and the mother said, "I'll get for you later." But I got the indication that there was no milk. And here was this father who was willing to spend money to put a roof on the house, when it was more important to me to see that the kids had the milk. Coming from poverty, coming from tough times, this hit home. And I just said, "Look, you could get by for another four or five years with the roof that you got. Save your money and see how things are by that time." I wished them well and I walked out. Then I packed in Tyler Roofing.

I thought to myself, "Now, let me try something else. Let me take a shot at Electrolux." I started selling Electrolux vacuum cleaners. Well, in the morning, they'd get you all fired up with a good salesman who would tell you how great the product was and that it came from Sweden. It was going to do this – clean the house with very little effort. The product really was good. It was a good vacuum cleaner and you could go out in the field and start selling it. That was interesting and fun job, really. And I tried that for a while. I stayed with that for maybe ten months, maybe a year. I forget now.

Then a job opened up in Sheffield farms for a Route Salesman, and I took that job over in Jamaica – there was a big Sheffield's plant over there. We used to go around and try to build up the milk routes for the deliverymen. Well, we'd go around to an area where a guy's section was not too strong, go pound on the doors, and try to get the people to have milk delivered to their houses. That was the way it was done in them days. You would have the man go around the back yard and put the milk in the containers and so forth. That was an interesting job. I tried that for a while, and I enjoyed that. That was the only time in my life that I was bitten by a dog. A housewife opened the door and the cocker spaniel ran out to bite me. It ripped my pants and I took them off so this woman could sew them for me.

While I was doing that, I also had a job with the RCA people at night. I was selling renewable contracts on their TVs. It was a service contract that they put out for two or three years at a certain fixed figure, and for every time we sold a service contract, we got a commission. So, I was working days and I was working nights trying to make some money. During the course of this time I met one of the top salesmen by the name of John Metelski. He and I became close friends and I'll tell you the story about him later on. John and I worked together for quite a few years.

John was a great guy with a lovely family; two kids. He was the sales export manager for Pfizer Chemical on 42nd Street, which was quite a big job in them days. He lived in Oceanside and he tried to survive in a world with engineers all around him and it was a difficult time for him. I can remember going to the Engineers Club on 41st Street to see him and meet him for lunch. He would make friends with a certain waiter, and take good care of him. In return the waiter would carry a make-believe "urgent" message for "Dr. Metelski." This waiter would run around paging, "Dr. Metelski, Dr. Metelski," and that was for John. He wasn't a doctor – he was trying to impress people. Then this waiter would come over and give him the "message." I would say to John, "Was it anything important?" He would say, "No, but I gave that guy the watch that he is wearing so he would come over." So I asked, "What's with this doctor business?" He replied, "Bill, the place is full of doctors and professors. This helps me a little bit. They think I am a doctor; but you and I both know that I am not."

John was a big help to me in the years later on. In fact, I named my son William John Otto after him. But, he was a tough nut and I enjoyed his company. He actually saved my life. He was very helpful to me. I'll tell you more about him later on.

During these periods I kind of became very close to my mom. She was a great gal. We would sit and have long talks. She told me about how the family came over in 1793 from Kilkenny, Ireland, and the story she heard was that everybody on the boat was drinking a lot, including the crew, and that they were supposed to land in New York but most of the crew got so drunk that they wound up in Albany. And a lot of her family settled in Albany. Some were successful and got into the real estate field. Uncle Andrew got into the real estate field. He was also a musician. I had another aunt who married a man by the name of Nolan who was the chairman of a big chemical company in Albany called Eastman Chemical Company. I saw them periodically when I was younger, but as I got older, I never got a chance to get back up there.

My mom was the type of person who could have two nickels in her pocket and you would never know it. She never asked for nothing. She just accepted life as it was. After being married to my father all those years, I guess it was just something that she learned to live with. She was happy just to have a cup of coffee and a piece of toast and sit and talk. Some people are uppers and some people are downers, but she was an upper – God Bless her! We would split a can of Campbell's soup together and be happy. She was a great gal. I miss her – miss her – terribly.

I had a friend of mine named Mike who worked for Olympic TV, so I went over there and applied for a job. I got a job testing the TV sets. I gradually did so well that I moved up the ladder. They made me Supervisor of what they called the CRT department. My job was to see that the big tubes were running clearly and were separated on the assembly line. I came back and packed up the boxes and shipped them out. They gave me a raise and treated me good. I was happy.

Well, there was a wise ass named Juan. He just kept breaking my balls – he wouldn't stop. So, I confronted him one day and with this he flips out a knife and he stabbed me on the lower left side by the ribs. I'll tell you the truth: I didn't even feel the knife going in, but I knew the knife was in me. I grabbed his hand and I grabbed him behind the neck and I pulled the knife out of me and turned it around and stuck it in him and twirled it around in his stomach. Well, I could see the look on his face and could tell I was hitting some good spots. He backed off and ran out holding his guts. We never saw him again – he just took off. He never filed a complaint or anything. I went to the first aid place and they examined me. They asked me if I wanted to go to the hospital. I said, "Well, it's only bleeding a little bit. It was a very thin, narrow knife, so it seems to be alright." He said, "Why don't you just take the day off and go home and rest." I said, "Alright, fine." They bandaged it up, put some disinfectant into it and I was fine. The next day I was back on the job. I carry a small scar from this incident. The knife I still have.

Mike and I had a lot of crazy times together. Some, I can't tell you. I can't even put it down on tape. We wound up getting a place in Jackson Heights together. It was in the basement. He had a '47 Chevy convertible and we used that car to have a lot of good times. I remember one night in Jackson Heights – we had a hell of a blowout in a bar called The Orchid Room.

It was a nice place that had two entrances in the front; one for the bar and one for the restaurant. Mike and I had our girlfriends with us. We were eating pizza, drinking beer, playing the jukebox and dancing. These two wise guys came out from the bar and wanted to cut in and dance with our girls. We said, "Get the fuck out of here." But they kept on coming back. We pushed the girls away so they wouldn't get hurt and these guys came at us. The fight started. Mike looked like Anthony Quinn, and then you have me – 6'5" and 180 lbs, tall, lanky and strong.

There was an archway in between the bar and the restaurant. These two guys had to come through the archway to get to us. Every time they came at us, we would push them back through the archway. But then four other guys from the bar joined in. Mike and I knew we had our hands full, so I yelled to my girlfriend Doris, who was a big blonde, "Get out of here and get the car started." We had to get the hell out of there. It was like a John Wayne movie. We were so outnumbered and we were getting tired. So I said to Mike, "Go for their eyes, and we've got to get out of here." The car was a convertible so it was easy for all of us to jump into and take off quickly. We were lucky to get out alive.

Then he and I got a house out in Bayside. We were listed as *"engineers"* with everybody. We worked out of Bayside, and we had girls coming in and out. We had a hell of a time. We used to have a regular run that we would make over in Flushing with the Holiday Inn Bar. We used to hit there first and see what we picked up and then we went out to Bayside – we had another spot over there that we stopped off at. We got involved with a lot of crazy things.

Well, the breakup came when I could realize he was sooner or later going to get into some serious trouble, and I was going to be with him. I came out of the house one morning and he said, "C'mere Bill, I wanna show you what I've got." The Chevy had a way that you could take the cushion and drop it down and behind the cushion he had two loaded guns with wires in the back of the seat. He said, "Bill, you never know when we are gunna need a fast gun." I said to myself, "I have to get away from this guy because he is going to be in big trouble sooner or later." I did. I got away from him. I found out later that he did get in big trouble – for all I know he is still in jail. He was sentenced up to a place near Canada, a place called Dannemora Prison. That was the last I heard from him.

> ***You have to go look for the***
> ***Good times***
> ***The bad times will find you***

Chapter Three

"U.S. Army"

My two sisters were married. My brother was in the service. I soon moved back in with my mom, and then I got a notice from the draft board to appear. I went down and got examined and sworn in. Next thing I knew I was in Camp Dix. I went through the process – got shipped around to a lot of different camps. I got in in January 1953 and got out in January 1955. It was during the Korean War.

I had an interesting situation in the Army. A lot interesting things happened. Because of my size, they made me an Assistant Platoon Sergeant. This means that you have no rank, no authority, but they want you to keep the boys in line. This is not easy to do. We had a bunch of boys from New York and I got a reputation. They called me "Balls Otto." I can remember one of the things I did. There was a fellow who used to play the piano for Judy Garland – his name was Bobby Cole. Bobby Cole was the band leader at the Non-Commission Servicemen's Club. When he would see me come in, he would stop the band and play my favorite song "It Had to be You". We would wave and acknowledge each other. In fact, he used to play at Jilly's Restaurant on 58th Street and Frank Sinatra was always there. Well, Bobby was breaking my balls one day. I said, "If you don't get out of there, I'm going to fan your ass." He kept on breaking my balls and then he took off. I took off after him. I ran after him, caught him, grabbed him, turned him upside down and I fanned his ass! Well, I don't think he ever forgot that, and I don't think I ever forgot that. Even today, God Bless him, he'll remember it.

I remember another time when everybody was getting duty and we had a shed in the back yard and it was tipped over in a thirty degree angle and the sergeant said to me, "Bill I want you to straighten up that shed." I said, "Well, if I straighten it up, can I go on pass?" He said, "Yeah, you can go on pass." I said, "Okay, fine." I went down to the motor pool and I took a two and a half ton truck, drove it out to the shed, and leaned it against the building. I put the truck in low gear and gradually pushed the building straight back up. Then I took a brace on that side, took a rope on the other side, pulled it over, hammered it in, backed off the truck and the building was straight. Now I took the truck and brought it quietly back into the motor pool, went over to the Sergeant and said, "Sergeant, can I have my pass?" So he said, "You're not going to get a pass, Bill, until you get that shed straightened up." I said, "It's already done." He said, "C'mon," not believing me. I said, "Well, c'mon and take a look." So he came out and he looked at it and said, "How the hell did you get it so straight so fast." I said, "That's a secret." He said, "Okay, I said you could go on pass, you got a pass." I took the pass, and I was gone.

Another time I was working around the tanks. They put us in the Seventh Cavalry. I liked the tanks – they were a good piece of equipment. I was a tank driver for a while and then I worked my way up to gunner. In fact, I can remember one time we were up at Fort Meade in the gunnery range firing the guns, and we had the shell in the chamber and the breach wouldn't close. Well everybody jumped out of the God damn tank and ran like hell and I went with them. The Company Commander said, "What the hell is going on?" I said, "Well, the breach won't close. We are afraid it is going to explode inside." He said, "Well, then you'd better stay over here and see what happens." Then it dawned on me that if I ran inside and took a shovel and smacked it on the bottom it would close up and fire. That is exactly what I did. This is down on record. So I jumped down into the tank, hit the bottom of the breach, it closed up and the shell fired. I said, "Okay guys, c'mon back inside the tank." We went back to the tank and that was it.

One time we were in the mess hall. We were served spaghetti and meatballs. Well, the spaghetti was bad enough, but the meatballs you couldn't even cut. They were so hard they were actually difficult to eat. So I said, "This is bullshit! We work our ass off all day long! You think we're going to eat this kind of garbage?" I took the meatball, put it in my hand and I walked over to the Company Headquarters. I walked inside and said to the Sergeant, "I want to see the Captain." He said, "What about?" I said, "About this God Damned meatball." So he said, "Well, just a minute."

I walked past the Sergeant, walked into the Captain Oliver's office and there were a couple of Lieutenants there and I saluted the Captain and said, "I want to tell you something Captain. You know, we work our asses off making these tanks look good for you and we want to have something decent to eat. We can't eat this garbage. I mean look at this meatball – you can't even cut it." I put the meatball on his desk. He looked at it and he tried to cut it. He couldn't cut it. He said, "I can see what you're talking about Otto. Let me see what I can do about it." I said, "I really appreciate it, Sir." As I went out the door, he put the meatball down for the dog and I said, "Sir, I wouldn't give that to the dog." I walked out.

The next day we went to the mess hall and the Mess Sergeant Hughes clicked the glasses and said, "Attention please. Some wise ass went to the Company Commander and complained about the food in this company." So I picked up my tray and held it about two feet up from the table, and I dropped it. Everybody turned around to look. I said, "Sergeant, I want to tell you something. I am going to walk down this isle if you don't apologize for calling me a smart-ass, and I am going to belt you in the mouth and then I am going to go to the Stockade and I don't give a fuck. That's what you are going to get."

I got up and started walking toward him and he backed off because he knew I wasn't kidding. He said, "Alright Otto, take it easy. I am sorry for what I said, but I've got my hands full." I said, "What do you mean, you got your hands full? You cook the food – what kind of food are you cooking?" He said, "That's why my hands are full. I've got a problem. If you want to back off for a minute, come in the kitchen and I'll show you what I'm talking about." So he took me into the kitchen and he said, "Look, I give you guys meatballs. If I get good meat, you get a good meatball. If I get garbage, you get a garbage meatball. That's all that I have to work with. Look at the stuff I get."

He showed me the fat and the grizzle that he mixed together and tried to make a meatball out of. I said, "For Christ's sake, what the hell is the matter here? Where is this food coming from?" He said, "This comes from

Blackstone, Virginia. The meat is distributed into Blackstone. The Captain picks out the meat that is supposed to be sent to us and that's how we get the meat." I said, "Well, something is wrong." He said, "I know something is wrong. I think somebody is making some money out of this, but what can we do about it?" I said, "We are going to get the Inspector General on the phone." That's what we did.

We got the Inspector General on the phone and we talked to him. As it turned out, the Captain had the meat coming in from the Commissary and he had it separated so that all the garbage when to the companies in the army and the good meat was picked up by the butchers in the local towns. He was making money on the good meat and giving us the garbage. Needless to say, they took good care of him. He lost his rank, was discharged, and they put him in jail. I think he got six years. And there was a big write up about it in the paper at that time. Blackstone, Virginia – a very interesting town.

There was an interesting case in Blackstone where this guy's wife fooling around with a cab driver, in the back seat. He somehow, quietly, while they were in the back seat of the car, ran a rope around it, with his friend, and tied the car doors closed. Then he broke the glass, put gasoline in there fast, lit it and burnt the two of them to death. It was a terrible story, but that was what happened in Blackstone.

I eventually became Tank Commander. I ran my tank – kept it in mint condition. In fact, the Battalion Commander wanted me to be his Tank Commander and I turned it down and said, "No, I like working for my company, Company C." And, it was a great tank. It was called a T-25. It could go 52 miles and hour and that tank could weigh 25 tons. From a quarter of a mile away you could hit the hubcaps on a car. It was a great piece of equipment.

We played with the tanks and then all of a sudden, some of us got an order. No one was supposed to talk about anything. We were going on some sort of secret mission. So, we packed up our gear and headed to the airport.

Two airplanes went in two different directions – south, then across the south back up Texas over to Nevada. Then they finally told us what we were going to be doing. We were going to be guinea pigs for the nuclear testing of the atomic bombs. Well, we went out there and they told us about the bomb and what we were going to do and how we were going to protect ourselves and see to it that we tried to survive.

I'll tell you quite frankly, it was a very interesting experience. We went through three of them. A lot of things happened, but they won't tell you it was down on record, but some of the guys knew.

We got out there and went in a trench that was 2,500 yards away. I was carrying a Renkins counter. The Lieutenant was carrying a Geiger counter. He was at the end and I was next to him. What would happen was that they would count down from eighteen and then the bomb would go off. Well, one of the guys got scared and he started running to the back. Over the loudspeaker they said to him, "Get down! Get down! The bomb will pick you up!" Well, the kid didn't know any better and he kept on running because he was scared to death and figured, "Let me get the hell out of here." Well, he got out there, all right. When the bomb went off he disappeared and they never found him. I understand his name was Green. I don't know what happened to the issue on it – nobody pressed it. It was something that they kept quiet, like a lot of things they kept quiet. But he disappeared.

We were in the trenches and they would tell us to close our eyes and cover our heads and a blinding flash would go off. It would be a flash as if you had your eyes closed and someone flashed a very bright camera into your face. The light was very strong. Then you would wait and you would count to twelve and then the blast would hit. When the blast hit, the man on your left, you could hardly see him, because he was either two feet behind you or two feet in front of you and he was wiggling around – the whole God damned trench was wiggled. It shook you up and then you settled down. The dust settled down. Then they said over the loud speakers, "Rise." We all got up.

The Lieutenant went first with his Geiger counter. He picked up the nuclear waves. When it got too strong, they switched it over to mine which was the Renkin's Counter. We had two parts on that Renkin's counter. It went from zero to two hundred in the black and then when it got to two hundred I switched the controls and then it would go from zero to two hundred in the red. When it started to climb the red that meant that you were in trouble. We had to get out of there.

The first time that we were going up there we were up to about seventy in the black and we noticed that car motors had melted into the tires and we came across these sheep that they had tied up and although they were a little burnt, they were in pretty good shape and were standing up. It was amazing how they got through that. We went further up and he closed off the Geiger counter and the Renkin's counter that I had went from zero to two hundred in the black. I switched over to the red and it immediately went up to fifty in the red. I reported it to the Lieutenant. The Lieutenant blew the whistle and he said, "Vacate! Vacate the area!"

We all turned around, all five thousand of us, and we started running like hell to get away from there because it meant that the nuclear particles, whatever the hell they were, were coming at us. They would pick us up in the trucks and we would go back to the base.

When you got back to the base you would strip yourself nude – everybody took his or her clothes off. They gave you a bar of brown soap and you went into the shower. You could be standing next to a Colonel or a General, who the hell cared? And you washed yourself down with the brown soap. Then you came out and they checked you again. The basic areas that you had problems with were under your armpits or your groin. So if the clicking sounded loud under your armpits or in your groin, you had to wash yourself again until the sound went down. You had to do this several times until you had clearance on the Geiger counter.

Then we left got dressed, had something to eat and had a truck take us into Las Vegas. We saw the action, saw what was going on, and we spent three months out there with this.

There was one bad part that we heard about later. They had taken a truckload of guys on the second bomb and they dropped them at 750 yards away from the bomb, in an open field and said that they were coming back to pick them up. Well, they didn't come back to pick them up. There were about 17 guys who heard over the speaker that the bomb was going off, and what were they going to do? A couple of the guys were pretty sharp, pretty smart and they said, "Dig in." Then they dug themselves in to face the bomb, lengthwise, got their heads as low as they could possibly do it, all lined up, pushed dirt over their heads, over their helmets, and the bomb went off.

All these guys survived. I don't know what they're doing today. Whether they are cripples, or they're dead, or what, but they survived that blast. That is an interesting concept: if you face the bomb, lay down prone, and dig yourself in as close as you can to the ground, you have a chance of surviving. We learned that from those fellas. It was very nice of the army to use these guys as guinea pigs to see how they would make out. Anyway, that was some of our experiences with the atomic bombs.

We came back from there and I was sent to Camp Pickett, Virginia. They really didn't know what to do with us. They put us in a field house and some friends of mine and I got together and we took the job of taking care of the swimming pools. Well, we had a ball with that. We used to close up the pools at 6 o'clock at night and the girls would come over and we would have a great time. There were four swimming pools and we had parties at all of them.

In the field house we didn't know what to do with ourselves. We had some time to kill. We had a boxing team there. A friend of mine, Bob and I used to go into the ring and punch each other out a little bit. It's amazing how you can get so banged up and you don't realize until you get out of the ring just how many marks you have on you. I can remember one time with this fella Captain Jones, God bless his soul. I don't think he is alive, and I hope he is not. But Captain Jones was a black fella, classy guy, sharp, and he had a way about him. He came past the shop one day and I was working inside and he stopped and he said, "What are you doing Otto?" And I said, "I am working on something." And he said, "Oh, yeah," and he walked into his office.

The Sergeant came over and said, "Otto, the Captain wants to see you." I said, "Okay, fine." So I walked into his office and said, "What's up, Captain?" He said "Otto, you have to find yourself something to do – keep yourself busy. You only have a short time to go before you get discharged, but find yourself something to do." I said, "Wait just a minute Captain. Can I talk to you man to man?" He said, "I am going to say yes Otto, but I hope it is alright." I said, "It is going to be alright sir. You have to understand something. I am an intelligent individual, and sometimes I think to myself: No, I am not working with my hands. But, I am working with my head and sometimes that is necessary to plan something, to figure out something, to make something, to do something for the shop, or to

27

make something for the field house. You just can't keep yourself busy with your hands. You have to use your head a little bit and that's what I was doing at that particular point when you came past. I was thinking about how to make a big cabinet, because somebody needed a big cabinet and I was going to put it together and work on it and so forth." And he said, "Otto, you always have an answer." And I said, "Well, it's a legitimate answer, Capt, and I happen to be right."

I saluted him and I walked out and I said to myself, "I have to do something for this Captain." First of all I remembered that he swiped a set of golf clubs and he had them put away for himself. Well, now I swiped those golf clubs – so what was he going to say? "Who swiped the golf clubs that I swiped?" He couldn't say nothing. They were McGregor's and that is what I played with. We were playing golf down there a lot and I didn't have any clubs, so I used his clubs.

We were getting ready to get discharged and I said to my friend, Buddy, "Let's fix the Captain. You know that soap dispenser that has concentrated soap?" He said, "Yeah?" I said, "Let's open his car and take the windshield washer out. He has two motors there, one that puts it on and one that takes it off. Let's take the water out and fill it with soap, then let's take the off motor off." He said, "But then it can't go off – it will stay on." I said, "Then when he is driving along and it is a very bad day and he puts the windshield washer on he will get a gallon and half of pure suds and if the water comes down on that – I could just picture the car." Captain Jones, I don't know if you are alive today, but we were the ones that planned that surprise for you.

When I was in the Army, in Camp Pickett, they were trying to see what they could do about making me an un-commissioned officer. So they gave me the job, and the responsibility of taking the company over to a lecture hall. This is a big group of men – 144 men. I marched them over and it was, "Left column; Right column," and so forth, until we finally got to the area which was twelve blocks away.

During the course of this journey there was always some wise guy in the crowd making remarks about me. Now, I kept it to myself until we got outside the lecture hall, then I lined everybody up, the whole company, and I said, "Gentlemen, about face." So now they were facing away from me. I said, "Would the wise ass that's making all those remarks at least have the decency to take a step forward and a step right, come around to the corner, make a turn and come around in front of the company, and address me? The rest of you, stay the way you are." Well, the snickering stopped and nobody took a step forward to come out and face me. I guess that's how I got the name, "Balls Otto."

Anyway, I told them all to turn around and we got back to the barracks and this one guy named Smitty – he was a tough piece of work – he came over to me and I knew he was one of the wise guys. He started mouthing off and I grabbed him by the throat and pushed him up against the wall and said, "Shut your fucking mouth or I will break your face." He threw a punch at me, but I locked his arm and he couldn't move. I said, "Do you want to talk, or do you want to fight." He said to me, "What are you going to do when you get out of the Army?" I said, "I don't really know."

We talked for about an hour. He said, "There is a situation coming up where they want to take over control of the shrimp industry in Panama." There was a president down there by the name of President Ramon. Smitty said, "We have 15 guys going down there and we need one more. Would you be interested in it?" I said, "What do we have to do?" He said, "You're going to go on the tug boats and you're going to take control of the shrimps. You'll get a 45, you'll get $300/week and you'll join in with the rest of the boys and see what they do." I had a pretty good idea of what they did. I said, "Well let me digest this a little bit. I'll let you know." I found out later that President Ramon was killed and thirteen of the fifteen men who went down there from my crew were killed.

Chapter Four

"I'm a Civilian Again"

I finally got discharged and had $386 handed to me. That was a lot of money in them days. I went down to the main street in town to figure out how I was going to get home and what I was going to do. The first thing I wanted to do was to get myself a nice steak and a nice bottle of bourbon or Jack Daniels. That was my favorite. I was walking down the street to a restaurant and as God as my witness this is what happened: along came a duck. This duck was just walking down the street towards me and I was walking towards this duck. We were approaching each other. There was nobody around. I looked at this duck, and it looked at me. That duck did not get out of the way – I had to go around the duck. It just kept on going and it struck me as very odd. Where did it come from and where was it going? A little further up I came to the restaurant and I went inside and said, "I want one of your best steaks and put a bottle of Jack Daniels on the table. I want to work with it."

I managed to hitchhike back to New York. I got to midtown and took a cab over the 59th Street Bridge to Long Island City. I got in to see Mom. She was glad to see me. I was glad to see her. We had a long talk and I helped her out with some money and spent the next couple of days doing nothing. I was trying to figure out where I was going to go and what I was going to do.

When I came out of the Army at that point, I was looking for a job and had a tough time. I didn't have an education, I didn't have a background, and I really didn't know where to go, so I figured, let me take a shot at this thing.

I called Smitty up and he told me to go down to the Chantilly Club on 1313th Street and he said to say goodbye to everybody. He said, "These two guys will walk in, they will say hello to you – you'll know who they are. They will say that they are going to make a trip to Panama and you'll leave with them. That's it. Once you are in with them, you don't get out." I said, "Just like that?" He said, "Just like that." So, what the hell do I have to lose? I was going no place. Three hundred a week sounded pretty good to me.

I went down to the Chantilly Club – it was on 13th Street, off 6th Avenue at that time – got there early. I figured, "Jeeze, I am going to be gone. Who do I have to say goodbye to?" So I went to the phone booth, and I called my good friend John Metelski, who was the Sales Export Manager at Pfizer Chemicals at that time. (His name will keep coming up in my life, as we go along).

I said to John, "Hello John, how are you?" He said, "Who's this?" I said, "Don't you recognize my voice?" He said, "It sounds like Bill Otto." I said "That's who it is." And we talked. He said, "God Bless you Bill, I haven't seen or heard from you in so long. I often think about you and wonder what you are doing." I said, "John, I am down at the Chantilly Club phone booth and I am going to meet a couple of guys and we are going down to Panama to take over the shrimp industry." Well, he knew that I knew of some of the situations with people before, and he says, "Bill, don't get back into that nonsense again. You got out of that a long time ago. Stay out of it." I said, "John to tell you the truth, two guys just came in and they are sitting at the bar." He said, "How far are you from the bar?" I said, "About twelve feet – over at the phone booth." He said, "Can you get out?" I said, "Well, I would have to bend down, tip toe, and walk out. I mean, I would have to bend all the way down to get the hell out of here." He said, "Do it Bill. Get a cab and meet me up at the Stork Club uptown and we'll have a drink and we'll talk. I'll get you something." Well, I bent all the way down, and these guys weren't looking at me; they were busy at the bar and I managed to get out. Just as I got out a cab came past and I jumped in. This cab took me to the Stork Club and inside was John Metelski at the bar. Well, we had a few scotch and sodas, and we talked, and we talked. We drank. We wound up drinking all night.

We went to the Sheridan Hotel – at that time it was on 33rd Street. They used to have a massage place there where you could get a massage, and then you could go to sleep and sleep it off. That is exactly what we did.

The next day he said, "Bill, get yourself straightened out and come up to the office and see me. I am going to make a couple of calls." Well, he called one of the top people at Philips Petroleum to see if he could get me a spot over there. They were on 42nd Street, if I remember right. I went over to see them, but they were, well, it's not that they were snobbish; it's just that I wasn't qualified. They wanted an engineer to handle the work. So I told John, "John, I don't fit into that." He said, "Let me see what else I have for you."

He put me in touch with a man by the name of C.C. Wong who was a very well-known, very powerful man in Formosa. He said that he could get me something down there; but again, it would be well, not so much strong-arm work, but enforcement work. I said to myself, "Hell, I am back to where I started from." So, I said, "John, let me try some of the agencies and see what I can do." He said, "Well, if you are going to try some of the agencies, go to the top one – Maud Lenox, over in Rockefeller Center. Give them a shot. See what they can do for you."

I went over to Crawfords. At that time you used to be able to get two pairs of pants with a suit jacket for $29. I got some shirts and ties, got myself fixed up, and started going around to the different agencies looking for a job.

Well, I was going around to these different agencies and I figured, "Hell, if I am going to look for a top job, let me go to a top agency." I went to the Maud Lennox Agency in Rockefeller Center. This was a very classy outfit. I walked in, filled out an application, the woman called me in and said, "You know, Mr. Otto, you don't have a college education and you don't have too much of a background. It's going to be difficult placing you." I said, "Well, try to get me something that I can fit into or that I can adjust to. I am not afraid to work. I am not afraid to talk to people. Try to give me a shot at something." She said, "You know, there is an interesting job that we have not been able to fill. I don't know whether or not you can sell yourself, but let me see what I can do.'"

She got on the phone, called this man up and said, "I have a young man here. He is not an engineer. I know you are looking for an engineer, but we don't have one, and I think perhaps maybe you could work with him. Do you want to meet and you can talk to him?" He said, "Fine, send him over." So, she sent me over to the Harvard Club on 44th Street.

I met the Division Manager, Mr. Ed Baker – a very classy Englishman of the Quaker State Oil Company. He met me and we talked and then he said, "C'mon, let's have lunch." We had lunch, talked some more. Three hours later, he said, "Bill, I am going to give you a chance. I think you can do it. But, I want you to get familiar with the products, work out of Oil City for a while, and see how the oil comes out of the ground, so you know what you are talking about. Let's give it a shot."

Well I spent a month at that. He gave me a car, a nice new Ford. I came home with the new Ford and mom was tickled to death. She said, "Boy, that's great, Son." Then I was dressed pretty nice – I was doing good. I got a salary, I got expenses and I traveled all over New Jersey, Pennsylvania, New York, and Long Island as an oil refinery man.

I will give you a typical example of how it went. I pulled up to a Buick dealer – they were using the Quaker State products. I walked in with cards my company printed up and I introduced myself. "Hello, I am Mr. Otto from the oil refinery." He said, "Boy, Mr. Otto, am I glad to see you. We have a terrible problem with our hypoid gears. We don't know what to do and how to get them to run smoothly to stop them from burning up. We have tried the different greases and oils, but it hasn't worked out right."

Now, here was a question that I did not have the slightest idea of how to answer. I did not have the slightest idea of what a hypoid gear was. So, now I had to back off. I said, "Listen, Tom, I'll tell you what. Call me Bill. I have to make four stops today. I am going to make the stops, but I am going to schedule you for tomorrow for lunch and we can take these things apart." He said "that would be great." I said, "You pick out the restaurant, expenses on me, and we'll have lunch."

I needed to get back to the hotel where I was staying. Well, I got back, got on the phone with Oil City, and I got a hold of one of their engineers. He told me to go to catalog gears, pages so and so, and it referred to a hypoid gear. They used to have stenographers in the hotels in them days, so I called down, and she came upstairs. I asked her to confine everything I was going to dictate to her on a small little card. And that is exactly what she did. She took the information down, and printed it out on a small, little card, nice and neat. I had that, took care of her, and the next day I was off again.

Well, I made it my business to get to the Buick dealer about a quarter to twelve, and I walked in. "Hello, Tom." He said, "Hi, Bill. Good to see you. I am glad you came over. I got a great restaurant picked out." I said, "Let's go." So we went to the restaurant, had a few drinks, relaxed and talked about generalities. And then, I said to him, "I have to run to the bathroom."

I ran to the bathroom and took out this card and reviewed what it said to do with hypoid gear, and now I had it down in my mind. I went back to the table and said, "Tom, I almost forgot. We had some problems the other day, what was it about? You were talking about a hypoid gear, I think?" And, Tom said, "Oh, I am glad you brought that up. I was having such a good time, I forgot all about it. Yes, we've got a terrible problem with the hypoid gears. I'm afraid I'm burning them out, I'm afraid I'm not using the right type of grease, and I don't know what to do." So I said, "Tom, I'll tell you what. Quaker State Oil has what they call sulfur-chlorinated grease and it has a tremendous ratio of 9 x 1 attaching to the gears and I would highly recommend that for your problem. It's not expensive. Give it a try on a couple of them. I think it will solve your problem with the hypoid gears." He said, "Gee, that's great Bill. Could you send me a small drum of it so I can try it out? I said, "I'll send you a thirty gallon drum. Try it out and see what you think. If you like it we can always order more." He said, "Gee that's great." And then we finished off our lunch, I took him back to the showroom and said goodbye.

I was off again to the next stop. When I was in Pennsylvania, I was snowed in at a diner in Allentown and I wound up sleeping in the end-curved booth with Arlene, the waitress. We had a lot of fun.

I got into trouble a couple of times because when you are on the road a lot, you're all by yourself and you get lonely. I usually found that the best place to go to was the local firehouses. They always had dances in them days. You could go to the local firehouse and walk in and you could always pick up someone to dance with and have a good time with, but you had to be a little careful. Those were interesting times.

There was one man that took me around in Pennsylvania. His name was Gustafson. He was the oldest Quaker State Representative they had on the road. At that time, it was what was classified as old. He must have been about 70 years old and today, 70 is nothing. But I can remember him taking me around in Pennsylvania. He was known all over Pennsylvania.

The two things I remember about him. One was the local whorehouses. This guy knew everybody. He knew the madams. They would see him and smile when he came in – he had a great reputation. Then I went along with him and we had some fun. Then, the second thing that I remember is that he had great hands. We came to a stream and he said, "Hold it, Bill. I want to show you something." Then he took me down to the stream and said, "There are trout in that stream." I said, "Gus, I don't see any trout in that stream." He said, "I'm telling you Bill, there are trout in that stream. Now, you just stay where you are. Don't come near the stream." He would walk over to the stream, slip his hands into the water and pop up a trout. I said, "For God's sake, how the hell did you do that?" He said, "They hide out on the shore line and they lay in there. If you don't approach them fast and scare them, they are so nice and pleasant. You just have to caress them, and let them know, just like we caress the women in the whore house. It's the same thing – you have to handle them nice like that."

Well, we had a good time with Quaker State Oil and I spent three years there. I can remember in Allentown, Pennsylvania and the head of the Chamber of Commerce asked me, "Can we do something about getting industry into the area?" The poverty was so bad in that area at that time. The coal mines were closed and people were out of work.

A fellow by the name of John L. Louis, with the big eyebrows, he was the head of the Coal Miners Union. A heartless bastard, but I guess he had to be in those times. He was constantly fighting with the President, Franklin Roosevelt. The strip mines were having a difficult time, the shaft mines were having a difficult time, and there just wasn't any work to be had in those areas. He asked me if I could get some industry into the area and I said, "I really don't think that I can. I don't know what I can do to help you."

He took me to a couple of homes and showed me how tough things were and how bad things were with these people. I said, "God, it's terrible, but I don't know what I can do for you."

One of the women showed me into the second floor of her old house. She said her husband was trying to do some work, trying to make a few bucks for the house, and the union men came in and they threw him out the window. She showed me where he landed down below on the concrete. I don't know whether he died or what. But that's how things were in them days. People were out there scraping out coal to keep their houses warm. There was no work, little food in the stores, and it was tough times in them days. Very few people would understand what those times were like.

It stayed in my mind, the poverty. Poverty always seemed to stay close to me. Every time I saw it, I always remembered it.

Chapter Five

"Off the Road"

I stayed with Quaker State Oil and then, to tell you the truth, I got tired of traveling all over the place.

Before I found Quaker State Oil I came across a man by the name of Ed Singleton, who ran the NY Floor Finishing Company which at that time was on 18 East 41st Street. He told me if I didn't find what I wanted to come back to him and have a shot at being a salesman.

After three years I went back to Ed Singleton and I said, "Ed, is that job still open for me to stay in New York as a salesman and sell cleaning and floor waxing and all that stuff?" He said, "Yes, Bill, I could really use you." I said, "Okay. I am going to quit my job with Quaker State Oil and I am going to come and work for you."

That was a big jump because I had a solid income, a nice job, and a good car. Before I get off the subject of the cars, let me just tell you one thing: I had to make a trip up to Albany. When I made the trip up to Albany the idea was for me to come back from Albany, back to New York, at a break neck speed. Well, I was doing 90 – 95 miles an hour and in them days that was a lot of speed. I was going like hell. The idea was for me to get stopped by the police and then to tell them that, "I couldn't help it. I put Quaker State Oil in my car and I could not hold it back." That was the whole idea. Well, I tell you. I drove all the way down from Albany to New York, I made it in record time, and *I never got stopped*. I was so disappointed. Here was the one time I wanted to get arrested and I didn't.

Well, getting back to Quaker State Oil, I called Ed Baker, and I said, "Ed, I am thinking seriously of resigning." He said, "Oh, Bill, don't do that. You're not an engineer, but we have high hopes for you. You have done a tremendous job and you are well liked and we want you to stay on. We have some good ideas for you in the future. You have to stay with us, Bill." I said, "Ed, I am tired of being on the road all the time. I am tired of sleeping in the hotels and getting into trouble, and all the problems that come up with that idea. I am going to take a shot a New York and try that out."

We stayed on the phone for three hours. He was trying his best to get me to stay and I don't know what would have happened if I had stayed. Maybe I would have been one of the top executives. Anyway, I decided that I was going to make a move and I left and went to work for the New York Floor Finishing Company on 18 East 41st Street.

My job at the New York Floor Finishing Company was to go out and get accounts, schedule them, and then have Oley, who was a Swedish fellow, set up the schedule for the men to go out and do the cleaning, and waxing. That was basically what we did – cleaning and waxing. But, that turned out to be a very good business.

What I would do was go into a building and sometimes I would talk to the superintendent and make a deal with him, or sometimes I would talk to the starter and make a deal with him. I would get the "leads" in the building of the tenants who were having trouble with the floor waxing. In them days, most of the people had tile floors and they required to have the floors cleaned and waxed at least once a month – weekly if it was the elevator lobbies or corridors. When you think of the thousands and thousands of square feet of tile in the Manhattan area, there was a hell of a demand for this.

I would go into a building, pick a tenant, go upstairs and say hello, and introduce myself. Most times you would ask for the office manager, or the purchasing agent. If you got a chance, you were able to go inside and talk to them and explain the fact that you were from the New York Floor Finishing Company, a very prestigious outfit, and you had a fine group of men and very competitive prices.

Sometimes you were able to find out what prices they were paying, and then you could undercut them and bring the men in and get the job. A lot of times I would just approach them hopefully and just say, "Listen I don't know what you are paying, but I'll do better." They would give me a price and I would say, "Let me look at the bill." Then they would show me the bill and if the bill was $350/month I would say, "Alright, we will do it for $300 a month." We were still making a good profit. In them days you didn't have a big union headache like you do today.

I kept going around to the different buildings. For example, I went into 250 Park. I didn't have anything in there, but by the time I finished I had about 80% of the building. I went in to 342 Madison and I had just about all the tenants in the building.

I was scattering all over the place. I had accounts like ABEX Corporation and Link-Belt. I had accounts in 530 Fifth Avenue and 230 Park. In 250 Park there was U.S. Industries and St. Joseph's Lead.

One of the days I was in 250 Park, the starter said to me, "Hey, Bill, guess who is in the building?" I said, "Who?" He said, "Jimmy Hoffa." I said, "Jimmy Hoffa, are you sure?" He said, "Sure. I know Jimmy Hoffa and what he looks like. He's up on the eleventh floor." I said, "Where?" He said, "In a company called Greenberg." I didn't know what the hell they did – some public relations work I think. Well, I was going through the building and I was on the tenth floor and I noticed the elevator was coming down and who do I get in the elevator with but Jimmy Hoffa. I looked at him and I was very impressed with the man. In fact, I even said to him, "Mr. Hoffa, I have always been impressed with you. You have been a tough fighter and a tough leader. Can you give a young guy like me any pearls of wisdom?" He looked at me and he just said, "Kid, you gotta do what you gotta do." And that was all he said. He got out of the elevator when we got to the main floor. I thought, "That's a hell of a strong statement." It meant a lot. And, in real life, when you get down to it, "you gotta do what you gotta do."

I have an old antique pewter lamp that I got from a very old, dear, wonderful friend, Albert Cornewal, of Abex Corporation. No words could describe this man – he was just a beautiful human being. The lamp had in old Latin, "Vivivo et Armis." For the longest time I never knew what it meant. One day Father Carey, a Jesuit priest, came up to the office. We were having a cup of coffee and I said to him, "Father, can you make this out? What does it mean?" He read it, and he said, "You go through life by force." And I said, "Boy that is a strong statement." I still have the lamp. I also still have the lion that Al gave me on a piece of marble.

Al was one hell of a guy. I could tell you stories about him and me all day long, but I'll just give you a few. Al and I always used to have a joke for each other when we met. We had lunch at least once every week at a different place. One week he would pay, next week I would pay. I can recall us standing on the corner of 44th Street and 5th Avenue, and I said, "Al, I gotta tell you this joke." So, we stopped right by the bank, and I told him about this Italian guy who was working on a construction crew with a chainsaw. It slipped and cut his arm off – his right arm, right by the elbow. He grabbed the arm, and ran into the building. There was a doctor there and he said, "Doctor! Doctor! You gotta sew my arm back on!" And the doctor looked at him and said, "It'll cost you $1,500." He said, "$1,500?!" So he ran out, ran to the next building, which wasn't as nice, but it had a doctor. He said, "Doctor! You gotta sew my arm on! How much will it cost?" The doctor said, "$200." He said, "Do it!" So now he had his arm sewn on, went down the block, saw the first doctor, and he said, "Hey doctor, remember me? You wanted to charge me $1,500 to sew my arm on. Well, I had it done for $200!" And he gave him the Old Italian expression, with the hand over the elbow, and said, "So fuck you!" and with that his arm flew up in the air! Al and I were on that corner laughing. He was such a great guy.

Another time, it was his birthday and I wanted to do something special. My accountant, Martin Hershey, took care of a lot of night clubs. A new place opened up on 55th Street between 2nd and 3rd Avenue. It was called The Crystal Room. I said to Marty, "I want to throw a nice luncheon for my friend Al Cornewal." So he said, "We'll set it up at The Crystal Room." We took a cab over, and I had the driver go past the converted house where The Crystal Room was, about three houses down. We got out, and I said, "Come on, Al!" And we walked back, nice and easy, to The Crystal Room, which had a small little awning outside, and two steps down. We opened up the door and walked in. The first thing we saw was the hat-check girl. She was completely nude. And was she built. Al stood there and didn't know what to say. I said, "Check your hat and coat, Al." With that, a hostess came over with just a little tiny apron on. And she said, "Are you Mr. Otto?" I said, "Yes." She said, "We have your table ready." As we were going down to the stage, our table was right up front by the stage. On my right side we passed Mayor Impelleteri and Sammy

Salerno – old friends. We got down to the stage and there's Marty and his friend, and we sat out facing the stage. Well, the girls knew it was Al's birthday, so when the music went on, the girls came out with nothing on, and then did a number in front of Al. I only wish that I had a camera to take pictures of the expressions on his face. That was one hell of a lunch.

There was one other time worth mentioning, when I took Al to the Playboy Club up on 59th street. We were both at the table eating, having a drink, and the waitress on Al's left dropped the bill. She bent down to pick it up, and I motioned to Al to look on his left. All he sees is the bunny with her rear end sticking up with her little tail. Well, Al started to choke, and choke, and it scared the hell out of us. A guy came over and grabbed him from behind, lifted him up, and he came out of it. That was one scary experience.

There was another great guy by the name of Owen Cottle. He was a hell of guy, too. He was the treasurer of the ABEX Corporation. He had a budget of $200 million to work with.

Anyway, I kept going around, getting the business. It got to the point where I was bringing so much business that I was making a salary and a 5% commission. Well, Ed had a tough time paying me because I was bringing in so much business that he couldn't take care of the accounts, and well, he couldn't take care of it all. So, I said to myself, "Jeeze, this has got to be something worthwhile. Maybe I'll take a shot at this myself." So, I went and I got a name incorporated. It didn't cost me much – I think it cost me $8.00. It was called U.S. Cleaning Company.

I liked the name. It sounded impressive. I got the stationary, but I didn't have an office or any equipment. So I thought I'd figure something out. I was down at 11th and Broadway and I said to John Metelski, "Let's have a drink together, my last buck." So, he met me down there, and I said to him, "John, I am going into the cleaning business by myself. I am going to take a shot at being the boss." He said, "Good for you, Bill." I said, "This is my last buck, and I am going to buy us two beers." He said, "No. You take that buck and put it away and never spend it. I am buying the beers." Well, I've got that buck and it has been on my desk. In fact, I had it embossed in plastic and it is still here with me. That was in 1957.

From there I took the subway uptown, and went into a building by 342 Madison. Up on the ninth floor was a paint company. As a representative of the New York Floor Finishing Company I went around and I had introduced myself. There was a fellow by the name of Morris Skelly. Morris was a little Jewish man who worked his ass off and always tried to make a dollar and take care of his family. He was a beautiful, beautiful man. I'll never forget Morris. His company was called Skelly Paint Company. Well, Morris had two offices: one that he used and one that was empty. So, I went and approached him and I said, "Morris, I would like to out rent the office next to you. How much would you want for a month?" He said, "How about thirty-five dollars?" I said, "That's sounds pretty good. But Morris, I need a little help." He said, "What's that Bill?" I said, "I need you to give me six months free." He said, "Six months rent-free? I think I could manage that. It's been lying there empty; it would be good to have somebody next door to me. It would be good to see you get started and maybe you'll make a success of your business. You work hard, you'll be alright." I said, "Morris, I need one more favor." He said, "What's that Bill?" I said, "I need to borrow five hundred dollars from you and I'll pay you back with interest in six months." He said, "Wait a minute Bill. First you want the office, and then you want six months free. Are you going to pay me that rent in six months?" I said, "I'll make it up to you Morris. I am a man of my word. You are just going to have to live with that. But I need the five hundred dollars because I have to buy some equipment. I need to buy a little used desk, too." Morris said, "With that kind of drive you'll be successful. You got it."

That's how I got started in the cleaning business. I had a little office, bought a used scrubbing machine, a bucket, a wringer, some finish, some stripper, and some pads – everything I needed. I got the equipment and I got the office. Now, all I had to do was get some business.

Well, in the course of going around with the New York Floor Finishing Company, I made some contacts with some people. I had a pretty good idea of some of the people who I did not swing over to the New York Floor Finishing Company and I started pressing them for the business. The first big account I got was Zurich Insurance Company, down on 110 William Street.

Now, I didn't have a car. So what do I do? I went down and I approached Gus, the manager. He said, "Bill we are moving into this whole new set up. It is 23,000 square feet. I have to have the whole place ready for when they come in Monday morning." I said, "You do, huh? I will have my men here and they will have everything in shape. They will have it all ready for you." This was Friday.

I went back to the office, changed my clothes, and took the subway downtown. I brought all the equipment upstairs. Now that's a ticklish thing, taking all that equipment onto the subway. You have to take your buckets, your stripper, and your wax, and you have to tie it all on to a scrubbing machine. Then you have to roll it into the subway and down the streets, and it is not an easy task. Anyway, I managed to get the equipment down there. There was a subway stop right at the corner of the building. So I was able to take the equipment from the subway right up into the building. I told the security guard I was bringing the equipment into the building and so forth.

National Cleaning Company had the whole building except for Zurich Insurance Company. They weren't aware of the fact that this guy Gus didn't like the National Cleaning Company and he was anxious to give me the business, which he did. We signed the contract. I was supposed to do it every month and I got $325/month for it. Now, $325 in them days was a lot of money. Today it would be equivalent to maybe $3,000. It was a nice job, so I couldn't turn it down.

Meanwhile I got on the phone Friday night, called my brother-in-law, Pete, and asked if he could help me. He couldn't help me. He was busy. I called my brother. He couldn't help me. He wasn't around. I didn't know who I could get to help me. First of all, I didn't have any money to pay anyone – I was a little tight on cash. But, I started doing the job. You know, after construction you got debris and garbage. You've got to sweep the floor. Then you've got to scrub the scuff marks and get the floor clean. Then you've got to put down finish. Sometimes you have to put down a double coat on the corridors to try to make it blend in. You have to swing that mop back and forth, open it up and flange it out so that it covers the ground. Fortunately, I could run the scrubbing machine with one hand and I would have a cup of coffee in the other, so it didn't bother me using the machine. But getting that finish on the floor, that takes time and that takes effort. I worked all day Saturday until late at night, slept over, and all day Sunday. Well, I finished that job, at about three o'clock Monday morning. It was seven floors and about 23,000 square feet. Anybody who has worked hard knows what I went through. I went back uptown, washed myself up, changed and put my suit on. I went downstairs to Chock Full O' Nuts, got myself a cup of coffee and a couple of donuts, and took the subway back downtown to Zurich Insurance Company.

I walked in there at 8:30 in the morning and I said, "Gus, how did the boys do?" He said, "Jesus, Bill, they did some hell of a job. The place really looks beautiful. I am really pleased. I am glad that we got you guys." I said, "Well, this is the kind of service that you will get all the time." He said, "Get me the bill right away; I'll get you a check right away." So I got him the bill and he cut me a check and I was in business. That's how I started out.

There were a couple of guys in Staten Island. One was a fellow by the name of George Francis, and the other by the name of Carl. First I hired George Francis – had him on the payroll. I was giving him $65/week, which was a good salary. He was an experienced man. He knew how to run the machines and everything else. He was clean cut and he was a pleasure to have around. The only thing was that he drank coffee. Boy he would drink about 14 – 15 cups a day! We brought his buddy in to work from Staten Island, and that was Carl. That's two of them. Now I had two men on the payroll! And I started.

I started getting accounts. Then I hired another man and then another man. I hired five men. Then Morris Skelly saw the men coming in and out and he said, "Bill, you are going to make it. I see what you are doing. You are going to be alright." Well, it got to the point where I started doing very well and I needed a bigger office. I said, "Morris I need a bigger office, so I'm squaring up with you." Just as soon as I squared up with him, God rest his soul, he was coming up the subway steps carrying a TV for his family. He got a heart attack and dropped dead. Right there on the subway at the top of the stairs. I was heart broken. I miss that guy. He was a wonderful man.

Anyway, I went on from there and I took another office on the seventh floor, opened that up, and started a new business. Hired a girl – she worked in the office. The girl was named Diane Bergmanson. Diane was not only a beautiful girl, but a tough piece of work. She was Swedish and Armenian. She had something about her. Nobody fooled her and nobody gave her a hard time. She knew what she wanted and what she stood for. I can remember the union guys giving her a hard time later in life and I can remember her saying to them, "Shut the fuck up and don't tell me what to do. Who the hell do you think you're talking to?" They backed off. They didn't know what to say to a woman who was talking this tough to them. She handled things great. She was great in the office. She kept the records in shape and the books in order. She was a blessing, boy believe me.

Chapter Six

"It's Who You Know"

I had a little problem. The National Cleaning Contractors had the whole building, except for The Zurich Insurance Company. National was run and controlled by M. S. I don't care if he is alive today and if he hears this, but he was the most miserable son of a bitch you ever want to know. This was a piece of garbage. Now, I got a call from Gus at the Zurich Insurance, "Bill, what happened to the men?" "What do mean what happened to the men?" He said, "Nobody showed up last night to do the job and we found this bucket and a mop over by the elevator." "You've got to be kidding." "No." I said, "I am coming right down." So, I jumped on the subway and I got down there and the job wasn't done. It was a mess.

I called up one of my men, George Francis, "George, what the hell is going on here?" "Bill, last night we got a call telling us to get off the premises. We didn't know what that meant. We had a visit from a man by the name of Mr. S and a man by the name of McGee. Mr. S was nasty enough, but McGee was almost bigger than you, Bill, and he seemed like a rough bastard. He said he was from the Union. He told us, 'You guys got twenty minutes to clean up this shit and get out of here or we are going to throw you through the window.' Well, he kicked over buckets and threw mops around and he scared the hell out of us. We got off the premises and we left." I said, "For Christ sakes, why didn't you call me and tell me what was going on?" "Bill, we just went home. We were disgusted and tired and we just went home. I am sorry that we didn't call you. We should have called you." "Certainly you should have called me and told me what the hell was going on so I would know what to do." Well, that really pissed me off. I was really aggravated.

I went up to National Cleaning Company and couldn't find Mr. S. They said he wasn't coming in today. I went up to the Union Hall at 57th Street – at that time it was called 32J. At the reception desk I said, "I want to see Mr. McGee."

The receptionist said, "Do you have an appointment?" I said, "No, I do not have an appointment. And I would like to see Mr. Perry." She said, "That's my boss. Who are you?" I said, "Never mind who I am. I want to see McGee or I want to see Perry. I want to see somebody here and I am not leaving until I do." She said, "You're not going any place." I said, "I'm not, huh?"

She had a reception door – the kind that you put your finger underneath and click with your finger and open up the door. Well, my foot opened up that door and I could see the private office in the back on the right side there. I just ran into and smashed that goddamned door. Nobody was there. Then, I figured they're all inside in his office – Perry's office. Well, that door opened up nice and easy with my foot. I went inside and he wasn't there. Now I had nobody inside and I felt like a goddamned fool, but I was really pissed and I was looking for some action. So I came outside and I said, "You tell that fucking Perry and that cock-sucking McGee that if they ever come near my men again I'll break their fucking heads!"

I was really pissed. And with this I needed to make an impression, so I started throwing a few typewriters around. There must have been twelve or fourteen people in the office. Everyone was scared to death because they thought I was crazy. I was a big guy anyway and usually people didn't bother me. So, I threw the typewriters around and said, "Tell those fucking bums if they come near my men again, I am going to break their goddamned heads."

Everybody was scared to death. Nobody moved. I left, and went back to the office at 342 Madison. That afternoon I got a call. Ed Singleton, from the New York Floor Finishing Company called me. He said to me, "Jesus Christ, Bill, what the hell did you do?" I said, "What do you mean, what did I do?" He said, "The word is out that Perry is going to knock you off. He is so fucking aggravated with what you did. You went to his office and broke a couple of doors and threw some typewriters around, and all that shit? Well, now he's gonna kill you." I said, "Is it serious, Ed?" He said, "Bill, this guy don't fool around. This is a top union guy and he don't give a shit for nobody. He's got a lot of friends. He could be talking to you and the next minute somebody else does it to you." I asked, "It looks bad, huh?" He said, "C'mon downstairs. Let's have some coffee."

I met him downstairs at Chock Full O'Nuts we had a coffee. He said, "Bill, you're in big trouble. You can't even go up there. If you go up there then you're liable not get out of there alive. You have got a big problem on your hands." I said, "That's great. Now, what the hell do I do?" Then I said, "Ed, I'll figure something out."

I stopped on 16th Street at the St. Francis Xavier School down there and I saw Father Phil Carey. Phil Carey was involved with Father Courigan on making the picture *On the Waterfront* with Marlon Brando. In fact, I still have the cross from Father Carey hanging from the lamp on my desk.

I stopped in to see Father Carey. Father Carey was instrumental in saving my life. A long time ago I had given him an etching on canvas that was in the family. It was titled "Veronica's Veil" and it was of the crucifixion of Christ, and Veronica, who took a towel and wiped Christ's face, which left His imprint on the towel. This etching on canvas had the Pope's seal on it. It was a very valuable piece, and the only thing I had that was worth while, but I felt that Father Carey deserved it. Since then I've tried to trace it back to see where that picture has gone. It's disappeared. Somebody's got it. It would have been nice to donate to St. Patrick's Cathedral and put it on the left side where they have the copy of the "Veronica's Veil".

Well, I went in to see Father Carey and he said, "Hello Bill. How are you?" I started talking to him. I told him what happened with Zurich Insurance Company and that I made a little mess in the union hall. Father Carey said to me, "Bill, you are in big trouble. Where were you going when you came in here?" I said, "I was on my way downtown to see the ex-Governor Dewey. He said, "What are you going to him for?" I said, "I figured I'd get some help from him and he'd pull the mob off me."

You can't go to see Dewey.

What do I do now?" He said, "Let me think for a minute. Let me think." After a while, he said, "I am going to make a call, Bill. I don't know if it is going to do any good, but I am going to make a call. Let me see what I can d, just keep quiet."

Father Carey called Jim Earley. At that time, I didn't know who Jim Earley was, but I found out later that he was the *Irish Godfather*. He was a tough piece of work.. Jim made his reputation many years ago running liquor back from Canada, in tractor-trailers. Jim was the reason that Harry Helmsley was able to expand so much. Jim was his vice president and took care of all his problems. I mean *all* of his problems.

One of the guys Jim was associated with, which very few people know about, was a man by the name of Joe Kennedy. His son later became President of the United States. Joe Kennedy was very friendly with Jim Earley. They broke bread together.

They used Frank Costello to pick up the liquor and have it distributed to the different places. In fact, they used to have boats running them up and down the East River. This is why when you recall when Frank Costello getting into problems later on, they treated him very nicely. In fact, he didn't want his face to be shown, so they just showed his hands at Senator Kefauver's hearing. It was also understood that he would never be deported as long as there was a Kennedy alive. Well, that's another story.

Going back to Jim Early – Father Carey said to me, "Bill, he is up at 60 East 42nd Street, up on the 55th Floor. I want you to go up there and talk to him. Tell him the story and let's see what he can do. Meanwhile, I am going to call him and tell him a little bit about your background while you are on your way up. Get up there now."

I jumped into a cab and went uptown to the Lincoln Building at 42nd Street. I took the elevator up to the 55th Floor – Helmsley and Spear. I told the receptionist, "My name is Bill Otto. I am here to see Jim Earley." She said, "Yes, he is expecting you. Go all the way down to the end to that private office down there. Eileen is his secretary. She'll take you in." Well, I walked down and introduced myself to Eileen, a real Irish gal. She said, "Come on in." Then I went inside and got my first glimpse of the great Jim Earley.

Jim was about my size, but about thirty pounds heavier, mean-looking, and a tough piece of work. He said, "Sit down, kid." I sat down. He said, "You have got a great friend in Father Carey. I just had a long talk with him. He thinks the world of you. He wants me to see what I can do to help you. Let's discuss this problem and let's see where we are going to go from here."

I started to tell him what happened. I said, "Mr. Earley, I just went into the cleaning business and I am trying to make a living. It's not that easy. I'm having problems here and problems there. One of the big problems I had…" And with that, the phone rang. Eileen said, "Mr. Earley, it's Mr. Perry, do you want to take it?" He said, "Yes."

He was talking to Al Perry, the president of 32J Union on 57th street, and the guy that I just went up on. Mr. Earley said, "Just a minute, Al, just a minute." Then he covered the mouthpiece and he said to me, "Did you break the reception desk?" I shook my head and I said, "Yes." So he went back to talking to Al Perry and he said, "Is that right? Is that a fact? Just a minute I've got another call." Then he covered the mouthpiece and he said, "Did you break Al Perry's door?" I said, "Yeah." And, with that, I figured I was in big trouble. He went back to talking to Al Perry and he said, "What? C'mon for Christ's sake, he didn't do that, did he? Just a minute, Al, I got another call. Hold on a minute." And he once again covered the mouthpiece and he said, "Did you throw fucking typewriters up in the air?" And I said, "Yeah." He laughed. And he went back, took his hand off the phone, and he said, "I'll tell you what, Al. I know this kid, Bill Otto. In fact, he is sitting right across the desk from me and if he did all those things, he's my kind of guy. He's got a lot of balls to do that, to pull that off. I like this kid. He makes a nice appearance. I think he is going to go places. I want you to do me a favor: lay off the kid. Drop everything. I will consider it a personal favor. Do you understand me, Al? I don't want nothing to happen to this kid. He comes under my wing. Yeah, I'll take care of it. Don't you worry about it. You just have a nice day, Al. Forget about it and we'll move on to other things. *Leave the kid alone.* Okay?"

He hung up the phone. He looked at me and he said, "Come out kid. Let's go have some lunch." We went to the Uptown Club, which was in the building, and we had some lunch and we talked. He asked me about my background. I told him that I didn't have a father. I told him where I came from: poverty, hard times. The fact that my mother's maiden name was "Walsh", an old Irish name, that didn't hurt because he was a rough Irishman. From that time on we became very close friends. Closer than friends. I was almost like his son. He was my size and we looked good together. I always dressed nice – he was never ashamed of me. I watched the way I spoke, watched the way I handled myself. With him I met a lot of people, people that you read about in the papers. He knew everybody. He was a hell of a guy. He was the great Jim Earley. Boy, do I miss him.

Jim's office was in the Lincoln Building. I went to see him all the time. In the course of doing this, I was going with this blonde girl, no sense in mentioning names, and we would meet in the cafeteria downstairs, and have our coffee and Danish. There was a dark haired girl in the next booth always there with another blonde fellow. One day, in the subway, I was coming into Grand Central, and this dark haired girl was in the same car with me. She looked at me and smiled. I smiled at her. I got out and she came over to me and I said, "Don't I know you from someplace?" She said, "Yes. We see each other in the cafeteria in the morning. I am with the blonde fellow and you are with the blonde girl." So I said, "Isn't that interesting. I'll tell you what. Tomorrow morning, let's let the two of them meet by themselves and the two of us will meet and have coffee." That was how it started.

That girl was Pauline. She was my Greek beauty. We started going out together. We met the families. She lived in Flushing with her sister, her sister's husband, and their two kids. The kids would ask me, "What should we call you? Should we call you Uncle Bill?" I would say, "No, no, I am not an uncle. Just call me Bill, plain Bill."

We went out for quite a while and I finally said to Pauline, "Look, I am really not interested in your family or how they feel, and I am really not interested in my family or how they feel. I think we should get married. I owe about $4,200 in debts. I don't know what you have in the way of cash." She said that she had $250. I said, "Let's take a shot. I intend to make a lot of money. I intend to see that you are very comfortable. I am a very hard worker, and I think I will be a very good husband." She agreed.

We rented an apartment in Bayside on 212th Street. It was a lovely little apartment with three and a half rooms. The rent was $94 a month. When we had the apartment I said, "Let's go up to Connecticut to get married." Heading down Northern Blvd, she said, "I don't have any flowers."

We stopped at a florist on Northern Boulevard. The cat in the florist just had kittens. I picked up a corsage for Pauline and the woman said, "Would you like a kitten?" I yelled out to Pauline, "Would you like a kitten?" She said, "Yes." So I said, "Okay, fine. We're going up to

Connecticut to get married. We'll pick it up on our way back." The woman said, "Fine, no problem."

We went up to Connecticut, got married and stayed at the Motel on the Mountain for two nights. That was our honeymoon. Then we came back to our apartment in Bayside.

On the way back we stopped off at the florist and picked up the kitten. We called the kitten Cleo. It was a beautiful little cat. We brought it up to our apartment and it became part of the family.

I said to Pauline, "Look, I don't want you working. I want you to stay home. Somehow I will make a living and we'll get by. Here's two dollars. I want you to go out and buy the silverware with that. You have five dollars to buy some dishes and pots and pans. You'll have to go scouting around see what bargains you can get." She did work for about a year and a half until we got on our feet.

We didn't have any furniture – we had suitcases. I can remember going out to the incinerator and finding an old vase that somebody threw out and boy that was a treasure. I brought that in and painted it and fixed it up. I can remember going down to Canal Street and buying metal cones and I bought wire and I made a hanging lamp out of that. We somehow managed to get by and started to develop the apartment.

Jim said, "How are you doing with the business?" I said, "I am having a tough time, Jim. We're getting there, but it's taking time." He said, "Look, there is an opening at Harry Helmsley's. The partner, a fellow by the name of Erwin Wilson, is putting up a building at 100 Church Street. How would you like the job as a night superintendent there? I can get you $135 a week." I said, "Wow." $135 a week in them days was big, big money. Guys who were president of a bank were only making $5,000 a year. And I was going to make $135 a week! I said, "I'll take it Jim." I went downtown and met the people.

I met Charlie Holmes and Bob Campbell, who was a hell of a guy. We went to work setting up 100 Church Street. We had, at that time, I think, almost 142 people there. Later we took over the immigration building behind it, and we had that as well. There were about 189 people I was responsible for every night. I had to lay out the schedules, lay out the program, see that the floors were maintained, scrubbed and waxed, and that the carpets were cleaned. I had to see that the general cleaning was done, that the women coming in were doing their job, and so forth. I covered about 1,400,000 square feet each night and earned my salary.

It was a very interesting job. I used to go down there and start at 4:30 p.m. and I would be down there until 1:30 in the morning. So that by the time I left there and went out to Bayside, it was about 2:30 a.m. Then I would be up again the next morning and start all over again at 7:30 a.m.

We started to expand. We wound up taking most of the work at 250 Park, most of the work at 342 Madison. We were into 230 Park, into 530 Fifth Avenue. We were downtown at the Zurich Insurance Company. We started to move around.

I was all over the place working very hard, and took many accounts. One of the buildings I was told to stay out of was 250 Park, and I went into it. I took over U.S. Industries, St. Joe's Lead, Sullivan and Cromwall the Law Firm, United Tanker and whatever else I could get. I must have taken over 80% of the business. Then I went across the street to 299 Park Avenue, which was another building I was told to stay out of. I got a big account there—three floors. It was called Norton Simon. In fact, when Norton Simon closed up later on, the manager said, "Bill is there anything you would like? We are getting rid of all the furniture." On Norton Simon's desk was a big piece of gold in a stone and a magnifying glass in front of it. And I said, "Yes. I'd like to have that piece." And so she gave it to me, and I have it to this day.

I started most of my work at 342 Madison where I had my office. I was in and out of that building all day long. 342 Madison was purchased by the Purdy Family for the Christian Science Organization, many years ago. These were two great gals and they ran a tight ship. They knew what they were doing and they were there all the time working hard and they kept the building in great shape. We had some fantastic tenants in that building.

One of the accounts that I took over was Harry Macklowe on the third floor. I can remember I was charging him $32 a month to clean and wax his floors, and he was having difficulty making the payments. He was working his ass off. I'd pass him on the way home sometimes at 9-10 o'clock at night and he'd still be working. He's a multi-billionaire today and he deserves it.

Down below on the 6th floor I had Victor Riesel. He was a newspaper reporter who was blinded over on Broadway by one of the mob. Stories like that were in the papers all the time. He was a nice guy. I used to stop in and sit and talk to him and there was always a man sitting on a couch on the right carrying a machine gun. He was assigned by the district attorney's office to protect Victor Riesel so nothing would happen to him. He was a little guy. His face was a little banged up from the acid they threw in his eyes. But, there were some great people in that building.

I took over American Break Shoe at 230 Park. Then the company swung over to 530 5th Avenue and I went along with them and took over the three floors they had there. There was another company called the Link Belt, I took them over too. I had a lot of great accounts and met a lot of interesting people.

At 530 5th Avenue American Break Shoe I met some great people there. One was the manager by the name of Al Cornewal who became one of my dearest friends. To this day I miss that man. I have his picture and I have his flag from his funeral in my bedroom (he was in the service). There was another great guy there too, Owen Cottle. Owen is still alive today, thank God, and I still talk to him. Great people. I don't think they make people like that anymore.

During the day I was making contacts for my cleaning business and getting new accounts. I was calling on everybody and laying out the schedules for my own men. At that time, I don't recall how many men I had but I must have had quite a few – ten or fifteen – and that was expanding. After I got my men lined up and squared away then I would head downtown and take over the crews at 100 Church Street and set them up. This is what I did for seven years.

It was a tough grind, but I can remember when they were building outside of 100 Church Street. They had these big pieces of granite, I would say they were about 2 feet by 4 feet, and I said to one of the men who was putting them on, "Jeeze, that would make a hell of a cocktail table." He said, "It certainly would." I said, "Do me a favor. Here is $5.00. One of them is going to disappear tonight. Don't make a stink." He said, "It's as good as done."

I got that piece of granite, but it was heavy as hell. How was I going to get it home? I called up the night manager at 230 Park Ave. His name was Sandy Mahr. He worked for Jim Earley too. I said, "Sandy, I've got this piece of granite and I want to get it home. Can you help me out?" He said,

"Sure Bill. I'll come down." He came down with a wagon and we loaded it in and we managed to get it home and that was the start of our first piece of furniture, really. Sandy was a hell of a guy and a rough piece of work.

I can remember him and I being in the bar at 37th Street and Lexington Avenue, and there was a wise guy at the end of the bar making a lot of noise. He was on the telephone screaming and hollering and the bar tender looked at Sandy, and Sandy gave him a look and went with his finger across his throat and pointed to the guy at the telephone booth. Sandy nice and quietly got up and walked over to the telephone booth. I don't know really what he did or how he did it but he hit this guy a shot, the guy got quiet and didn't move. He closed the telephone booth put a chair over in front so no one would use the booth. He came back over and sat down with me and I said to him, "What the hell did you do to that guy?" He said, "Bill, my job when I came out of the service was to get all the veteran mental patients that escaped from mental hospitals. I didn't carry a gun so I learned to use my hands. So I became very adapt at using my hands and straightening people out." And he did, he was very adapt, believe me when I tell you: he straightened that guy out.

Sandy's gone now. God bless him. I miss him. There was a little suspicion about how he died. But, nothing was ever done about investigating it. We sort of just let it pass. That's what happens in life. Things happen and you just let them pass.

After the granite table I got some wood and made a bookcase that we had on the wall. That came out pretty nice. Then little by little we started adding. I found a picture and we had it framed, or somebody would throw something out on 100 Church Street, and I would get it and bring it home. Gradually we put everything together.

Pauline became pregnant. We had Tina. She was a blessing, my little angel. We became concerned with the cat, because the cat was very attentive to me and we were concerned that the cat might take it out on Tina because of the affection I had for Tina, and the cat could sense it.

The doctor came over one time, examining Tina, and he suggested that we get rid of the cat. It was a shame, because this was the smartest cat I ever saw. We used to go out at night and we would put the cat into the bathroom and we would lock the door. Then when we came home I would open the front door and the cat would jump up into my chest and greet me. I would say to Pauline, "I thought we put the cat in the bathroom." She would say, "We did." I would say, "How is this cat getting out? It's hard to believe that it can get out that door. I'll tell you what. I am going to inside with Cleo and lay in the tub and take a bath and you call out to Cleo, 'Cleo, come and get your supper; come and eat, Cleo.'" Cleo would tear down the wall to get at this supper.

We closed the door and the cat was inside the bathroom with me and Pauline yelled out, "Come on Cleo, come and eat." Well, the cat jumped up on the toilet seat, jumped up on the tank behind it, got on the railing where the towel was, and the left paw would turn the knob, while the right paw somehow squeezed in and pushed the latch open and pushed the door open and dropped down.

I am sorry to this day that I did not take a movie of that because it's hard to believe that the cat was that smart to do that. But that cat did it. It was a very intelligent cat. Unfortunately, we had to get rid of the cat. The cat was heartbroken, but it was necessary.

We had our problems with Tina, and Pauline had a sense that she wanted to get Tina examined by another doctor. So, her sister had a doctor in Flushing, called Dr. Dilello. We went down there just for a casual examination. The doctor laid her out on the table and said, "What's the matter with her hips?" We said, "What do you mean, what's the matter with her hips?" He said, "There is something wrong with your daughter's hips. What does the report show?" We said, "What report? We don't have any report?" He said, "What about the doctor who is examining her now?" I said, "That's a Doctor in Bayside." He said, "Well, you have a problem here and we are going to need to take X-rays."

Tina had what they call "displacia of the hips" – the hipbone was not going into the socket properly and was off like a centimeter or something. Although it was nothing at that point, it would have become more noticeable as she got older and she would have walked with a little bit of limp. As she crawled she dragged one leg a little behind and it was cute, but as she gradually got older, she would have been a cripple.

Needless to say we were very upset by it and I went out to see thre Doctor.. His office was very crowded and the nurse said to me, "I'm sorry, Mr. Otto, but you are going to have to wait." I said, "No, I am not waiting. I want all of Tina's records. We are getting out of this office." Then I looked at the people in the reception room and said, "If you people are smart, you will do the same thing."

The Doctor came out and said, "What's all the excitement?" I said, "You have some hell of a nerve. What you did to my daughter – my daughter would have been crippled for life because we didn't realize what was going on. You didn't tell us what the problem was with our daughter's hip. We went to another doctor to get an examination, to find out that the X-rays showed she has displacia of the hip! You have been examining her for eight months and you didn't come up with anything like this. I want all my records. I am getting out of here now." He could tell I was very upset about the problem, so he gave me all the records. I said, "It doesn't make sense to be here. My daughter could have been crippled."

Thank God we got out. We went on from there. Meanwhile, about three or four weeks later we understand that the Doctor closed his office. He got such a bad reputation in the area. Where do you think he wound up? He wound up at Mt. Sinai Hospital on Fifth Avenue, teaching pediatrics. That was a hell of a twist. He nearly screwed up on one child that I know of, and how many others were there. Now, he is teaching pediatrics at Mt. Sinai!

Tina had a cast on and she used to walk like a duck – her legs were stretched straight out. She had a problem with that, especially on hot days, but little by little it got better. I remember Jim Earley saying to me he was upset about Tina having to wear that cast in the hot weather. He said, "You need an air conditioner for the house." I said, "I know we do Jim but we can't afford it." Jim told me, "Get a hold of Sandy Marr."

I called Sandy up and said, "Jim said that I should see if you can find an air conditioner for me that I can take to the house for my daughter, so that she can be cool in the apartment." He said, "Well, I've got some of these big console units. They look like a big radio or television set. How about one of them?" I said, "Well, how do they look?" He said, "They look beautiful. Take one of them out there." I said, "That sounds great. How are we going to get it out there?" He said, "I'll help you out." So we put it into the station wagon and boy, it was heavy. We got it out there to Bayside and took it up one step at a time – it was really heavy. I think that thing must have weighed almost four hundred pounds.

We finally got it up to the apartment and we got it inside, set it up in the apartment, plugged it in, and it didn't work! Well, what we didn't realize was that it was running on DC current and we had AC current in the Bayside apartment. Now what do we do? We made a deal with the superintendent that he could have it if he took it out. And, he took it out. He got a couple of his men and they got rid of it. Jim managed to get us a window unit. We had the window unit installed and it was nice and cool.

We had a nice apartment in Bayside. Good time there. I can remember one time when Pauline was pregnant, she said to me, "Would you go down and do the wash?" So, I went downstairs and I just poured the suds into the machine, and I poured the whole box of suds into the machine! I didn't realize that you are just supposed to put a small amount in. Well, if you could picture the whole basement, and this was a big basement, it was covered with suds. The machine popped open and water came out and the suds were all over the place. What a mess! I learned my lesson from doing the wash that time. We got it cleaned up and that was all right.

Pauline and would take Tina for a little walk over to the park on Sunday. One time, we have it on movies, Tina bent down and picked up a flower. She gave it to me and I put it in my lapel.

We would always walk to the park and to the market to do our shopping. Those were pleasant days.

Family Love

No matter what the future holds
Let's all hold on to each other

Chapter Seven

"Syosset and the Greeks"

Pauline was pregnant again. We had been there for a couple of years and we felt it was time to make a move. We got all our money together, as best as we could, and we scouted around and found a place out in Syosset. That was our first home. It cost us $21,600 for the home. Today the house is worth about $350,000.

It was a lovely little house. We worked hard on that and did a lot of repairs to get it the way we wanted it. When we bought it from these people, we didn't realize that they had a lot of different paint. They would paint the walls and the paint would fall down onto the floors and they would just move the carpets over the spots with the paint. We had to get the paint scraped off and the floors cleaned.

When my Son was born, we had a lot of problems because Pauline wasn't well. Yayia, Pauline's mother, came into the house and she helped us. She took care of my son and Tina. I was still working fifteen, sixteen hours a day trying to make money to get us on our feet, which we did.

At 100 Church Street, Ebasco Foreign Power had these terraces on either side of their office. They bought this beautiful furniture, from California. This was put out on the terraces in the summertime. Nobody would sit out there because it was too hot. In the winter, everyone sat inside. They took these beautiful tables and chairs and brought it all down to the basement. So now, with the house we had in Syosset, we needed furniture for the backyard. I had an idea. I contacted Mr.Grant, the CEO, and asked, "is it possible that I could buy some of that outdoor furniture that you had? I could use it for my house in Syosset." He said, "Why not? Go down and speak with the office manager. Tell him that you are interested in buying some."

I went down to speak to the office manager.

"How many pieces do you want?" I told him that I wanted two long tables and two round tables, a couple of long benches, and some chairs.

"Well, that's pretty expensive. What do you want to pay for it?"

"Well, it's just laying there and you're not using it – how about $135?"

"What? One of those chairs alone costs $135."

"I know, but they are not being used, they are just laying down here. Here is a chance for you to get some of it out."

"Not for a $135." I said "Okay, fine," and walked out.

A couple of days later I met Mr. Grant. He said, "How did you make out with the furniture?"

"I spoke to your office manager, and I made him an offer, but he felt that the offer wasn't high enough."

"Well, I'll tell you what. Give him a day or two and then ask him again."

"Thank you, Mr. Grant, I appreciate it." I knew that he was going to see the office manager on my behalf, and talk to him, which he did. The office manager said to me, "You got a hell of a deal here, Bill. $135 for that furniture, but that's the deal. You got it." That's how we got the patio furniture out in Syosset.

We were in Syosset for ten years. We fixed the place up with the shrubs. I can remember one time when Jim Earley was coming out I had just bought twenty plumosas. They were about four feet high. I knew that Jim was coming that afternoon. It was raining like hell that morning and I wanted to get everything done before he came over.

I lined up all twenty plumosas along side the curb, where I wanted them, all in a row like soldiers. Then I dug a hole for the first one, took that dirt and put it in a wheelbarrow and took it all the way down to the end where the last one was. I dropped the plumosas into the first hole, dug the dirt for the second hole and used that fill in for the first hole. I followed that pattern all the way down until I got to the end. When I finished the last one, I didn't have any dirt, but I did have some left in the wheelbarrow, so I just poured that in. It worked out great. In two hours, I actually planted twenty plumosas! I was very pleased with that job. I saw them recently and they must have been thirty feet high.

We had all kinds of dogs. One of them I named after a friend of mine, Sam. Sam and I used to go fishing all the time. He got a call from a guy at a gas station over on Queens Blvd. He said he had a little white puppy that had just been born. I said I was going to go over and take a look at it. I looked at it and I brought it home and Pauline looked at it and she said, "That dog is going to shed. It will be a headache." I said, "Well, we'll keep him outside." She said, "I think you ought to get rid of him." I said, "Well, I'll tell you what. We'll keep him for a couple of days and if you don't want him, I'll get rid of him."

I figured if you kept him for a couple of days, by that time you get attached to the dog, you know? And she did. We called the dog Sam. What happened was, my friend, Sam, came over the house one day and I called, "Sam, come here," and, he said, "What do you want?" and I said, "No, I wasn't calling you, I was calling the dog." He said, "What do you mean, you were calling the dog?" I said, "Well, we named the dog, Sam, after you." He said, "You've got to be kidding." Well, I'll tell you, he was so insulted that I named the dog after him that he got up and he walked out of the house. I never saw him again, except for one time later on when he said, "I'd like my sailfish back." He had given us a sailfish that I had put in the den in my house. So now he wanted it back. I had it wrapped up and ready for him. I didn't want to be there when he picked it up. He picked it up and he left. That was the last we saw of Sam. He and I were very close and he was a hell of a fisherman.

I can remember fishing with him off Block Island. We had a 53-foot boat and the boat kept coming out of the water. The Captain said, "Hold on. A storm's coming. We're going to have trouble." Well, that boat kept spinning. The prop would be out of the water and then would be back down again. Everybody was down below and they were sick as hell. I was getting sick. Sam was saying to me, "Bill, listen to me. I'll tell you what to do. Do you have any pound cake?"

"I have some coffee cake."

"Well, take the coffee cake and eat it." Boy, it's tough to get down when you are being banged around like that, but I did.

"Do you have any bananas left?"

"Yes, I have two good bananas."

"Get the bananas down, and get them into your stomach. Here's some coffee. Get that coffee down into your stomach and you'll be alright." And, sure enough I was. I ate the coffee cake, the two bananas and the coffee on top of that I was fine.

We lost a lot of the equipment – it was swept overboard. You couldn't go down below because there were eighteen or so men down below and they were throwing up all over the place and the smell and the stink was enough to make you sick anyway. We finally got home that day, it was an experience, but we had a good day. Block Island has always been a tough place to fish.

Later on I had my throat operated on. I had what was called a salivary gland that was becoming bad. I had to have that cut open and taken out. I needed a throat doctor. My other friend Sam – Sam Salerno – recommended a Dr. Shultz at the Roosevelt Hospital. He did the job on me. The nurses in the hospital said that he was very good with a knife. Sam said he took care of a lot of the boys. I used to kid everybody and say, "Boy, a lot of guys would love to cut my throat, and I had to pay a doctor to do it."

Sam was the guy who used to dance with Pauline at the Round Table Night Club. We were all there one night during the week with Jim Earley and his wife, Sammy and his girlfriend, Saul Lindner and his wife, and Pauline and I. We had a great time. The Round Table was a fun nightclub. Sammy would Jitterbug with Pauline. When we were getting ready to leave, we were all standing around the coat-room and this other couple joined in with us.

We said that we were going to Ruben's to eat. Well, this couple came right along with us and nothing was said. We started out as eight, but at Ruben's we were ten. This couple joined us and sat right in the middle. The night went on and we all talked and had a good time.

When the bill came, as usual, Jim Earley, the big Irish Godfather, picked up the tab. Outside, we were all saying goodnight. Some of us were going in different directions. The couple left. I turned and said to Sam, "You're friends seemed very nice." Sam said, "They're not my friends. I never saw them before. I thought they were friends of Saul and Mary." So, we asked Saul and Mary. They didn't know them either. They thought that they were friends of ours. It turns out that nobody knew who they were. They just freeloaded on our table. It was quite unusual because they were not aware of the influence that this group had. They were lucky that they got off for the night – had a free dinner – and we all laughed at it. Freeloaders. They had a lot of nerve. If this couple only knew who they were sitting with.

We had good times in Syosset. It was a little house, but very cozy and warm. We had a finished basement where we had a fireplace. We put a copper hood over the fireplace, which added a lot of charm. We also built a bar down there. We had good times and parties down there and at Christmas time, all the guys used to come over, and I'd bring out a bottle of whisky and some glasses, and we'd put the Christmas carols on, and they'd all help me decorate the outside of the house, and we had a great time.

We had a neighbor across the street. He was a sweetheart. His name was Tyle Hayden. He used to come over our house almost every Saturday and Sunday through the back door. He would say, "Willie, how are you doing?" We would sit and talk and have a drink. He would tell me about his day and the problems that he had. He was a good guy and I missed him when he died.

I lost a lot of people around that time. I got a call from John Metelski. He was telling me that he just bought this big house out in Spring Lake, New Jersey. He said, "I like that patio furniture you got, Bill." I said, "Let me see if I can get you some the same way." I went back to the manager at Ebasco Foreign Power. I said, "Look, do you still have another batch of that furniture laying there? Can I get that out and take care of that for you?" He said, "Yes." So I got that for John for $135 and he had all the furniture he needed for the house. But then, something happened with John. John had some problems, I don't know what they were, but he was having difficulty in business trying to make a living. Some men just don't get a spot where they can develop themselves. John had that problem. He wound up having trouble with his wife. He was gone for weeks – moved into a place in Bayside. They found his body. It was suicide. He had taken some kind of chemical. I don't know what the chemical was, but it bloated up his body and made it black. John lost his daughter in a terrible car accident, and he never got over it. He was a tough marine, but with all his business problems, and then the death of his daughter, I guess it drove him to suicide.

John was a hell of a guy. I can recall when My Son was being born, we went to the Flushing Hospital, and they examined Pauline and they said that there was a growth coming out from down below. They didn't know what it was and they were concerned about it. The doctor had to perform a caesarian operation and they came out to me and said, "Mr. Otto, is there anything we can do for you?" I said, "Yes. I need about three or four fingers of bourbon. I'm really having a tough time getting through this." Well, that nurse came back out with three, four fingers of bourbon for me, and I drank that, and it relaxed me a little bit.

Pauline was inside getting the operation, and then they came out and told me, "We have a choice. Your son may be blocking the passage for your wife and we may have to make a decision." I said, "What are you talking about a decision?" He said, "Well, we may have to make a decision on pulling the child out. It may save the child, and it may cost you your wife. What's the decision?" I said, "There is no decision. You save my wife. That's the most important thing. And we'll go on from there – you do what you can." Well, they were able. They had five doctors and they spent a lot of time working on her. They opened her up and took the boy out. He was premature but he was about 7lbs. 8oz, I think. He was a good size at that time. And they worked on Pauline. She had cancer of the bladder, and they cut out twenty percent of her bladder, sewed her up, and they came outside and told me what she had. I said, "Look, don't ever tell her that she has this. It will break her heart. Let's keep this to ourselves and let's not report it."

Well, John Metelski came over that night at the hospital to pick me up and take me out to dinner, and he said, "What are you upset about Bill?" and I told him what happened, and he said, "Alright Bill, look, let's keep it to ourselves. Nobody will ever know that Pauline had cancer." And no one knew for a long time – until My Son was about 17. We were going to see Dr. Khoury, the one who operated on her, and he said, "Well Pauline, all your cancer has cleared up." Pauline said to him, "What cancer?" The doctor looked at me and I said, "Doctor, no one has ever told her until now." He was sorry, but it was done. Anyway, it slipped out, and Pauline realized the fact that she was over it 16 years ago. She was able to live with it, and we went on from there. My Son grew. He got to be a big, strong, strapping boy, and Pauline was fine, and her bladder expanded enough to maintain itself so she didn't have a problem at a later date.

Then I had another good friend, Martin Hershey; he was our accountant, and he was some piece of work. Pauline used to do some work for him years ago, so she knew him. She said she needed a new accountant and thought he would be a good guy. I got him, and he was a hell of a guy. He had Polio problem with his leg. He used to drag one leg, come along, but what a hell of a man he was. A lot of good people I knew over the years.

I can remember Marty was going to a restaurant in the village to do his accounting work. He wanted to play a game on the owner. He showed me a badge that the IRS agents carried. He gave it to me and this is what happened:

I went into the restaurant and asked to see the owner. I knew his name and I asked for him by name. The manager came over. I explained to him that I wanted to talk to the owner and I showed him the badge and told him that I was with the IRS. I said that I would like a quiet table somewhere in the corner where I could talk to the owner.

Marty had already told me some of the areas where he was hiding money through his business. The owner came out, we ordered drinks, and I told him that we had heard a story about money being hidden in the business. Well, he stepped back, became very nervous, and said that he didn't know anything about this cheating. I said, "I didn't say anything about cheating. But somehow, somebody is taking money that should be going to the government." Well, I milked this dry for about fifteen minutes. It was timed perfectly. Then, who walks in, but Marty. The manager brought him over to us. He looked at me and said, "Hello, Mr. Otto." The owner was shocked and was probably thinking, "How did Marty know him?" Marty said that he had worked with Mr. Otto on other cases. We kept this going for another half hour. The owner didn't know what to do. Finally, Marty and I looked at each other and laughed. The owner said, "What the hell is going on?" Marty tells him the story. He said, "You son of a bitches." We all laughed, had another round of drinks, and a nice meal. Marty and I left to go uptown after that. Martin Hershey was one hell of a guy and I will always miss him.

One of our neighbors was across the street, his name was George Stephanidis, and George Stephanidis was the strongest man I ever met in my life. I'm telling you, this guy was a powerhouse – a mountain Greek. He used to drive a big Perkins truck, and he had arms on him like most people have legs. I remember we went out one time to Shinacock, a water area on Long Island by Riverhead. He had this cigarette lighter that was chrome and had a Greek name engraved on it. It was beautiful. He used it all through his services when he was in service in the army. We were fishing for fluke, and we got a big fluke, and he bent over to get this fluke, and the cigarette lighter fell out and went into the water. Boy, I'll tell you – what a heartbreak that was. The water was about 30 or 40 feet deep so it was impossible to try and go down and get it. It's a shame, but he lost it. He was heartbroken.

I could remember one time when I was sitting with George in the backyard and his son came out, Gregory, and he said, "Hey Dad, I told him you can straighten this out," and he handed George a horseshoe. Well, George looked at the horseshoe, handed it me, and he said, "Hey Kovmbaros, see if you could straighten this out." Well, I took that horseshoe, and I couldn't bend it. I couldn't do a damn thing with it. And he took that horseshoe and twisted it and straightened it out and gave it back to his son. He said, "Here, now get out of here." And unless you saw it, you wouldn't believe it, but that's what he did with the horseshoe – he gave it back straightened.

The reason I say "Kovmbaros" is because when we wanted to have Tina baptized, the Greek Church wouldn't let us because of the fact that we were married in Connecticut. They wouldn't accept the marriage ceremony, so, they wanted us to get married out in Minneola, Nassau County. We got married there, took the papers back to Flushing, and they performed the marriage ceremony there. But on our way back down there, George had said, "Hey, who's going to be your best man." I said, "To tell you the truth George, we never thought about it." He said, "Well, I want to be your best man; I want to be your Kovmbaros." I said, "George, it will be our honor."

So, George and his wife Helen took off with us on the weekend. We got married and I'll tell you, we came out of the church, and George went over to the policeman, and he said, "I want to take my Kovmbaros to the best restaurant in the area. Where's the best restaurant I can take him?" He said, "Well, you're in Flushing. There isn't too much around here." He said, "There's a great place over by the LaGuardia airport. It's in the hotel over there; they have a great restaurant." He said, "Okay, so that's where we're heading."

So we got into the car, the four of us, and headed over to LaGuardia. George walked inside and said, "Where's this restaurant," and the guy said, "It's closed." George said, "What do you mean it's closed?" And the guy said, "Well, it doesn't open up until about one o' clock." He said, "Oh no. No sir. My Kovmbaros is here, his wife, my wife, myself – you're going to open that restaurant now." And George wasn't kidding when he said *now*, and the manager understood where he was coming from. We opened up the restaurant, and we had a great, great time. In fact, when we left there, we had a bottle in the car, and we were driving, and we were drinking, and we were having a hell of a time.

We were on our way to the Motel on the Mountain. We had reservations up there for two days. Well, we were all pretty drunk in the car. In fact, we drove past the Motel on the Mountain, had to turn around, come back down to go to the place. This was in October, so it was cold out, chilly out when we got there. We had so much liquor in us that George said, "Let's go swimming." They had a big pool there, and I took some pictures of him and me out on the diving board pushing each other into the pool, and we had a hell of a time. He was some man. How I miss George.

Anyway, we came back and settled in Syosset, had our Christmas parties, had our friends over, and became active members of the Greek Orthodox Church. Every Sunday, we went to church with the kids, and we had our parties with the Mr. & Mrs. Club, and our dances. In fact, I was on the board with the Greek Orthodox Church for nine years. I helped put the concrete in by St. Paraskevi. You'll see this, this concrete walkway, and over at one end you'll see B.O. That's Bill Otto; I put my name on it.

I can remember one time when I was with the board there. The Greeks are great people, they like to talk a lot though, but they didn't do too much in the way of action. So, they did a lot of talking, and I was getting annoyed because what happened was, we had a wooden floor that had to be put down as the dance floor. We had the wood all stacked up, and we had the cement and cans – five gallon cans, and it was laying there for God knows – almost a year. Nobody ever put it down. So finally I said, "Look, this weekend we are going to put down the floor," and they said, "Well, we're not ready for it." I said, "No, this weekend, we're going to put down the floor, and you'll see why."

The men on the board were cursing at me in Greek, but they knew I was really pissed off and I wanted something down with that floor. I went outside and took a screwdriver. I opened up some cans of the cement and started pouring and throwing the cement around on the floor– it was a liquid. They came in and started hollering, "What are you doing!?" I said, "Now, if we don't get the wooden floor in here this weekend, we're going to have to get a jackhammer and chisel up that cement." Well, they got all excited, and they said, "You're crazy. What did you do this for?" They knew I was pissed off at them and I wanted action! The end result was that we all got together that weekend, and we put the wooden floor down, and that wooden floor, I imagine, is still down. We did a good job. It worked out well, and we accomplished it very easily.

What interesting good times at the Greek Orthodox Church, following the priests. It's a tough job being a priest for the Greek Orthodox. You go to the board meetings and at the board meetings they can tear you apart. They'd say, "Why did you do this, and why did you do that?" And yet on Sunday, he has to get up there and preach and get everybody to atone for their sins, and they have to listen to him, and the whole picture changes. It's a tough job but we had some good priests, and we had some good men, and we spent a lot of good times at that church. We saw the opening of it, the building of it, and the expansion of it, and a lot of good dances we went to. Those were good days.

George had another good friend. His name was Stan Weizurick. Stan owned a bar down in Woodside. That whole area is changed now. It's all been torn up and the bar and everything else is gone. But Stan was a big Pollock and a hell of a sweetheart. What a great man. He loved to cook, loved to eat. We had some great times together. We went skiing together, fishing together, out to dinner together. Our other Greek friend was Jimmy Janoutus. He made up the foursome. We always had good times together.

I remember one night, we were sitting at the bar, and there were four guys at the end, and we were four guys – three of us and Stan (he was behind the bar). And these guys were really breaking balls. They wouldn't stop, and George, in his nice little way, he said to them, "Look guys, why don't you knock it off? You know, you're stepping out of line." And they said, "What do you mean, we're stepping out of line? And what are *you* going to do?" They didn't stop. So George, the strongest man I ever met, he took that half-dollar, held it on his nose, and he bent it, and he dropped the half-dollar on the bar. And he said to them, "You see what I did to that coin? That's what's going to happen to you if you don't get out of here." Well, they were a little bit nasty, we wound up in a fight, and Stan had to replace that front window. The insurance company covered the cost – we chipped in a little bit – and those guys didn't come back again. But what a hell of a man he was.

I never questioned the fact that George bent the half-dollar on his nose because he was so strong. But some time later, I went to the bank and got two half-dollar coins and I tried to bend one. It's impossible. I tired it with pliers and can't do it. So how the hell did he bend that half-dollar on his nose at that time? Either he was superman, or he already had a half-dollar bent in his pocket which he took out and threw down the bar. We'll never know, will we? God Bless you, George, wherever you are. Miss you.

George and Stan were such powerful men. Ironically, Stan wound up in the Veterans Hospital. He had to have an operation on his testicle. You won't believe this but what I'm about to tell you is true: they cut off the wrong testicle.

I went up to see him, and he said, "Bill, you won't believe what happened. They cut off the wrong testicle. Apparently depending on how the doctor was looking at me, it was supposed to be the left one, if he was looking at me, the right one would be the left. And that's what they cut off! The right one!" And now I got trouble here Bill." He had trouble all right. He died three months later.

George, my Kovmbaros, was one hell of a guy. I can remember going to the gas station one night. He was there with his friend at the Texaco Station on Jericho Turnpike in Syosset. They were both drinking. I always had a bottle in my car. I took that out, and we drank that bottle. Joe, the guy who owned the gas station, he took out another bottle. Between the three of us we killed a bottle of bourbon a bottle of scotch and a bottle of Canadian Club. Well, we all felt pretty good that day. It's a good thing he had a helper taking care of the pumps outside. Joe said, "Let's all go hunting this weekend." I said, "Great."

Joe owned a motel up in Hunter Mountain. They both had to work Saturday, so I went up Friday night after work and opened the place up. They told me where the key was and how to put the boiler on. I took a room in the area on the left where I could put the heat on. Then, I jumped in my car, went out to the supermarket, and did some shopping. I bought frankfurters, beans, hamburgers, cold beer, and a couple of bottles of whiskey – stuff that men like. I called the boys and to tell them everything was ready. I said, "I'm going out Saturday morning, hunting by myself. So when you guys get here, the food is all ready. Help yourselves."

In the back of the motel were apple trees and I knew the deer would be coming there. So I picked this spot up in the tree where I could get a good shot at the deer. I got out there about 6 o'clock. It was still dark, but I found my way around. I don't know what the temperature was, but it was cold as hell. I got into the tree and I sat there, nice and quiet, and I waited. Well, it must have been an hour that went by. I could start to see some motion. It was starting to get daylight, and in front of me were four deer: three does and a buck. I grabbed my gun, which was across my lap, and started to move to a firing position. I couldn't move. I was frozen. I never experienced anything like that in my life.

Now, what do you do? I was all by myself in this empty motel, nobody was there. So little by little, I started to move. I moved my eyelids, my eyes, very carefully. I tried to turn my body, little by little. I tried to move my hands and my feet. I started to get some motion and then the deer saw me and took off. It must have taken me 20-30 minutes to finally get mobile. I got off the tree, went back to the motel, and had a couple of shots of whiskey. I made some coffee, and I got back to normal. I called the boys. Both of them said they couldn't make it; Joe was jammed up with business and George had family problems. I said, "That's great. What the hell do I do with all this food now?" So I rested up, took it easy, and decided I'd go out in the afternoon and find a different spot to hunt.

I went deeper into the woods in an area I was unfamiliar with. Well, it started to snow like hell, and I lost my bearings. When the hunter's in the woods, he could look up and see the sun and figure out which is north, south, east and west, and trace his way out. I couldn't. So now what do I do? I picked a big pine tree, and if any of you hunters out there know, at the base of the big pine tree, it's like a little house inside. I went inside, relaxed, and didn't panic. There was nobody to come looking for me, I didn't know my way out, so what else would you do? In my hunting jacket, I always carried two frankfurters, and two pieces of bread. That was my dinner. I curled up and went to sleep. Snow was all around me, but it wasn't cold. It was beautiful. I woke up with the sunlight coming through, found a clearing, got my bearings with the sun, and knew which direction I had to go to get back. It's always a good thing when you hunt in the woods to carry two frankfurters and two pieces of bread. They can get you through the whole night.

George and I went hunting at a later date. We both got home from work, tired, and he called me, and he said, "What do you say we go hunting?" And I said, "George that sounds good." We packed our gear, threw a bottle of bourbon in the car, and headed north. We found a spot, nobody was around. We were on a little hill, so we could get a clear view of the area. We sat back to back with the bottle between us. I took a sip, and he took a sip. Well, we spent three, four hours like that, and decided we were going home. Now, both of us are extremely tired, so we took turns driving an hour a piece. And every so often I had to smack George in the face to keep him awake, and when it was my turn he'd smack me in the face to keep me awake. And that was how we got home. Those were great days. He's a wonderful, wonderful friend, and a great Kovmbaros.

George was the strongest man I'd ever met in my life. I could sit in a chair, and he could come behind me and grab the chair with one hand and pick the chair up with me in it. Boy, George was strong. Now, picture that. I must have been 200 - 220 pounds – I was no featherweight. He was so powerful, this man. I can remember another case. We loved to drink together, him and I. We drank many a bottle together. I said to George my Kovmbaros, "You know George, I got this stuff coming in from Haiti. They said it's fantastic stuff. It's very good for your sex glands, it's good for your body, and it's made out of the trees. The guys are smuggling in a bottle of it for me." He said, "Jesus, Bill, can I have some of it?" I said, "Are you kidding, who else is going to drink it besides you and me?" So I said to him, "As soon as I get it, I'm going to call you."

71

Well, the fellows brought that bottle in to 100 Church Street from the guys that got it from Haiti. It was a gallon jug, all white. Now I took it home, and I put it on the kitchen table. Pauline said, "What's that?" I said, "That's the stuff I got from the boys down at Church Street." I was home early for dinner, and that's unusual. But anyway, I got home in the house; I put it on the kitchen table, and I called George, and I said, "Guess what? I got…What the hell is that noise, Pauline?" She said, "The bottle, look at the bottle, the bottle is shaking!" I said, "George, I got that bottle here, but the damn thing is shaking! Hold on, hold on, it's shaking!" So I reached over and grabbed a towel and took the cap off, because I was afraid that the damned thing was going to blow up. When I took the cap off, the whole thing sprayed up against the ceiling. What a mess! So now I said to George, "George, you'll never guess what happened. It exploded all over the kitchen ceiling. We've got a hell of a mess here." George asked, "How much is left?" I said, "About a third of the bottle." He said, "Don't touch it, I am coming over." And he came over and we drank that third of a bottle that was left, and it was good.

Chapter Eight

"The Man that Rocked the Boat"

While I was at 100 Church Street, I also became active on the St. Francis Xavier Labor Board. We used to sit down and try to solve problems between management and labor unions. It was a very interesting group of people. You heard me talk about Father Carey; well, he was on the board. Father Carey was a hell of a guy. He used to go out to the churches out on Long Island. He would do mass on Sundays at Our Lady of Grace in West Babylon, and he'd stop off at my house in Syosset and have some dinner with us before he went back to St. Francis Xavier. We did that many times. This man saved my life. He gave me his rosary beads. They are on my lamp on my desk. He died in May, 1989.

Father Carey introduced me to Bill Keating. He was the assistant district attorney under Hogan. Bill and I had many a drink and dinner together. While I was running 100 Church Street for the Irish Godfather, he used to come down there and say hello when he was in the downtown area. Bill was a tall, rugged, handsome man. One of his best friends was Little Brownie. Some of the old timers, maybe you remember Little Brownie. He may have been little, but he was a tough piece of work. Anyway, Bill Keating and I were out having dinner one night over in Lee's, a Chinese Restaurant over off Canal Street. We were having a nice dinner and a few drinks, and we were getting ready to leave. The owner always walked around with what looked like a water glass, but that was not water, that was vodka. That's what he drank all night long. As we were leaving, we saw two guys at the bar, one guy had his head lying on the bar, and the other guy was trying to get him up. Lee was having a problem. So we walked over and said to the guy standing up, "What the hell's the matter with you? Can't you see this guy's out cold? Leave him alone for Christ sake." Lee shook his head, and the other guy said, "I can't leave him." So, we said, "Why not?" The guy said, "Cause he's gotta drive!" He was out cold on the bar, and he had to drive! We just laughed and left them.

Bill Keating wrote a book, and he wrote several articles, but the one that they published and made a movie out of was *The Man that Rocked the Boat*. Richard Eagan played the lead. We saw each other on and off as time went by, and then I got a phone call from Father Carey about Bill. They were having a barbeque in the backyard. It started to rain, so they all went inside. Then they figured the rain stopped so they could go out and start the barbeque again. So Bill took a can of his lighter fluid, stood there by the barbeque, and squeezed it onto the hot coals. The flames ignited, ran a path up the can, the can exploded, and blew his stomach apart. It killed him. What a hell of a way to go for a man like that.

Because I was the night superintendent and the boss of 100 Church Street I knew everybody, and I was in the position to do people favors. There was a company called Ebasco American Foreign Power. They were the energy company for Cuba and they lost everything when Castro took over. They had their hands full. Anyway, at that time, the chairman of the board was a man by the name of Mr. Grant – beautiful man – and he had this great automobile. It was a two door gray Buick with a white top and red inside. Every once in a while I'd get it cleaned up for him. I said to Mr. Grant, "If you ever want to get rid of that car, boy, keep me in mind." And he said, "I will Bill." Well it wound up on a later date I got the car from him. It was a classy automobile.

I can remember down at 100 Church Street, we had a guy by the name of Joe Granadas. He bought this old '56 Pontiac. He said to me, "Bill, do you think I could bring it into the garage once in a while and wash it off." I said, "Of course you could." We had a great big garage down there. He would bring it in once a week to wash it off. I spoke to some of the guys in the night crew and here's what we did. We would send a guy down to the gas station to get a five-gallon can of gas. He brought the gas can back. Nice and carefully we poured the gas into his car. Joe would come in and say, "You guys can't believe this. I am getting 32-33 miles to the gallon on the gas in my car." I would say, "Oh, c'mon Joe. You can't be doing that.

You can't be getting that kind of mileage." We would be choking inside, because he never realized that we were pouring gas into his car. We kept this up for about three months with him. He was going crazy. He would said, "I am never going to get rid of this car. I am getting such gas mileage. I might have to put it in the Hall of Records, or something! This car is fantastic!" And, then we finally we had to tell him. We told him one night, "Joe, we've got to tell you a story..." When we finished, he said, "Boy, you guys are something else. I can't believe what you guys did." He got a big kick out of that.

There was another great man in that building. His name was Harry Lipsig. He was a world renowned negligence lawyer. In fact, he was the biggest negligence lawyer in the world from what I understand. Everybody respected and everybody admired him. We used to sit and do a lot of talking. He'd be there late at night and I'd pop in to see how he was, and we'd talk, and we got to be very, very close. He always said, "Anything you need, Bill, in the way of legal work, papers or anything else like that, you come to me and I'll take care of it for you."

I remember my daughter – I used to bring her into his office. We used to take pictures of him and my daughter. And he became a real help and he was a real guidance for me. I miss that man. I went to his funeral. He died at 93 – that's another story. I can remember when I stopped in his office one day to say hello.

He said, "Come here Bill, I want you to meet somebody. This is Beverly Addland. She's Errol Flynn's girlfriend." And then he took me aside and said to me, "Can you do me a favor?" I said, "Mr. Lipsig, anything you want." He said, "Would you take my car, or your car, and get her up to the Astor Hotel quietly and safely? She's meeting Errol Flynn, Rocky Graziano, and Martha Ray there at the bar on the second floor." I said, "Don't worry Mr. Lipsig. I'll take good care of her." He said, "I know you will." So I took her suitcase, took her downstairs, put her in the car and drove her up to the Astor Hotel. It was difficult to park, but I got a little spot there. I ran her inside, up to the bar, and there they were, Errol Flynn, Rocky Graziano, and Martha Ray. I said, "Are you okay now Beverly?" She said, "Yes, thank you very much, Bill. I really appreciate it." I said, "Have a great time, take care of yourself." And then I left.

Harry Lipsig was almost like a stepfather to me, always there to advise me and help me. Over the years I got to know him very well, and he was always there.

I remember at 100 Church Street, they took over the building behind them, which was 20 West Broadway. That was the Immigration Building. So now I was running 100 Church Street and The Immigration Building for The Irish Godfather, running my own business; I was on the go from 7:30 in the morning until 1:30 the next morning. I did this every morning for six years. We got on our feet that way. I gave Pauline the money and she put it away. We were able to get our first house in Syosset. Those were tough days, but good days.

I was doing pretty good with getting accounts. One of the accounts, United Tanker, was my dear friend Jack Coakley. He was the President of United Tanker – big, rough, tough looking guy.

Years ago Jack was one of those Navy Seals; he was also a football player. He was involved in a lot of things. In fact he got his start running the Todd Ship Yards, and what happened was the guy was on the crane and he wasn't handling the load properly and Jack gave him hell. He said, "Either you handle that load differently, or otherwise you gotta get the hell outta here." So they guys said, "Is that so?" So he pulled the crane over, got down, and headed over to Jack, threw a punch at him, and Jack knocked him on his ass. He was out cold, the guy. Jack was a rough bastard.

Now, a guy behind him, dressed all nice, yelled, "Is that the way you treat the help?" So Jack turned around and said to this guy, "Listen, if you don't like the way I'm treating these guys, too bad. They are gunna do the job right on this pier or they're gunna get the hell outta here. And that includes you! Now you get the hell outta here!" And with that the guy turned around and walked away.

About two weeks went by and Jack got a call from the main office. He went over to the main office, walked inside, and the secretary said, "Mr. Todd will be with you in a moment." She took him inside, opened up the door, and there was the guy who was all dressed up, looking great, that Jack told to get off the pier. It was Mike Todd, owner of the ship yard. Mike said, "Jack, sit down. I want to talk to you. I've gone over your background, your resume, and I know a lot about you. I think I could use a man like you. And I'll tell you what I want you to think about and consider: I want you to come on the board with me. I need some strength, and I need someone who doesn't play games." Well, Jack accepted it, and got on the board with Toad Ship Yards. Along came United Tanker – they offered him a fantastic job. He took that job and became the President of United Tanker.

Jack was a hell of a guy. He was a big game hunter. He had the big six, five times over. He had a place in Kilimanjaro, Africa. And he used to hunt with Bill Holden, the actor, and Robert Ryan, the actor. They were both hunters over there and they belonged to this club. They used to ask me to come over, and he had his own airplane. I said, "I can't go Jack. I'm so busy. I'm up to my neck in business and I can't walk away from it." He said, "Alright, if you can't, you can't."

I can remember Jack telling me one night that he knew I was having some problems with threats and some wise guys giving me a hard time. He said, "Bill, if you run into a bad problem, come into my office. You have the keys to my office. Take the key from under the statue, and on the left hand side of my desk, open the top drawer – there's a 38 in there. Don't let nobody push you around. If you get boxed into a corner, you come in here and you take it and you use it if you have to. It's ice cold. Just clean off the prints and lose it." I said, "Thanks Jack, I appreciate it."

Jack and I used to have great lunches together. We met a lot of great people we met. Them were good days. Jack was also the guy that was involved with John Wayne. They made a movie called *Atari* about wrestling rhinos. He was also involved with the hunter who was attacked by the lion. The lion jumped over the embankment and grabbed the hunter and had his head in his mouth. Jack was only a couple of feet away and the only thing he could do was shoot the lion in through the ear to kill him instantly. He saved the guy's life. It was in the papers and magazines. He was a hell of a guy, Jack.

I stayed at his house out in Sedona, Arizona. He bought Frank Lloyd Wright's house. On the living room table in his house was a big piece of black cut marble with a stand. On it it said, "Jack, we had a hell of a trip. Keep in touch. Regards, Frank Sinatra". What happened was he made a trip with Frank Sinatra, Gregory Peck, and other famous actors and they went over to Israel for some kind of meeting over there. Frank sent him this piece of marble and he kept it on his table. I was hoping to get it if anything happened to him, but I never got it. I don't know what happened to it – it just disappeared.

I can remember up in my office at 342 Madison, and I was breaking my back trying to get business. I got the business and I sent my men out to work. I went over and checked the work – the work was lousy. A couple of the men weren't doing the work. This one guy in particular, his name was Juan, I went after him and I was almost killing him. The guys were pulling me off, saying, "Bill, you've got to cut this out. You've got to get some release – you're too tensed up." So I went up to the uptown Athletic Club, 59th Street, and I asked them if there was some way I could join the club and maybe do some boxing – get some steam out of my system. They said that there was nobody heavy enough. I was about 240 pounds at that time. The guy who was running the gym was about 160 pounds. Anyway, so a couple of days later I was on the subway, and I saw a sign that said, "Jerome Mackey's Judo School: The Art of Self Defense. Release your frustrations. Come in and try it." So I did. I started playing judo three times a week. I did it, and did it, and did it. I wound up doing it for fourteen years. I figure I must have had about three thousand matches and I wound up getting a black belt from the top judo school in the world: The Kodokan – it's in Japan. They had the Japanese instructors coming from the Kodokan and they gave us a test at Rutgers University in New Jersey that took twenty minutes. I must have lost five pounds taking that test. I trained for three months and my university test score was 92, which was high! Judo is a great sport.

When we moved into Syosset, I got my son, involved in it. He had a problem. First of all, he had an asthmatic condition. We went to a specialist and he said he couldn't cure it; he said that my son was going to have to take these injections twice a week. Every time we brought him to get his injections, he would run around the office, and we had to catch him and hold him down. He hated that needle. He was petrified every time he had to go get the needle. We did this up until he was about six. In between that time, sometimes when he was three years old, or four years old, he would have difficulty breathing at night, so I would pick him up and take him over to Bayville and we would walk along the beach. In fact, one time, a cop stopped me and asked me what I was doing. I told him that, "My son can't breathe, and I had to take him down here to the beach for some fresh air." And he understood. He said, "Just be careful." And we were. All the cops knew me there and I never had any problems. We did this many times to get him some fresh air. We'd get home around 2:30 AM. Then, I'd take him up stairs, give him a warm bottle of milk, and tuck him in. Then I'd have a drink for myself, go to sleep, then off to work the next morning.

When he was about six, Jerry Mackey opened up a judo school on Front Street in Hempstead, Long Island. I thought it would be a good way for him to get exercise so I enrolled him in the judo school and started taking him there. In the interim, we again went back to this Dr. Dilello, who saved Tina, and we explained to him what the problem was. He said, "I am going to inject your son with something from the bull." I think it was something with the urine or something. He said, "I am taking this from the bull and I am going to inject it one time. Then I am throwing away the needle and I am not going to do it anymore. He is going to get better." And, so help me God, he did. He injected this stuff into him and that was the last time my son had the needles. He was better. Every Saturday morning I was always taking him over to judo on Front Street and he had judo for a couple of hours. He was six years old. We went to the Hempstead Outdoor Store to get him his judo uniform, his *gee*, and that's when I met Herb Terowsky, owner of the Hempstead Outdoor Store. We hit it off right away.

Herb became one of my dearest friends. He still is to this day; he is a beautiful human being. Everybody should have a friend like Herb. Everybody. He is always there for you, never lets you down, trustworthy, honest, just a wonderful person. Over the years, Billy kept playing judo and we kept going back and forth to the Hempstead School.

On Saturday morning we had a ritual. We'd all get in bed and watch Fireball XL5 and then Pauline would go downstairs and she'd make a big stack of pancakes and sausages and call us when it was ready. We'd go downstairs and have a beautiful breakfast, then Billy and I would go upstairs, get dressed, and we'd head over to the school and I'd take him to his judo classes. That was our ritual. It was nice; we enjoyed it.

We had picnics and barbeques out in the backyard. I was still running my own business. I was running the buildings downtown. I had a crew of 189 people for the Irish Godfather, and I had 65 of my own people. I was running a good sized crew – 254 people to worry about every night. That was enough to keep me busy, believe me. That was some headache. I was on the go constantly; I walked miles every night.

I remember one night at 100 Church Street I got a call from Anne, the boss of the cleaning woman. She said, "Bill you better come down to the lobby. There's some trouble down here." I said Anne, "I'll be right down." I took the elevator, went down, walked into the lobby, and there were over 100 people in the lobby. I said what the hells going on? Anne said Bill come over here with me. She took me to the front of the lobby and said to me, This is from the crew to celebrate the birth of your daughter Tina. It was an atmos clock, self-perpetual, and it was a beauty. It was inscribed on the bottom, From all the crew at 100 Church Street. Today the clock is worth about $2,500. I have it in the condo in Florida.

Chapter Nine

"The World's Fair"

Then, in my own business, a situation came along. A fellow by the name of Abe Gold, he was a public relations man and was well connected with everybody, and I mean *everybody*. He came to be interested in helping me get into The World's Fair in 1964. I said, "I thought The World's Fair was all tied up?" He said, "Yes, it is all tied up. That's why I am coming to you – to see if you would be interested in a shot of going against everybody." I said, "But that's Allied, and it's Pinkerton. They've got everything locked up." He said, "Well, it's up to you. You have a chance to make a name for yourself, a chance to expand, and make some money. Some of the people that I represent will want to get a little piece of the action." I said, "If I'm making money, I don't mind spreading it around."

I went out to the premises one night and I met the Commissioner General Miguel Garcia De Saez of Spain. He had six men around him – bodyguards. I guess he was concerned that something was going to happen. I don't know what. He was a handsome man, although he was gay. And he kept his overcoat over his shoulders. He said to me, "I understand that you would be interested in taking over the Spanish Pavilion." I said, "Well the Spanish Pavilion is a beautiful spot. Though, if I took it over, I could wind up with some problems. Before I do that, let me see your contract." He clicked his fingers and a man brought out a contract. I said, "I'll tell you what. I am going to meet you back here the day after tomorrow. I want to go over this contract carefully and see what I can do. I want to find out about the labor, what the union problems are going to be and so forth. Let me see what I can do. I will meet you back here at the same time." It was eight o'clock at night.

I met him back there at the scheduled time. I said, "Commissioner, Allied has control of this whole fair. They have abused the people. They were abusing you on the contract that you have. I can probably save you five or six thousand dollars a month." He said, "Five or six thousand dollars *a month?*" At that time, that was a lot of money. I said, "Yes, I probably can. But we are going to have some problems." He said, "What do you need from me?" I said, "Commissioner, I will draw up the contract for you; but more than that, you are a nobleman from Spain, and I would like to have your hand. Look me straight in the eye and I will look at you the same way. If I have any problems, I want to know that I can come to you for help and I may need those five or six guys that you have behind you because it could get a little rough." He said to me, "You have my word." We shook hands, looked at each other and that was the bond. A wonderful man named Manuel Artunio from the Spanish Embassy, also the general manager of the Spanish Pavilion, helped draw up the contract. We presented the contract to the Commissioner and then he signed it. So I prepared to bring my men there and go to work.

All hell broke loose. I got a call from Judge Poletti telling me that I could not go into the Fair – I had to stay out of it. He said that the Fair was controlled by Allied and Pinkerton. I knew Mr. Pinkerton because Mr. Pinkerton had given me two of his clubs when I opened up the fountain for the poor kids at 100 Church Street. By the way, my "fountain" idea is now used in a lot of buildings, like PAN AM, and so forth. That was my idea way back then. The idea was to collect toys and put them in the lobby fountain for the underprivileged children to have on Christmas. Mr. Pinkerton liked the idea and he gave me two of his clubs, he thanked me, and he had a nice write up about me in his paper. But anyway, Poletti said to me, "I want you to stay out of the Fair. It is being controlled by Mr. Pinkerton." I said, "Well, I will see what I am going to do." I noticed what had happened was that Allied and Pinkerton had really taken control of everything and were really overcharging everybody. There really wasn't much you could do about it.

I got a call from Bob Moses who was a big shot in the highway department and was supporting them and he said, "I want to talk to you over on Randall's Island." I said, "Randall's Island?" He said, "Yes. I want to talk to you privately there." I said, "Okay, fine." So I drove over the Trioborough Bridge and swung around and got on down to Randall's Island and went over to Bob Moses' office. I might tell you ahead of time though, that we were getting calls over at the house. My wife, Pauline, was getting calls saying that, "You had better be careful. You could get hurt. You have two babies. They could get hurt. You're husband could get killed." They knew my children's names. My life was being threatened. It became a very dangerous situation. Pauline was a little nervous but she was tough.

Anyway, Bob Moses and I met and he said to me, "Mr. Otto, I am a representative of New York City. We don't want any trouble at The World's Fair. We want to control everything quietly and peacefully and I want you to back off with your contract at the Spanish Pavilion and walk away from it." I said, "Why?" He said, "Because of what I am telling you. If you don't walk away from it, you are going to have some serious problems." Well, we were alone in the office and in them days I was kind of headstrong. So I said, "I'll tell you what, Mr. Moses, you don't know me from Adam, but I don't give a damn about you, your authority, your position, or that you're such a big shot. But I'll tell you this: if you bother my men, or you bother me, I am going to jump over that desk and kick you right in the fucking head. Do you understand me? Right in the fucking head and if I take your eye out, that's your problem. Don't ever tell me what to do and what not to do and what to stay away from because I am not going to do it. With that, you can go fuck yourself, Mr. Moses."

I walked out of the office and got in my car. Now, he was a big shot there, but I figured I was going to have some problems, so who do I call? I called the Irish Godfather. I told him what I did. He said, "Jesus Christ, kid. You're always getting in trouble, but God Bless you. Keep it up. You got the men lined up to go in?" I said, "Yeah." He said, "This is what you do. You have the men come in from all different directions, and you've got to get equipment in there. Once you get the equipment in there and get the equipment running, they can't get you out. But, I want you to go through the gate with a tough piece of work." I said, "Who's that?" He said, "You are going through the gate with Sol Lindner."

Sol Lindner was the bagman for Tony Provennzano – the unions over in New Jersey. Sol was a wonderful guy. Sol was the guy who helped me later with Manhattan College. He helped me in a lot of places. Anyway, Sol and I loaded up the truck, we drove over to Fowler Avenue gate, and they were waiting for us. But, what we did was this: we drove right into to the Allied yards – we knew where it was. They had cars going out over to the Spanish Pavilion for us. We followed the cars, got over to the Spanish Pavilion, and drove right up the steps of the Pavilion. My guys were all there. We had told them all to meet us there at ten o'clock. We unloaded the equipment. I said, "Get the equipment moving. Start throwing water around. Once the equipment is going, they are not getting us out of here."

I stayed there three days. Sol left. I thanked him. We didn't have any guns. We couldn't carry a gun – it was a bad scene. But, we had Harry Lipsig on tap. Harry Lipsig was standing on the outside and he was in the United Nations – he lived over there. He had what they call a "show cause injunction" to get us out if we couldn't get out physically. Jim had arranged through Sol to have 25 teamsters on the outside to come in and get us if we needed it. It was going to blow the whole thing wide open. This is a very unusual story, but this is the way it went.

At 2:30 in the morning I called Mr. Lipsig and I said, "Mr. Lipsig, call off everybody. We are in. We got the men running. I am going to stay here and sleep here. We are taking over The Spanish Pavilion." He said, "Okay Bill, I know if you said it's okay, then it's okay. I am going to sleep. You keep me posted." I said, "I will." We worked straight through and got the pavilion in top shape. We really worked hard at it.

Now we were working on The Pavilion, doing the job. Manuel Artunio said to me, "Bill, can you help us out with the engineers?" So I said, "What are you talking about, the engineers?" Well, what happened was they had an engineering plant to run the Spanish Pavilion, the air conditioning and so forth. The problem was that the engineers union sent one engineer over and he said to Manuel that he needed an assistant. And then they were telling him now that they were going to send over a supervisor to watch the two men. So he said, "I can't go for that, Bill. That's about $1,700 a week." $1,700 a week in them days was a lot of money. So I said, "Let me see what I can do."

I went into the engine room and these two guys were sitting there and having coffee. I closed the door and I picked up a lug wrench and I said, "Guys, I want you to leave quietly and get out of here. Your job is finished. I want you to leave *right now*. Get your personal stuff and you are going now." They said, "Who the hell are you to tell us what we are going to do or we are not going to do?" So, I took the lug wrench and I smacked it against the pipe. I said, "That's what I am going to do to your fucking head if you don't get out of here. Now what do you want to do? Do you want to walk out, or do you want to be carried out? I don't give a shit. You can go either way. But, you are leaving now." They saw that I wasn't fooling around and they left. They got out, but they reported it to the union right away. Meanwhile, I got on the phone with Jim Earley, and I said, "Jim, what are we going to do?" He had a guy named Walsh, which was my mother's maiden name, and Walsh was with Local 30 of the teamsters engineers and he said, "That's all you need is the one guy to run the plant." But, the plant was designed very badly. It made all kinds of noise. Well, what happened was then, I was called over to Columbus Circle to attend a meeting. I thought I was going to walk and see Manuel Artunio there with a union representative from the engineers and that's the way it was going to be – just the three of us. It wound up there must have been twelve guys around that table and they were all ready to break my balls. I was the "scapegoat".

They all started talking, one after the other – they all had something to say. They were unhappy with the way the thing turned out. I said, "Manuel, the plant is running. You got your air conditioning. It was a lousy design to begin with, but we are running it smooth. Are you satisfied?" He said, "Yes." I said, "Well, then the rest of you, you can go to hell. I have an engineer in there by the name of Walsh, Local 30. He is doing a good job. We are not going to change it. We are going to leave it alone. If there is any dispute, we are going to have serious problems here, because I am going to go right to the newspapers. That's the way it's going to be." Well, they talked back and forth, back and forth and they felt that what was it – one guy? But I am surprised they had so many there for that meeting. There was one guy that was involved. They were going to lose two guys on that whole job, but they had the rest of the goddamned Fair locked in. They were making a ton of money on the rest of the Fair. They figured that they didn't want to blow this thing wide open and they could see that I meant business. So Manuel Artunio, his assistant and I walked out and left. I thought that was the end of it.

Now what happened was that Allied also had the garbage industry. They collected the garbage for the World's Fair. So we noticed that the garbage in the back of the Pavilion was just lying there and it wasn't being picked up. So I said, "This is nice." So, I got on the phone and I asked for Allied's office. I said, "This is the Spanish Pavilion. The garbage has to be picked up. It's not being picked up." They said, "As long as you have U.S. Building Maintenance doing the cleaning for you, and as long as you have Bill Otto on the premises, we are not going to pick up the garbage." I said, "You're not, eh? Okay."

I got on the phone with Judge Poletti. He was the guy who was like a liaison for Bob Moses. And I said, "Judge, this is Bill Otto." He said, "Oh, more trouble, eh?" I said, "No, no trouble. Trouble for you. I have got the garbage in the back not being picked up. I have 60 people in the Spanish Pavilion working here and I'll tell you what I am going to do. I am going to have each person take a tray and fill it with garbage and we are going to line up around the Unisphere. At twenty minutes after two I will give the command and we are going to dump the garbage into the Unisphere. And, it is going to be on TV, because the next thing I am going to do is call Channel Five, and I am going to call the New York Times, and the Mirror, the state department and attorney general and anybody else I can call in the press! I am going to tell them what is going to happen, and the publicity is going to make this fair stink and it's going to be your fault because you are not stopping it. Now, you need to correct this and get this garbage out of here, otherwise my men at the Spanish Pavilion are going to start marching out." Well, that was twenty after two that I told him we were going to start marching out. At 12 noon they had two trucks pull up with twelve men and they grabbed the garbage, so, we got rid of that.

Two days after that, they had what they call like an ansel system for the restaurants to put out fires, and stupidly, it was rigged on the outside of the building. Well, somebody got a hold of it when all the food was prepared and ready to eat and they pulled the system and all this powder and fire prevention stuff came down all over the food and we had a hell of a mess. But after that, they left us alone and we just functioned, ran the

Pavilion, did the job, kept it clean, maintained everything, and everything went fairly smooth.

We did have a problem trying to get the valet for Commissioner General. We ended up hiring someone from the Armenian Embassy who was leaving. We got them to take the job, and they came over.

We had some very lovely parties over there at the Spanish Pavilion. I can recall that Mrs. Kennedy was there, Johnson's wife was there. We had dinners and they always did everything up elegantly. Gold plates and everything was top of the line. In fact, one night we had a very formal affair there, and we were sitting around with Manuel from the Embassy, and there was about twelve of us at the table. Everybody was in gowns, formal tuxedos, and they had six wine glasses out. You had a different wine for each part of the meal. It was really top drawer. I said, "You know, Manuel, this table looks like the United Nations." He said, "What do you mean, Bill?" I said, "Well, it's like the United Nations because we have you, the Spanish people, here, we've got a Jewish couple over there, we have a Polish couple over here, you have American, me, here, and you've got my wife, who is Greek." There was a little guy in the end who had his head down, he wasn't saying anything, impeccably dressed, and he lifted his head up and he said, "Greek, who's Greek?" I said, "My wife is Greek." So he looked at Pauline. He said something to her in Greek and she answered him in Greek. And that was the end of the story – after that these two were inseparable for the rest of the night.

This guy was Gustav Camborus. Gustav Camborus owned 25,000 acres in the Canary Islands. Very wealthy and powerful man. And, he was the godfather to Onassis's son, Alexander. He told us all kind of stories. The night went on and at the end of the night, Manuel came over to us and he said, "Bill, Mr. Camborus is very taken by you and your wife and he would really appreciate it if you would take him home. He would rather not go home in a cab." He didn't have a limousine with him. So I said, "Fine, we'll take him home. Where is he staying at?" He said, "He is staying at the St. Regis." So, I said, "Okay, fine." That was at I think 53rd Street at that time. It was the end of the night, about 3:30 in the morning and he said, "C'mon, I am going to buy you people a drink. You are going to have a drink with me, by ourselves, and we'll talk."

We got back to the St. Regis Hotel, a very affluent hotel, and walked inside and he asked if the manager was there. He knew him by name; I don't remember the name. He said, "The manger is upstairs in his room." Mr. Camborus said, "Tell him I want to see him." He said, "Mr. Camborus, it is 3:30 in the morning." He said, "That's alright. I want you to open up the bar so my friends can have a drink." The man said, "But the bar is closed. The lights are out." Mr. Camborus said, "I want the bar to be opened so that my friends can have a drink." He called the manager and he talked to the manager on the phone. The manager put on his robe and he came down. He said, "Mr. Camborus, how can I help you?" Mr. Camborus said, "I told my friends that I would buy them a drink and I intend to buy them a drink. Now open up the hotel bar and I want a bar tender and I want a waiter." He said, "All right Mr. Camborus." See, Mr. Camborus could buy the hotel, probably out of petty cash if he wanted to. He was very influential in getting what he wanted. We just went along with everything. We had a booth inside and we sat there until 5:30 in the morning. We talked, had a few drinks and he told us about Maria Callas and Onassis, the boats and all the parties, Eisenhower coming over, meeting General Patton, and he was impressed with this one and impressed with that one and he told us all these stories. Pauline and I listened to all these stories and we were fascinated by this man because he was extremely impressive. At the end of the night, we said goodbye to him and he said, "Please be my guest and come to the Canary Islands. Come and see what I have over there."

The next day I got back late in the afternoon to the Spanish Pavilion and I told Manuel what happened and he said, "Yes, when he wants something, he gets it." I said, "But tell me Manuel, the stories he was telling us about Onassis and Callis and Eisenhower and all these different stories, is this so?" He said, "Yes it is so. He is a very powerful, very famous man and he owns a large part of the Canary Islands and a lot of areas in Greece. He is a very strong political man, a very influential man and he is worth a fortune. You were in good company." I said, "We really had a good time. He invited us over to the Canary Islands." He said, "You really should go. You would never forget that trip." I said, "Manuel, with all the problems I have with the Pavilion and the business and expansion – I am working night and day trying to keep up with everything now." He said,

"I know, but it would be a great trip for you if you could make it." Well, unfortunately, we never did get a change to make it. I was just too snowed under with work.

One time I invited Manuel over to the house in Syosset with his wife Lola. So, to impress Manuel, I went over to the liquor store and I said to the salesman, "I have some Spanish people coming for dinner and I need some good Spanish wine. Can you make any suggestions?" At that time, I didn't know much about Spanish wine. He said, "I only have these two bottles." I said, "I'll tell you what. I'll take them both." I took them home. We had the Spanish music playing, Pauline set up the dining room nice and I said, "Manuel, I have two bottles of wine here, Spanish, which one should I open first?" And he looked at them, and he made kind of a face. I said, "Manuel, tell me, is this good wine or bad wine?" He said, "Bill we are going to drink this wine." I said, "But tell me, you know wines from Spain. Are these wines good?" And he started to laugh. I said, "What's so funny?" He said, "Bill, in my country, we would use this wine for mixing cement." I said, "Holy Christ, it's that bad?" He said, "No, we are going to drink it. You bought that wine special for us and we are going to drink it." Well, we drank it at the dinner.

Now, George Stefanitis, my Koumbaros, he was four houses down so he called me up and said, "Bill, how are things going?" and so forth. I said to him, "Why don't you come over and meet Lola, Manuel's wife?" So, he came over, and he said, "Have you got any scotch? I'd like some scotch." And, Lola said, "I would like some scotch, too." Well, Lola and George sat down and they drank a bottle and a half of scotch between the two of them. We had a very nice time, had a very nice talk, but I found out that Lola was a very heavy drinker. I already knew George was.

Lola told us a very interesting story. She told us how Franco, who was this little man with a very high squeaky voice, got into power and took over Spain. And this particular story she told us was about Franco and her father:

When the Spanish people took Morocco, they had the French Foreign Legion there. They were a bunch of tough, tough eggs. These were killers from all over the world who joined the French Foreign Legion. They were like rebels and tough people to deal with. They all lined up and Franco was addressing them and talking to them, and then he went down to see the troops. He walked up the isle and he looked at the men and he said to one man, "How do you like the food?" And the man said, "It's fine, sir." Then, he walked a little further down the line and he said, "How do you like the food?" And he said, "It's alright sir." Then, he went down a little further and he said, "How do you like the food?" This guy spit in his face. He didn't say nothing and the guys around him went to make a move towards him and Franco said, "No. Don't do anything." He wiped his face, kept on walking down the isle. He went back up to the podium and said to Lola's father, "Would you please call that man up who spit in my face?" So they called him up. The sergeant went down and got him. They escorted him up to the podium and Franco said to Lola's father, "Take your pistol out and shoot this man between the eyes." Lola's father took his pistol out and shot him between the eyes. Well, the French Foreign Legion men, who were tough bastards, saw this and said to themselves, "Well, this guy's got some balls. If he can do that in front of us, that's the leader we want." That's how Franco took over the French Foreign Legion, the Spanish Army. He took over everything and became the dictator of Spain.

That was Manual, Lola's father, he was in the Spanish Embassy. When the fair closed they moved the restaurant over to St. Louis and put it under the archway. I don't know if it's still there.

While I was doing the Spanish Pavilion, my other business was expanding; I was running all the time. My contact, Abe Gold, told me that he was involved with some of the boys and they felt they weren't getting a good enough return on the situation. So, I said to Mr. Gold, "Listen, I am breaking my ass trying to take care of things out there. I've had to threaten men, throw men out, and deal with unions. I'm going with tough pieces of work at the Fair, and I've had bodyguards standing by to get me out. I've gone through things with Harry Lipsig standing by. I've gone through a lot of shit over this thing and there isn't enough money left around to take care of everybody. The small piece that's left over—you're getting whatever we have to share around." He said, "Well, they don't feel it's enough. They feel that maybe something is wrong, and they are coming up to see you." I said, "Who is they?" He said, "You know who he is: Tommy Lucchese." He was also known as Three Finger Brown. He was one of the "boys" and a well-known character.

I told my accountant, Martin Hershey, "Marty, I want you here when they come in." "Bill these are very tough people. They are bad news." "That's okay, the tougher they are, the better. We'll talk to them straight with no nonsense and tell them exactly where we stand with everything."

Marty and I were in the office waiting for them. At about 7 o'clock, the doorman downstairs called me and said, "Mr. Otto, I've got three men downstairs here who want to come up and see you." I said, "Send them up." Two minutes after, he called again and said, "Mr. Otto, they are on the elevator. Are you all right?" I said, "Sure." He said, "Do you want me to call the police?" I said, "No, unless you hear gunshots. I think everything will be alright."

The doorbell rang, and Tommy Lucchese came in with two tough looking guys. I said to Tommy, "Things didn't go exactly the way we wanted. We had a lot of problems there. This is my accountant Marty; if you have any questions, ask him now. Don't hold anything back; I want to get this cleared up. If you want to see the books, they are right in front of us. You can see anything you want. Would you like a drink?" He looked at the other boys and said, "No." Meanwhile nobody sat down. Tommy seemed nervous. He walked around the office and he looked over and he saw the picture of Jim Earley. He said, "Is that Jim Earley?" And I said, "Yeah." He said, "How do you know Jim Earley?" I said, "He's like my father." He said, "Wait a minute. Are you the guy they call the kid?" I said, "Yeah, I'm the kid." He said, "For Christ's sake why didn't they say so?!" He said to his boys, "Sit down on the couch and relax. We're gunna have a drink." We had a couple of Jack Daniels and relaxed. I told him about all the bullshit we went through at the fair, all the threats, all the aggravation. I showed him the payroll and what we were making on the job, and he said to his boys, "This guy's not fucking around. If he was fucking around we wouldn't be talking to him right now."

A little while later he got up, we shook hands and he said, "Don't worry kid; we'll make it up some other way. Take care of yourself." And then he said to me, "Jim speaks very highly of you." I said, "Thank you," and then they left.

Marty was beside himself. He couldn't believe what happened. He said, "Bill, I don't believe it. What happened here tonight? Did you see those two guys he had with him?" I said, "Yeah," and we laughed. I said, "Marty, let's have another drink," and we did. He stayed a little while and then we called it a night. When he left I thanked the doorman downstairs for his consideration on the meeting.

· That year at The World's Fair was a tough nut. Lot of problems. Lot of headaches. But it had to be done.

The second year came up and I was getting calls from Bob Straile and he said, "C'mon Bill, I want you to take over the Belgium Pavilion for me." I said, "Bob, let's have a talk." He came out to the house and we sat and we talked.

We were sitting at the bar in my house, and Bob Stralie was married to Zsa Zsa Gbor, and he was telling us some crazy stories about her and we had a good laugh. But anyway, he wanted me to take over the Belgium Pavilion. I said, "I can't take a chance on that, Bob. I run on six month schedules for both years and the last month is usually when I am picking up my money and I could wind up on the short end. I can't take a chance; I'm gunna have to pass. The Japanese Pavilion asked me to get involved, but they are not backed by the Government. You are not backed by the Government." He said, "Well, why are you doing the Spanish Pavilion?" I said, "The Spanish Pavilion is backed by the Government, that's why. I wouldn't touch anything that wasn't backed by the Government. As a matter of fact, I am getting a call now from the Masonic Lodge Pavilion. I have to meet with the Judge Froessal, Charlie Frossel and that's backed by the Masonic Lodge. That's almost like being backed by the government; they don't play games." Anyway, we had a couple of drinks, talked a while and they left.

I went over to see Judge Froessal about the Masonic Lodge. I had to meet him downtown; they had the main headquarters on 14th Street. Meanwhile, they gave me the specs on what he wanted, what he didn't want and what he was paying for now. He said, "This is what I am paying for now, Bill. See what you can do." I went over the specs and I looked at them and he said to me, "Bill," and then the phone rang and he said, "Just a minute." He said on the phone, "Yes, Bob, I know." He was talking to the mayor, Bob Wagner. He said, "I know, we are short $19 million for the Fair. Nobody can account for it, eh? Isn't that great? Alright, we'll see what happens." And he hung up. So I said to the Judge, "Judge, if you are connected with these types of guys, then you don't want me in there. It's only going to be a problem." He said, "Bill, I want you in there. Forget about Bob Wagner. Forget about anything else. I want you to do a good job and keep that Pavilion clean and I want you to save me some money. That's my job. The Masonic Lodge does not have a lot to spend. I want you to see what you can do. Now, do me a favor. Take the contract out of the desk over there, take a pencil and sharpen the point a little bit, alright?" I said, "Okay, fine." So I went over and figured out where I could cut there and cut here and so forth and I came back and I said, "How's that figure?" He said, "Now you're talking. You got the contract."

While I was in Judge Froseeal's office, the phone rang, and it was Jimmy Carter running for President. He said to the Judge, "I want to take my oath of office and be sworn in on the George Washington's Bible. I understand, Judge, that you have that Bible." He laughed and looked at me. The Judge had this conversation on the speaker, and he twiddled his thumbs and he said, "Mr. Carter, that Bible doesn't go more than 12 feet away from me." You could hear Jimmy Carter laughing, and he said, "I guess you're telling me you want to be there at the swearing in?" So you could figure what happened. If you look at the picture of Jimmy Carter swearing in as the President, you can see six guys over to the left, there's a man with a dark coat and a hat to the left – that's the Judge.

Well, we took over the Masonic Pavilion. Those were the only two that I did. There was a write-up in the Life Magazine about it. I don't know which issue; I've forgotten now. But anyway, we took over the Masonic Pavilion and from my contact with him, and I became very close to Judge Froessal.

He was a hell of a guy. He should have been President.

The Judge said to me, "Bill, please take good care of me at the Masonic Lodge, and I'll see what I can do with you downtown in the New York Law School. I said, "What do you got to do with the New York Law School?" He said, "I am the Chairman of the Board of New York Law School." I said, "Oh, now you're talking. That's great."

The Judge and I met many times, and he was kind enough to see to it that I got a chance to bid on the New York Law School, which I did, and I was awarded the contract. I took over the porters, the cleaning people, the engineers, elevator operators, window washers, you name it. It was a good contract. We had it for quite a few years. The Judge was very helpful to me. I appreciated all of his effort. As I said, we were very close.

So now when I tell you stories of the many incidents in my life involving these three men: Jim Early, the Irish Godfather, Mr. Harry Lipsig, the biggest negligence lawyer in the world, and Judge Froessel, Court of Appeals, when I say that they raised me, they pretty much did. With these three fathers looking out over me, I was in good hands. They kept me out of trouble.

Things were going well. So Pauline and I threw a party in the backyard of our house in Syosset. We had a lot of people coming over. We planned everything. We had liquor, we had wine, we had food, and we had music. We even took the pool table from inside the playroom and had the guys bring it outside. The guys carried it up at an angle and got it outside, and we were playing pool in the backyard. We were dancing. We even had a belly dancer. We were having one hell of a party. And this was at our little house on the corner in Syosset: 201 Nelson Court; that's where it was.

The cops came eleven times! Eleven times! It got to the point where the cops said, "Mr. Otto, what can we do? We have to answer all the complaints. We know you are having a party and they will ask us to ask you to please tone it down a little bit." So, every time the cops came I had to run outside and everything else. But, we kept having the party. In fact, I went out back and yelled, "If you can't sleep, put your slippers and your bathrobe on and come down and have a drink and join us!" It was a good party that ended about 4:00 in the morning. I said to my wife, Pauline, "We are going to get a piece of property that has a backyard where we can have some fun and enjoy our lives. So, let's look around for something else."

Chapter Ten

"Sands Point"

The Association For The Help
of Retarded Children

presents

A Spring House Tour

Wednesday, April 28th
10:00 a.m.-3:00 p.m.

The Otto Mast

The next morning I saw an ad in the paper that said, "2 1/2 acres waterfront property in Sands Point – 290 feet on the beach." I said, "Boy that sounds nice." So I looked at the price; it was $37,000 and believe it or not, that was a lot of money in them days. I thought, "Let me see what I can do." I called up the party. She said I had to go all the way to the end of Long Island to meet with them. I met with them, discussed the situation. I finally said, "Look, let's do a little better with the price. Let's make it an even number: $35,000 for the 2 1/2 acres, if I like it. I am going to go take a look at it." She said, "Well, take a look at it first before we discuss that."

I went down to the Hearst estate in Sands Point, right on the corner there. I was met by Mrs. Tunney. She said to me, "Mr. Otto, do you know anybody in the area?" At that time, it was very snobbish in Sands Point. I was a little offended by what she asked me. I said, "Why?" She said, "Well, it would be nice if you knew somebody in the area." So I said, "Well, I do know somebody, a prominent man, Mr. Frank Costello." She said, "Oh, he's one of our finest neighbors." Then I said to Mrs. Tunney, "The property looks good. It's what I'm looking for: 290 feet on the beach, 485 feet long, private, cul-de-sac. But I am not going to make a decision until my wife Pauline looks at it. I'll have her out here tomorrow and we'll make a decision at that time."

I thanked Mrs. Tunney and I left and headed back into the city, parked the car, went up to the office, and Dee said to me, "Bill, you got a call from Mr. Earley, so you better call him back." So, I called him back and said, "Hi, Jim, what's up?" He said, "What are you using *Mr. C's* name for?" I said, "What do you mean, what am I using Mr. C's name for? I looked at the property and they asked me if I knew somebody in the area who was prominent or if I had any friends in the area, and the only one that I could think of was Frank Costello." He said, "Yeah, but Bill, you don't go around using his name unless you get it cleared from him. It's not a good thing; it's not a healthy thing. You are probably going to get a call from him." I said, "Well, I'll tell him what happened and take it from there."

Well, about an hour went by and Dee said to me, "Bill, it's Mr. C." So, I said, "Hello, Mr. C., how are you?" He said, "Okay, Kid. What's going on?" I said, "Mr. C., I had to use your name when I looked at a piece of property on Half Moon Lane in Sands Point. They wanted to know if I knew somebody in the area. It seemed like they were kind of snobbish and I got a little offended and a little pissed off at them and I threw your name at them. I told them that I knew of a *very prominent* man down there, Mr. Frank Costello. They said that he was a great guy, and that was fine. So that was the end of it." So, Mr. C. said to me in that raspy voice of his, "Hey Kid, did you get the property?" I said, "No, not yet, Mr. C." He said, "I'll tell you what, kid; if those cock-suckers don't give you that fucking property, you let me know." I said, "Thank you very much Mr. C., I really appreciate it." He said, "It's okay, Kid. Take care of yourself. Bye bye." And he hung up.

Well, needless to say, we were working on the property and I went down to the building at 100 Church Street, which I was running at night, and I mentioned it to Harry Lipsig. He said, "Bill, you get that property, and the legal fee is my gift to you. I am going to have one of my lawyers take care of all the problems for you on the closing." I said, "Gee, that's great." Well, we negotiated the price of $37,500 down to $35,000. Can you imagine that? Two and a half acres of waterfront property, 290 feet on the beach, for $35,000? It's worth about six million today.

Anyway, Harry Lipsig said he would take care of all the legal expenses for me and he assigned me an attorney named Green. He went with me to the signing of the contract, we put everything in order and we thought that was the end of it. Now, we started doing some design work on what kind of house we wanted to build up there. We held the property for five years so I could gather enough money to have a house built there We had architects working on it – they went down to the property. We were pretty flush in them days. The architect's name was Jones. Ralph Jones. They were designing this and designing that. First, we had it looking like a cross. Then we had it with an atrium in the middle; we kept going back and forth. It was a very interesting task. We wound up with a pretty good looking design and then we were getting ready to file for a permit to build this house and Ralph Jones said to me, "Bill, I am just looking over your deed and you can't build this house there." I said, "What do you mean I can't build this house there?" He said, "Well, there is a covenant restriction; there is an envelope hanging over that property that says that you have to build a house within that envelope." I said, "What kind of bullshit is this?" He said, "I am telling you, Bill, that's what you got there." I said, "Well, why didn't the lawyer pick this up?" He said, "I don't know why he didn't pick it up. He certainly should have picked it up because you have a serious problem on your hands right now, and I don't know how we are going to resolve it." So I said, "Boy, oh boy. Now, what do we do?"

So, I called Judge Froessel and told him what the problem was. He said, "Well, talk to your attorney about it." I talked to my attorney, his name was Art Scolari. He's dead now. I told Art what the problem was. He said, "Bill, you've got this envelope hanging over the property and you're not going to be able to build that house." I said, "Isn't this great." So, I went back to The Judge. I said, "Judge, what the hell are we going to do? We've got a piece of property and we can't build a house on it?" He said, "Bill, you need a tough attorney. You need the toughest, political connected attorney in that area." I said, "Well, how do I get him?" He said, "Ask around. Try to find out who's breaking balls. Get the right guy."

I called up the Village. I got the secretary on the phone. I said, "This is Mr. Otto. I own that property down on Half Moon Beach and I'm considering building a house there but we are having a lot of problems with this pain in the ass attorney." She said, "You mean, Mr. Molloy." I said, "Yeah, *Mr. Molloy*. What the hell was his first name again?" She said, "Ken Molloy." I said, "Oh, yeah, that's the guy, that's the guy...is he in the Port Washington area?" "No," she said, "He's in Manhasset. He is a pain-in-the-ass. He doesn't let anything get by. He digs and digs and digs. He drives you crazy." I said, "Thank you very much. I'll look into this whole situation." So, I hung up with her and said to myself, "Boy, I've got the right attorney."

It was Sunday morning. I called up Ken Molloy's office and I couldn't get him. So I asked for the operator for the house number. A woman answered the phone and I said, "Can I talk to Ken Molloy?" She said, "Well, I'm sorry. Is it anything important?" I said, "Well, yes. I am trying to get a house built. I have a restriction on the property and I understand that Ken Molloy is the best attorney to handle this type of a problem." She said, "He is fantastic. But, unfortunately, my son, Ken Molloy, just left for the Bahamas for the week." I said, "Oh, Jesus, isn't that great." She said, "You seem very upset. But, don't give up. Don't worry about it. I want to put you in touch with my other son, Judge John Molloy. He is out in Westbury. You call him up and you go out there and tell him I said that he should take good care of you and see what he could do."

I picked up the phone, hunted around and got his Westbury number. I got Judge Molloy on the phone. Now, it's about 11 o'clock Sunday morning. I said, "Judge?" He said, "Yes, who is this?" I said, "I just want to tell you that I was recommended to you by a sweet elderly lady who said to me that you would take very good care of me and if you didn't, that you would answer to her." He said, "Oh, you spoke to Momma." Judge Molloy suggested that we meet at the Westbury Inn and have some lunch, which we did. He said to me, "Listen, I am not the best guy to handle this, but we have a good surveyor in our office. He is very prominent, very good, and very sharp and I am going to let him do the ground work for this, get it set up and then when Ken comes back, he can turn the matter over to him and let him work on it." I said, "Gee, that sounds great, Judge."

So, we had lunch, had a few drinks. I felt good about what we discussed. I was in touch with the surveyor that worked in his office. He came down to the property, looked at it, got some ideas, put it all together and then when Ken came back we had a meeting and discussed this whole situation. The surveyor came up with this idea and Ken backed it up and we thrashed it out. Now, it seemed what happened was this: The property stated that you had to go back 485 feet to the road. The Salgo property went way up on top of a hill. They had said to us that we could only build within a sixty foot radius from the road on our property. Mr. Nick Salgo did not want his view blocked from up above. Now, the idea that Ken came up with was that if you were going to buy The Grand Canyon, you wouldn't expect it to be filled in. You would buy it the way it was: empty.

With that idea in mind, we told Mr. Salgo that what we were going to go back on his property line go up to the top of his hill where his view came in, then from the top of the property go up sixty feet and then come down with the envelope, which gave us more than enough space to build a house. However, Mr. Salgo was demanding that we set up some sort of a frame to give him an idea as to what the house was going to be like. Well, we wanted to get along with our neighbor, as powerful as he was, and we tried to get along with him. We put up the frame, and he came down with his big Mercedes, looked at it, and then drove away. Then we found out that he felt that it was too big and it should be lower. He didn't like the idea that it was going to block his view on the hill. Very powerful man. He was really breaking our balls. His son, I believe his name was also Nick; he was a newscaster on TV. Very powerful family.

I set up an appointment to go and see him. He owned a six-story house on 72nd Street, just off of 5th avenue, and I went up to his office;

he was impeccably dressed, with slippers on. His office must have been 40 by 30 feet, and I walked inside and he had coffee ready, and I showed him what the idea was going to be like. He said, "Mr. Otto, I want to tell you something. I don't want that house built there. I don't like the way it's going to block the view from up on the hill. I am unhappy with it and I just don't want you to build it. I want you to build a ranch or something else." I said, "You can't build a ranch house on a piece of property that overlooks the Sound and the great New York view. You would loose all the benefit of the property. Plus the fact that you have to come up with the water table 8 1/2 feet. If we built a ranch house on that, we would have one hell of a looking house. No, I am afraid that the house is going to build the way we designed it, the way it looks." He said, "Mr. Otto, I already told you, I don't want that house built." I said, "Mr. Salgo, let me explain something to you. I stood on breadlines as a kid and I made up my mind that there are certain things in this world that I am going to get. One of the things I am going to get is this house built, the way we want it, on this property and there is nothing that you are going to do about it. I don't care what you attempt to do; you will only create problems for yourself. We are going to build that house and that's the way it's going to be." He said, "You are going to regret it, Mr. Otto." I said, "Well, I have regretted a lot of things in my life, but I keep fighting and getting things done, and that house is going to be built." With that, I said, "Mr. Salgo, I want to thank you for the coffee. You are a gentleman, but you just have to get used to losing once in a while, and you just lost. The house is going up." I got on the elevator and left.

I grabbed a cab. I was on my way down to the New York Law School and on 43rd Street and 5th Avenue, and who do I see looking for a cab but Mr. C – Frank Costello. I said, "Hey! Mr. C!" He said, "Hey Kid, what are you doing?" I said, "I'm on my way downtown. Can I give you a lift?" He said, "Yeah I'm trying to get a fucking cab and I gotta get to Penn Station." So I said, "Come on I'll give you a lift." I told the driver to drop him off at Penn Station first. Then we could go down to the New York Law School. The driver turned around, gave us a funny look, and then took off. I told Mr. C what was going on to the property and so forth and he said, "Okay Kid, you're doing good. If you've got any serious problems you give me a call." I said, "Thank you very much."

I took him down to Penn Station, dropped him off, and he grabbed his train out to Sands Point. The cab driver turned around and said to me, "Excuse me for asking, but was that who I think it was?" I said, "Yeah, that's who you think it was." He said, "Wow. I see him in the papers all the time, but I've never had him in the cab." I said, "Yeah. He's a hell of a guy." He said, "He seems like a nice guy. So now you want to go down to the New York Law School?" I said, "Yep. That's where I wanna go." So he took me down to the New York Law School and I had a meeting down there. It was a very interesting trip.

I went back to the office. Feeling pretty cocky, I called Ken and I told him what happened. I said, "What do you think?" He said, "Well, we've got a couple of problems. He is a very powerful man, but he made a couple of mistakes." I said, "What's that, Ken?" He said, "Mr. Salgo has had that property listed as part of a college trust, and that trust has about nine different members in it. All of these members are prominent businessmen, They took advantage of this trust. It was incorporated in 1958 and I have just been going through the records on this, and I don't see any place where they are going to contribute anything for this trust that is going to be used for colleges. So it appears that what they have done is they have committed an act which we call "self-dealing" which allows them to take advantage of a trust and no one gains but them in a tax situation. I said, "Isn't that nice. What do you think that we should do?" He said, "Well, I also heard that Mr. Salgo and Mrs. Salgo are getting divorced." I said, "You heard that?" He said, "Yeah." I said, "Oh, boy, maybe we can get Mrs. Salgo on our side." He said, "That wouldn't be bad, if we could do it." I said, "Let me see if I can set something up for us on a Sunday morning when she is home."

I called Ken on Sunday and said, "Ken, are you available?" He said, "Yes." I said, "Okay, c'mon over the house, we are going to force this issue." So, I called Mrs. Salgo. I said, "Mrs. Salgo, I am happy to let you know I am going to be your new neighbor; I am coming over to show you what the model of the new house is going to look like that is going to be down below." She said, "No, no, no!!! Don't come over. Nick will be upset. I don't want you coming to the house. Don't come to the house." I said, "Mrs. Salgo, don't worry about it; everything is going to be good. We are coming over in a little while." And I hung up. Now, Pauline, Ken and myself, we drove over to Mrs. Salgo's big house on the hill, rang the doorbell and we were met by Karl, he was a German Tank Commander. Karl said, "Mrs. Salgo said that she did not want to see you." And, with that, I sort of pushed my way into the door, and I said, "Hello Mrs. Salgo. How are you?" And there she is, sitting in the chair. So we walked over to Mrs. Salgo and I said, "Mrs. Salgo, I want to show you a picture of the model house; it is going to be down below. It is going to be a beautiful thing and you are going to be proud of it and it's going to be wonderful. You don't have to worry about anything." She said, "Why should I worry about anything?" I said, "Well, if Nick has to go to jail, it's not your problem; it's his problem." She said, "Well, what do you mean, if Nick has to go to jail?" I said, "Mrs. Salgo, you are not involved. It is nothing you should worry about." She said, "Wait a minute." Then, the German Tank Commander called her and said, "Mrs. Salgo, can I show you something in the kitchen?" So, she got up and went out into the kitchen with him and then Ken winked at me and I winked at him. Pauline winked at us and we figured we got him. Now she came back outside and she said, "Mr. Otto, what is this business about Mr. Salgo having to go to jail?" I said, "Well, I'll tell you what happened. In 1958 they formed this trust. And this trust was put together by all these big, prominent businessmen. They all took advantage of this trust. They all took tax advantages and they all made money on it. None of them contributed anything to the colleges. So, what really happened is that it was what you call "self dealing" because they were using this trust for their own behalf – nothing for the colleges. It would be that he may wind up going to jail over this because he has committed fraud against the government. But it doesn't bother you because you had nothing to do with it. You are clean and you are going to be our neighbor up on the hill and everything is going to be fine. I want to thank you very much for the day and I want to thank you very much for allowing us to come in and show you the model. I am looking forward to us being good neighbors." With that, we left.

We left and went to the local restaurant and had a few drinks and toasted our success. We beat Mr. Salgo because he didn't bother us again after that. We were moving pretty good in all directions. Ken Malloy, our attorney, was great. He was a PT Boat Commander, he was on the next boat to John F. Kennedy in the war. He became a judge. When I went over to see him at the courthouse chambers, we'd have coffee and look at the

PT boat model he had. His boat was about 16 feet long and 5 feet wide and it must have cost $50,000. When he died he put it in his will to have it donated to the Port Washington Yacht Club. It's there now for you to see.

Anyway, I got a bill from Ken Molloy for $11,700. I said, "Holy Christ," because $11,700 in them days was a big bill. But he did the job; he knew what he was doing. So now, I got this bill, and I go down to see Mr. Lipsig. "Mr. Lipsig, we got a problem." He said, "What's that Bill?" and I showed him the bill. "Boy," he said, "Is that what it cost, Bill? Why did it have to cost you that much?" I said, "Because the attorney you assigned to it, Mr. Greene, failed to tell us about the envelope that existed on the property. He should have picked it up at the title search or the closing or someplace, but he never did." So, Mr. Lipsig pushed a button and said, "Would you please have Mr. Greene come in here."

Mr. Greene came in and Mr. Lipsig said, "Mr. Greene, Mr. Otto tells me that there was an envelope on that property, a restriction telling you that he could only build a property with a house so high, and you failed to warn him about that." He said, "Oh, I told Mr. Otto about that envelope." So Mr. Lipsig turned around, looked at me and said, "Bill, did Mr. Greene tell you about that envelope?" I said, "No; never, never once." He said, "Okay, thank you. Mr. Greene, would you please leave?" And he left.

Mr. Lipsig was pissed at him. He said, "You know, Bill, you never lie. Now, how can we square this up?" I said, "Well, I laid out $11,700." So, he said, "How about if I give you a check for $2,500. Would that help?" I said, "I'll tell you what. How about you give me a check for $5,000? Then, you'd really help." So, he pushed the button down and called the girl and said, "Draw up a check to William L. Otto for $5,000 and bring it in to me." He said, "You know Bill, I wouldn't do this for the President of the United States, but I'm going to do it for you because I like you." The girl brought the check in; he signed it and gave it me. I thanked him, walked out, went home that night and said to Pauline, "Guess what I got?" Then, I showed her the check for $5,000; she couldn't believe it. I said, "Well, we are lucky; it worked out good. We got $5,000 back."

We spent two and a half years designing the house and it came out great. The architectural firm of Jones and Morgenson did a magnificent job.

We proceeded to get contractors, get some prices, and get some estimates. That was another headache. But, fortunately enough, we had the situation set up where the architect was smart enough to put a phrase in the contract and if the contractor failed to perform his duty we could not only fine him $1,000 a day for being delinquent, but we could also assign the contract to another contractor and make him responsible for the difference. A lot of times, I stopped off and got coffee and cake and brought it down to the construction workers. I figured the boys would be there, about five or six of them, but it wound up that nobody was there. I threw the coffee and cake up in the air; I was so pissed. I got on the phone. Now we had some action going and the boys came back down. The one guy's name was McDonald – good guy. He had a drinking problem, but he was still a good guy. Anyway, he had his hands full. We finally worked on the property, worked on the foundation, got the forms put up, and we had the topping out with the flag. We had a big party there, and it was moving along very nicely. We had the family picture there with everybody standing around with a gold shovel that we stuck in the ground. The house proceeded to be built, and that was the famous Otto house in Sands Point. A lot of great memories in that house.

Well, we built the house and started to use the water out there on the beach, and the water started getting dirty. I said to Pauline, "We're going to have a problem here. We're going to have to put a pool in. It's a shame. We've got the beach in the backyard, but we're still going to need a pool." So, she said, "Well, let's do it." And we did. So, we designed a kidney shaped pool, about forty-two feet long with an eight foot deep end, and we put a big rock on the top and had the water fall there and the water came over the rocks. It was a three ton rock, and we had that built up, and that really looked nice, and we had a light on it. It really looked beautiful.

Then, we put up a volleyball court. We used to have volleyball matches there. And then, we put up a garden in the back there. And then, we needed something on the beach because I said to Pauline, "We can't keep bringing chairs back and forth to the beach! I'm going to look around and see what I can come up with." I knew that over in Manhasset there was a big pile of telephone polls. They were creosote, which is the coating they put on logs that make them last forever. So I got a hold of Frankie Scobbo, the Police Commissioner, who was also a general contractor, and I said to him, "Do me a favor? Get these things brought over and dropped off at my house and just leave them there. My son and I are going to make a barbeque, and we're going to put some benches up there that are going to be permanent. They will accommodate about 42 people and will be there all the time in case you want to have a party."

I said to my son, "you and I are going to build a picnic area with tables and benches and a big stone barbeque with a sink, running water, and electricity." So I laid it all out. First, we built a bulk head, with a 16 foot opening in front of the mast to allow a boat to come through. This would work off the electric winch that would be attached to the mast. Then we had the creosote logs cut so that they were about 6 feet long. We put them 3 feet into the ground and had 3 feet up, and we topped that off with 2 x 10's of red wood running the length and side skirts on both sides. We built two big, long tables, using the creosote logs for support and the 2 x 10's for the tables. We laid out where the electric line and the water line would go and tied it in with the barbeque. Then we started to build the stone barbeque. We put 4ft x 6ft x 8 inches of concrete down as a base with the lines underneath. We still had a load of the builder's stones left over from the fire place. We used the stones and poured black concrete in between to tie in the design, and it really started to shape up.

Half way through the building the barbeque, everything stopped. There was an open area where we were going to pour concrete, and I said to everyone in the family, "I want you to go in a room privately by yourselves and consider putting something into a time capsule. Write a story about yourself, or the family, or anything you want! Put some little coins or trinkets, and items that we have in existence at this time or this year, so that someone will open it up 50 years from now and get a surprise!" I had a stenographer's court case to put everything in. It was very strong and would certainly hold up. So we took the money, the coins, the letters, the local newspaper articles, the story about the flag-raising, some family pictures and things about the Otto Family, and some other little trinkets, put it into the center of the stone foundation in the barbeque and filled the area with cement.

We went a step further. There was a great big tire that floated in. This tire must have been nine feet across. I figured we would take that tire because there was a big tree on the beach, and we would put that tire around that tree, and it would be great because that would be a nice place for the people to sit in underneath the tree. What a hell of a job we had to cut that tire. I didn't realize it had steel coils, like cables, inside the tire. We had to cut the rubber, we had to cut the steel cable and then after we got it all cut, what a job it was to open it up and put it around the tree. We finally did that and then we put a cable around it again and tightened it up with a clamp so it kept the tire back in shape.

So now, we had the barbeque built down there, and we had a place for sitting down. The only thing that was missing was a ramp going down into the water to hold a boat. Well, I went to design some steel work, got a hold of some steel people, some cross members and everything else. We ran a trolley line all the way down – 180 feet into the water. I designed a cradle to hold the boat. We had the cradle, we had the 180 feet going into the water, and we had this big mast made out of oak from Sir Thomas Lipton Shamrock that went up about 75 feet in the air. So, I got a hold of one of one of these electric wenches, which was attached to the mast. I knew damn well we weren't going to pull that mast down, and with that wench, we were set up there now to pull a boat down. I said, "Pauline, let's go out and buy a boat."

So, we went out and looked around and looked around and finally came up with this boat. It was a 21 foot cruiser. We had a couple of small boats before that. We had a 14 foot Applebee with a 6 horsepower motor on it, and we had a 24 foot Sea Ray that I didn't really like because it was too open. I wanted something that would be comfortable for the girls so if they had to go to the bathroom, they could have a place to go.

So, we bought this cruiser. We went in, looked around, and Pauline said, "Gee, I feel very safe. It has high sideboards, and a nice place downstairs to go to the bathroom, and the kids can take a nap down there." So, I said, "Okay, we are going to buy this boat." And we bought the boat. Now, what do you think we called the boat? We called it *Mekree* which means "little one" in Greek, which was what Pauline was – she was classified as the little one of her family. We called it *Mekree* after her. We had a lot of great times on that boat.

Now, we have this big house in Sands Point. We have to decorate it, furnish it. Some of the people I knew were very helpful to me. I had one dear friend, Al Cornewal. He had in the executive storeroom of Apex Corporation, a set of eight leather chairs from 1903. They were magnificent, like Queen Ann chairs. I said to him, "Al, you know, I really would like to have those chairs for my dining room." He said, "Well, we're going to do it; we're going to get them for you." And, we did. We took out a couple each every so often. Little, by little, I got the eight chairs.

Then a guy came in. I wanted to have a Travertine Marble table. I had him put a big piece of steel underneath the floor to support the table. And then I had a contractor stay there and build a table out of oak, reinforce it with steel on the inside and put this Travertine Marble on top. It was 9 feet long, 48 inches wide, 2 inches thick and weighed 875 pounds. What a job that was to get that set up there. It was done and it came out beautiful. Then he did cabinet work on either side with Travertine Marble, and that came out beautiful.

I had these two contractors. Well, not contractors really, but two guys who were really good workers. They were brothers, Vito and Tony. One did the fireplace. We got twenty-one tons of fieldstone from Delaware, and we used that for the fireplace. He worked on that all the way up the fireplace in the living room, which was fifty-four inches long and about three feet wide. It opened up on the living room, and it opened up on the dining room. And then we had that stone going all the way up to the top, and it opened up on the bedroom upstairs. It was quite a piece of work.

His brother did all the cabinet work in the bedroom upstairs. The drawers all had ball bearings; you just touched it and it rolled ride out. He also built a bar for me because Jim Early had given me a porthole to use in the house. I said to this fellow, "Do me a favor—incorporate this porthole in the bar, so you can look up through the porthole and see the New York skyline." It was a beautiful, beautiful set-up. He worked on that bar; we made it into four sections. It was made out of oak and black slate. It was a masterpiece with a sink, lights, a refrigerator and glass doors. It was a beautiful piece of work. He stayed there and lived in the house for three months. He did the cabinet work and his brother did the stone work. We finally got the house complete, decorated, and we had our boat in the back yard.

Next step was the wine cellar. I had a room downstairs all set up as a wine cellar. I had all the cabinets designed, and with Brother Gerard of Christian Brothers, we worked out a way of putting the air conditioner so it would keep a constant temperature in the wine cellar. We kept it about

55 degrees, and the cellar was set up to hold 177 cases of good wine. It was a work of art, and I miss that wine cellar.

Then we had a pool room put in downstairs, and we all used to go down there and play pool. Right next to that was a Judo room. As I told you, my son and I both played Judo, so we felt that it would be a good idea to have the Judo room, and we utilized that quite a few times. We had some great parties, some great times down there. When we didn't use the beach for an outdoor barbeque, we used the overhang area that extended out from underneath my den. In any case of bad weather, we were covered.

We had a tremendously big anchor in front of the front porch, where the driveway was, and we got that quite by accident. We went to this place that was closing up, and he had Maritime equipment, and he had this anchor there. I said to Pauline, "Jesus, that's the anchor for us." I said to him, "Look, what do you want for that anchor?" He said, "I'll tell you what: if you could get that anchor into your car, it's yours for $75.00." Well, I did all I could do to get this anchor into this car. It must have been about six feet long, six feet across and about five inches thick, and boy, was it heavy. I finally did it, got it into the car, and we drove off with it and put it in the front of the house. It would have taken two men to move this anchor. I don't know how I got it into the car by myself.

I also had a workbench in that garage. We had a great house there.

We did a lot of great things in that house, and had a lot of good times. At Christmas time, we had parties and sometimes, we'd have 125 people. We'd have a hell of a time. We would use the local Police Department to park the cars for us. I remember one time, we were having a Christmas party, and I couldn't get the waiter I wanted. I thought, "My Son is nine years old. What about him and his best friend, Dango?" I looked at them and said, "The two of you, come here. I want to talk to you. How would you guys like to run the party?" Dango said, "How are we going to do that?" I said, "Well Dango, you're going to be the waiter and Son, you're going to be the bartender." So he said, "I don't know how to make the drinks." I said, "I know that, but I'm going to show you. I'm going to give you a book, I'm going to give you the list, and I want you to get familiar with the different types of liquor. We'll set up the cutting of the lemons and this and that, and every night when I come home, I'm going to ask you to make me a drink, and inside of a month, you're going to become a good bartender."

Well, I did that. I'd come home at night and I'd say to him, "Make me a Bourbon Manhattan." And he would make me a Bourbon Manhattan. He would look in the book to see how to make it and so forth and I'd say to him, "You used too much Vermouth, or you used imported Vermouth, and you could taste the Vermouth. We have to get some domestic Vermouth so we could taste the Bourbon." He understood that. The next night, I'd come home and I'd say, "Make me a Vodka Martini." And he'd make me a Vodka Martini. I'd say, "You see the way you made the Vodka Martini? That's the same way you make a Gin Martini, same thing," and he understood that.

By the end of the month, believe it or not, he wasn't a bad bartender. He did a hell of a job. I bought the two kids white shirts, black bow ties red vests and black pants. Now, they both looked classy, they were all set up, they knew their jobs, and they handled it beautifully. There was only one little complication. As the drinks were being brought back, the both of them decided that they were going to take a couple of sips to see what they tasted like, and I was glad that they did. But boy, I'm telling you, I think that they got a little hung over. But we had a hell of a time; we had a good party, the kids were great, but my son lost his taste for any alcohol.

We had a lot of Christmas parties there, Thanksgiving parties, barbeque parties. It was an endless stream of parties. Then when we decided to build the pool, we had the pool parties, the volleyball parties, and we had some great times there.

I could remember one time when the guys were building the pool. Yayia, Pauline's mother, what a wonderful woman she was, God rest her soul, she was down at the beach walking with Sheeba. Sheeba was our Doberman; she was a beautiful dog. We had a Doberman and an Airdale. So now, she was on the beach with our Doberman. There were construction men coming, they were working on the pool, and all of a sudden Yayia decided that she was going to come back into the house. She had the Doberman with her, and the Doberman saw all the guys by the pool, and she started going after them. Well, all these guys jumped into the pool—they didn't know where else to go. So, they were all down in the pool, eight feet down, and there was the Doberman up on top barking like crazy. Yayia came over and started talking to the dog in Greek, and believe it or not, the dog understood. So the guys yelled out, "What is that language you're talking to the dog?" She said, "I'm talking to the dog in Greek." Some of the guys said, "Does that dog understand Greek?" Yayia said, "That dog understands four languages!" They said, "Oh my God!" Yayia was a corker. She was something I'll tell you. She took the dog in the house, and the guys kept working on the pool, and they figured that Doberman was one smart dog.

What a pool we built. We made it a dark pool so that it would reflect the sun and make the pool eight degrees warmer. We had a three ton stone mounted about eight feet up with a water fall so we could dive off. We also had a diving board. My two little grandsons, Wesley and Warren, would come over to swim. I had to watch Wesley because he had no fear at all and he'd run out onto the diving board. He was only a year and a half old so he could hardly climb up onto the board. He'd run out onto the diving board and jump into 8 feet of water. Wesley couldn't swim; he didn't know what the hell he was doing but he just enjoyed himself, and he kept on doing it. He managed to get to the sides, get out, go back on around and jump in again. I had a three ton stone mounted about eight feet up with a waterfall so we could dive off. Oh, we had a lot of great times with that pool, and a lot of great times at that property.

We had the mast there. The oak mast was from Thomas Lipton Shamrock from 1889. He brought it over from England and he was going to race in the American Cup. At that time the other yachtsman were using aluminum masts. He figured, "Jeeze, if I'm going to get the aluminum mast, what am I going to do with this one?" So he dropped it off in the Brooklyn Navy Yard. Well, it laid in the Brooklyn Navy Yard for many, many years. Carl Fischer came along in 1920. He picked up the oak mast, had it put into the ground, down by the water, 18 feet into the ground in concrete, 75 feet out of the ground up into the air.

He wanted to make Half Moon Beach into condominiums and build up that whole area. He had a lot of imagination, this man. The Village turned him down, so he went out to Montauk, and he built the Montauk Hotel. It's called the Carl Fischer Inn. He finished with that and got the railroads to make an express train going from Penn Station out to Montauk Point. He did a lot of great things. The biggest thing he did was that when he went down to Florida, he liked an area called Collins Avenue, and started buying up the street. He bought up most of Collins Avenue, and he built the big hotels on it, like The Fountain Blue and all the rest of them – that was all put in by Carl Fischer. He was a great man with a tremendous imagination.

We had the mast so I got a hold of Congressman Buckley, and I asked him to do me a favor. I said, "Can you get a hold of President Nixon and get me one of the flags that fly over the Capital so I could put it up on the mast?" Well, he was successful, and he got me the flag. Now, I got a hold of the telephone company to get all those climbers that they use on the telephone poles. They're about 20 inches long, and then you drill a hole, pound them in, and you keep running around, circling it in until you get the step. And I put the steps all the way up the top of the mast. Then I went to the Highway Department and I got traffic light holders. Their long arms project out about 16 feet. You'll see them along the roads as you drive around. I projected them on either side of the mast fastened in with 16 inch long bolts. The only thing that was missing was the eagle up on the top.

I called my friend Frank Kindt. Frank Kindt was a tough piece of work. I mean he was a tough man. I remember one time, he heard that I moved to Sands Point, and he knocked on the door, and I opened up the door and there's Frank with a cigar in his mouth. He said to me, "Hey Bill, your dog just bit me." That was the Doberman – he did bite him in the leg. He came inside and we fixed it up with bourbon and bandages.. He was carrying a depth finder, a CB and a telephone. He must have ripped them off the boats that were nearby the harbor, but he didn't take all the parts. So if I had a depth finder, I had a depth finder without the wires that connected to something else that could get it right, or I had a CB that didn't work because I had the other parts missing.

Anyway, I thanked him for all the great parts he got and I said to him, "Frank, I got to get this eagle mounted up at the very top of the mast. It's only about 16 inches around up there and I need a hole drilled in there so we could put the eagle through there and have that spin out like a weather vain." He said, "I'll come back," and he did and he got the equipment he needed. So, he took a big, long extension wire, must have been a hundred feet long, and he had the drill put on it. He took a line that went all the way up, and climbed all the way up to the top of the mast, and believe it or not, he stood on the top of the mast and drilled the hole. I was sick just watching him. He had no fear this man. He drilled the hole, stood there, dropped the line, and we sent up the eagle. We got the eagle weather vain up there and he stuck it into the hole. I think to this day - it's still there. He was one hell of a guy. I was just so happy when he climbed down off there. I was glad to see him touch the ground. Does he make you nervous, boy.

Frank was the type of guy that used to go around to punch-out joints, you know, where there's a little action going on and they need a bouncer. He'd come into the place with a cigar in his mouth and grab the guy and boom! That was the end of the story.

In fact, I still to this day have the over under shotgun that he gave me. It's a Winchester shotgun and it's still good; I still use it. He did a lot of ski shooting and trap shooting, but because he did so much of it, he lost hearing in his right ear. That was a problem for him, so he decided to give it up, and he gave me his favorite gun. And that was Frank Kindt.

We decided we were going to have a flag raising ceremony. This became an involved process. We sent out invitations. We had Senators, Congressman, Judges, and everybody there. We had the Marines there. That flag once flew over the capital. It was given to me by Senator Buckley from President Nixon. My son gave the flag to the Marines who hoisted the flag above. The music was playing. It was a great affair. Father Carey was there. He made the invocation and then I made a little speech. We had a great time. It was a great day.

The Flag Raising Poster

MR. AND MRS. WILLIAM L. OTTO

REQUEST THE PLEASURE OF YOUR COMPANY

AT AN OLD-FASHIONED FLAG RAISING

ON THE MAST OF

SIR THOMAS LIPTON'S YACHT

THE SHAMROCK I

SATURDAY, AUGUST THE TWELFTH

AT ELEVEN O'CLOCK

HALF MOON LANE

SANDS POINT, NEW YORK

Reply Card Enclosed   Rain Date: August the Thirteenth

The Ottos, with Tina, 14, and Billy

An Old-Fashioned Flag-Raising

By Virginia Sheward

Sands Point—The American flag, once flown atop the Capitol, was a gift from Sen. James Buckley; the Color Guard, a loan from the U.S. Marine Corps, and the 100 spectators, many of them public officials, were on hand as guests of Mr. and Mrs. L. Otto on Saturday morning to witness an old-fashioned flag-raising on the Otto's beachfront estate.

The unusual ceremony, complete with bugler sounding "Call to Colors," and a military-band recording of "Semper Fidelis," and "The Star-Spangled Banner," featured the hoisting of the ensign on a pole that once served as the main mast of the first English challenger in the America Cup yacht race of 1899. The yacht Shamrock, built and owned by Sir Thomas Lipton, was defeated by Columbia, the U.S. entry, a fate shared by Shamrocks II, III, and IV in subsequent races through 1920.

Guests, including State Sen. John D. Caemmerer (R-East Williston) North Hempstead Town Councilman Clinton G. Martin Jr., Charles Frossell, retired justice of the Appellate Court, and Assemblyman Jack Gallagher, (R-Bayside), stood at parade attention throughout the ceremony from the moment Otto's 11-year-old son, Billy, handed over the folded flag to the color guard until it was "two-blocked" atop the mast.

At the conclusion of the ceremony, Otto, who is president of the U.S. Building Maintenance Co. of New York, made a brief speech. He said: "I have been asked by several people just what is a flag raising. I will tell you. It's a bunch of God-fearing, law-abiding, taxpaying Americans who have gathered to do honor to our country's flag."

He spoke briefly about the Shamrock and the 70-foot mast, cut down from its original 120-foot stature when it was brought to it's Sands Point site in 1920 by Carl Fisher, millionaire developer of Miami Beach and Montauk Point. Otto said he had converted the mast into a flag pole and now was trying to have it officially designated as an aid to navigation.

Monday, August 14, 1972

Every year around July 3rd, 4th and 5th, which was my birthday, we'd have Al and Bertha Cornwall, and Owen and Betty Cottle come over and we'd celebrate The Fourth of July and my birthday. They'd come out, and the six of us would have a special three or four day weekend where we would eat and drink, raise the flag together on The Otto Mast, and take the boat out. We'd play pool and volleyball in the water, volleyball on the land, and have a lot of laughs. They were great people. Al is gone now. Thank God, Owen is still here; I still see him and talk to him. Burt's gone; Betty is still here, and life goes on.

Well, we enjoyed the beach and what we did a lot of times was we'd get a deep fryer down there, and I'd go out with some of the boys: Bob Campbell or Jim Earley or Dick Powell or whoever it may have been. We'd go out to Montauk and go out with Frank Mundus, the shark Fisherman. He had this boat called the Cricket, a 32 foot Cricket, and we'd go out fishing and come back with our sharks. A lot of times we would catch Blue Sharks, and we'd cut the blue shark open, and you had a big solid piece of meat that was about oh, 3 feet long and about a foot and a half wide and 6 inches thick. We'd cut it up in small pieces, like the size of your index finger, and we'd have some egg batter there and some bread crumbs, and we'd drop the piece in there with the bread crumbs and then drop it in the deep fryer. And boy, you put that on a plate, and everybody was eating and drinking, and everybody was having a hell of a time.

I can remember one time the Judge and Dr. Weary, who was the treasurer of St. John's University, came over for a barbecue. Dr. Weary wore a suit and tie and I said, "Doc, this is a barbecue. You come over with a sports shirt." He said, "I don't have a sports shirt. All I've got are shirts and ties." I said, "Okay Doc, open up your collar, take your tie off and relax." I bought him two sports shirts a little later.

Now what happened was that we had a 21 foot Aqua Sport. It was an open boat, and it had a 75 horsepower motor on it. So now the judge said, "You know, I have my friend George Gross around the corner on Sands Point. You go around the Point and he's on the inside." I said, "Well, do you want to go see him?" He said, "Yeah." I said, "Well let's all get in the boat, and we'll drive over there." So now, we drove over there, and we got to the house. It was the Judge, Dr. Weary, Jackie and Tony Lavero, Pauline and me. We were all in this boat, and it's pretty heavy; we had a pretty good load there. So we were going around the Point, and the Point was pretty rough at times. Anyway, we got around okay, and we got over to the Gross home and nobody was home. Gross was the guy that built the houses on 59th Street that project over the East River Drive. That was Gross's job. He was also very active with the Horace Mann School in the Bronx.

Anyway, he wasn't home so we turned around and we headed back. Well, the water got rough. The Judge decided that he wanted to sit up front. So, he was up at the bough sitting there nice with a cigar in his mouth. He said, "This is living." The boat was going up and down, the water was coming in, and I was trying to bail it out and I said to myself, "Well, the boat can't sink; it's all fiber glass. All it will do is level off with the water." With that, I saw my son come out from around the point with the Applebee, which was a 14 foot boat that was used to bounce off the rocks so you catch the blackfish and had this 6 horsepower motor with it, and he came over by us and spun around, threw us a line, and he grabbed our boat. Believe it or not, he damn near towed us all the way in.

We finally got the boat in and up to the spot where we lived. The boat was level with the water, so we just went inside, and I just left the boat there because there was nothing I could do. I pulled the drain on the bottom and let the water drain out and pulled it up on top and that was it. Then we went back and did some more drinking. We always did a lot of drinking then, but they were good drinks, they were good days and it's good to remember them.

We had a lot of great parties in the area. Then I had three tuxedos, and Pauline had about ten or twelve gowns. There were always formal parties. Sometimes we would be sitting and talking with Governor Cuomo and Matilda. So everyone was always dressed fancy. Some of the houses we went to had two Rolls Royce's in the driveway.

My next-door neighbor sold his house. He went out to California – that was La Pinto. He sold it to a fellow named Herb Carmel. Herb Carmel took the house and redid the whole thing. He spent a million nine just redoing it. He did a hell of a job, and he was a great guy. He went over to England, and he brought back a maroon Rolls Royce that he loved. Coming home from work I used to stop off at his house and have a glass of imported brandy with him because he always liked that. We'd have the brandy together, and then I'd go home into the house and see what was cooking.

My buddy Mike Cozzoli lived around the other side of the Point on Hoffstot Lane. He used to come over with a new sports car that he bought, or an antique car. He bought a 1933 Ford one time that he drove around, and he was wearing one of those old fashioned caps when he pulled up. We took it out for a spin. Then he came around with a two-door Rolls Royce. The hood of this car must have been about eight feet long. We tried that out, but it was too heavy a car to move, so we didn't enjoy it. I still go to his grave and every time I go, I stick a penny behind the stone in the ground so he knows that I have been there.

I remember Mary Lou – she was Eric Kirchhofer's wife. They were the people we sponsored from Switzerland into this country. Her father was Mr. Bussman, a very famous man in Switzerland who worked at The Hermitage Restaurant on Lake LuCerne. He was famous for his great wine cellar that had 40,000 cases there. He was known all over Europe for putting the marriage between the bottle and the wine glass.

He used to invite me over but I never had a chance to get over there. But, he finally came over to see us at our house in Sands Point and we invited him for lunch. He said, "It would be an honor to have lunch with you." I said, "Well, will you please select the wine for lunch?" He said, "I heard you have a great wine cellar; let's look at it. But first tell me what we're having for lunch." So I told him what we're having for lunch and then he said, "Will you please show me where we are going to have it?" So I took him down to the beach, then he said, "Okay, let's go to the cellar." He looked around and picked out a 1955 Château De Paupe – the Wine of the Pope. It was a great year. It was like velvet. After three bottles of this we settled down by the beach and we all had a great lunch. He was a very classy man with shocking grey hair and a silver turtleneck sweater.

Meanwhile, I was working like ten, twelve, fourteen hours a day. On weekends I was setting up schedules so we could get this fixed or that fixed around the house. There was so much to do around the property; the property was so big. And then we had this caretaker, Caesar, Caesar Tyberia. What a classy guy he was. He would come to the house like he was going to a party, and that is how he would dress. He would take care of the property, take care of the lawns, take care of the grass, take care of the shrubs, and then he would say to Pauline, "Mrs. Otto, what do you think I should do with this shrub?" And she would say to him, "Caesar, whatever you think should be done. I'll leave it up to you. You're the boss out in the fairway." So he was always happy with that. He liked that, and he'd get a big smile on his face, and he'd go about and take care of everything. He did a good job too.

We had a great piece of property there, and he took care of that. Then we had the cleaning women come in once a week to help Pauline. Pauline was very helpful with me because a lot of times we wanted to paint something or fix something up on high, and I never liked height. So, I used to put the ladder up, and Pauline would climb up, and I would hold her ankles and brace her so she could fix something that was high. Particularly, we had to change the light fixture in the entrance for the foyer. That thing was up about 30 feet, and I never liked that idea. So I used to put her on a railing and tie a rope around her waist and tie the rope on the stairway there. And then she could lean over and I'd hold onto her so she could replace the light bulbs.

The kids grew up in this house in Sands Point. It was a great life for them. We had a beautiful home where they could entertain their friends, we had a great big, beautiful pool, a volleyball area, three boats, 290 feet on the beach, and we were always having parties. We used the boat a lot. My son and I would take the 21 foot cruiser out and stay over night in Greenwich, Connecticut and do some fishing. We had a lot of good times on that boat – it was a solid craft. Pauline and Tina would be going to the beauty parlors and shopping and visiting their girlfriends.

Tina went to Our Lady of Mercy's Catholic Girls School and My Son went to La Salle Military Academy. Tina graduated with honors and Billy made platoon sergeant. We would go out to Oakdale on Sundays and watch them march. A lot of times we'd be with Mike and Lucille Cozzoli and Joe and Tita Monti. They had sons going to the academy too.

I can remember La Salle used to have their Father's Day. It was a great affair. I would take a table and then invite all my friends and they would have a comedian there. A lot of the wise guys had their sons going to La Salle. I can remember my good friend Mike Franco was at my table. His father in-law was Joseph Socks Lanza, the guy at the Fulton Fish Market, and when Mike would meet Tommy Gambino, he would bend down and kiss his hand to show respect for the son of the Godfather. It was the first time I saw that, and it really impressed me. I liked both of these men. They were both great guys.

Another time at the affair, this comedian started making smart ass remarks about the mob, and no one was laughing. I can remember Tommy Gambino whispering in one of the waiter's ears and then the waiter left. The next thing, two guys came out on the stage, picked up the comedian, each by his arm, and took him off the stage, and everyone applauded! We all were laughing and got a kick out of that.

I had a lot of great guests come over for dinner – senators, congressman and so forth. We had great times. One night Judge Froessel came over and he was supposed to get there at 5 o'clock. He came in at 3 o'clock. I said, "Judge, you're here a little early." He said, "I know, I know. I wanted to come over and have a few drinks before Harry gets here." I said, "Alright. Come over and sit at the bar," and I made him a Bourbon Manhattan. We always had 2-3 of them together. He said, "Bill, you made this terrible." I said, "What's the matter?" He said, "I can taste the vermouth." I looked and said, "God dammit that's imported vermouth. I gave you the best!" He said, "I don't want the best. I want vermouth, but I want to taste the bourbon." Well I took the pitcher I had made for him and I just poured it out. He almost had a heart attack looking at me pouring out this pitcher of Bourbon Manhattan. So I made it with inexpensive American vermouth that he accepted because it wasn't that strong, and then I put a little extra bourbon in there. He always liked Jim Beam or Jack Daniels. And then we had a few drinks.

So now Harry Lipsig came in with his chauffeurs. The Judge shakes his hand and Harry Lipsig jumps! I said, "What's the matter?" Harry Lipsig said, "You son of a bitch." And The Judge had one of those buzzers in his hands that comedians use to shock people. I said, "You guys are characters, boy." We had a great time. Look at the book pictures; the ones of Harry Lipsig and Judge Froessel are priceless. I was so lucky to have them as dear friends.

Unfortunately, a while later, I got news from Carol, Judge Froessel's secretary. She said, "Bill, we've got a problem. The Judge is in St. Vincent's Hospital." I said, "What do you mean he's at the hospital. What happened?"

She said, "He was downtown at the lawyers club having lunch with President Ford. He somehow slipped and hit his head on marble and he went down. Security took President Ford out of there because they didn't want the publicity, and they took The Judge over to St. Vincent's." I said, "Holy Christ. Carol, I'm on my way." I jumped in a cab and headed over to the hospital and went to the desk and said, "Would you tell me where Judge Froessel is?" She said, "Well, who are you?" I said, "I'm Bill Otto." She said, "Are you a family member?" And I said, "I'm closer than family." She said, "Are you a family member?" I said, "No, I'm not a family member." And she said, "Well then you can't go in to see The Judge." I said, "What do you mean?" She said, "Just what I said. We have instructions that only family members are allowed to see The Judge."

I turned around and walked outside, trying to figure myself out before I get violent. I was standing across the street I looked over and there are two entrances to St. Vincent's Hospital. So, I went to the other entrance about 100 feet down. I walked in and didn't say anything to nobody. I just walked right through to the elevator and took it up to the top floor. I climbed up to the roof door and put a stone there, in case I had to get back in, and walked across the roof to the other door where The Judge was. I grabbed the handle, turned it, and it opened. I said, "Thank God." I opened up the door, walked inside, walked down the flight of stairs, came outside on the landing, and grabbed the first nurse I saw – she looked impressive – and I said to her, "I'm Dr. Otto. Where's Judge Froessel? I need to see him." She said, "Right this way Dr. Otto," and she took me over to his room, and I said, "Listen, we don't want to be disturbed. Don't bother us." She said, "Alright Dr. Otto."

I went inside, and The Judge and I were together. I was the last one to see him. He died while I was talking to him, but he wasn't even talking – he was just laying there. I'll tell you I cried when that guy went. He was a hell of a guy. He was like a father to me, this guy. He was always there for me – him, Harry Lipsig and Jim Early. You're blessed when you have people like that around you.

Well, anyway, The Judge died. We had a big funeral. Carol really pissed me off, and she's gunna read this and be upset but I don't care, she had no business doing it. No one was closer to The Judge than me. Anyway, she had a dinner for The Judge. Ivanka Trump was there and her kids – there were twelve people. After I found out she had the dinner I said, "Carol, why didn't you invite me!?" She said, "Well, I didn't want to impose on everybody else." I said, "For Christ's sake! I can't believe you did that!" She said, "I'm sorry Bill. I really made a mistake, I really did. The Judge would have turned over in his grave if he knew you weren't there."

She called me back a couple of weeks later and said, "Bill, I've got all this stuff up here. Would you do me a favor? I know The Judge would say the same thing to you. Come up and take anything you want. What do you want?" I said, "Carol, I don't know. You have no idea how much I miss that guy."

He had an apartment in Forest Hills, on Austin Street. I parked the car, went upstairs, walked inside, and I said, "Look, give me something for my son." So I took all The Judge's cuff links. I don't know what my son did with them. I got my daughter a three-piece pewter set from Germany. And for my wife, I said, "What have you got for my wife?" She said, "I've got a set of dishes that Senator Keating gave him. It seats 18." So I went over to the dining room and there was a tremendous set of dishes. I said, "Jesus, they are absolutely magnificent!" They are probably worth $50,000 today. Anyway, I called up Pauline and I said, "Pauline, I'm over here at The Judge's apartment. I'm looking around. Is there anything you would like to have as a remembrance of The Judge?" There is a tremendous set of dishes here for 18 people. They are black and gold and…" She said, "Bill, I don't want them." I said, "Okay, what would you like?" She said, "Does he have a glass pitcher or something from Germany?" I said, "Let me ask Carol." Carol said, "In fact, he does have a glass pitcher from Germany from his mother." I said, "I'll take that."

Carol said, "Bill, I've got all these trophies and heads, and I know you helped him hang up some of these heads on the walls because they are so big." I said, "I don't want them. I'll tell you what. Let me have that." I pointed to The Lady of Justice that The New York Bar Association awarded him. The statue was beautiful. Then I said, "And you know what else I'll take? I remember Senator Keating gave him a yellow stone that he had mounted and he used to wear it all the time. I'll take that ring." She said, "Bill, I've got it in the vault." I said, "Okay, can I have it?" She said, "Of course, you can have anything you want."

Two days later I picked up that ring, and I wished Carol good luck, and I left. It was a sad time; I'll tell you the truth. Carol stayed there at the apartment. The Judge took good care of her – had her fixed up for life. I don't know if she's still there, or still alive, but their apartment was something else. It was filled with animal trophies. There were bear heads and tiger heads, and all kinds of stuff because he hunted all over the world. He was a hell of a guy.

Later on in life, when I was leaving Sands Point, I got a mechanic – his name was Ed Runbelow. He was the engineer of The Queen Mary. He used to come down and take care of my boat. He'd come down, dressed up, take his jacket off, take the motor apart every year and lay it out on the tables I had set up on the beach. He'd take everything apart, put it back together – he was just a master mechanic. We'd have him and his wife, Pauline and I, we'd launch the boat out, take the key and start it up. And we'd take them out on the water and have some champagne. It was nice. We did that every year.

Now, it came time for me to leave the house. I was going to lose it over foreclosure. I said, "Ed, come on, I wanna say goodbye to you." He came into my den and I said, "Ed is there anything I could give you as momentum? You've been so loyal and so good to us all these years." He said, "Is that from Judge Froessel, the Masonic Lodge?" I said, "Yeah that's him. That's his ring." He said, "You know, we're opening up a Masonic Lodge in Port Washington." I said, "You are? Would you like to have his memorabilia to put in a glass case or something?" He said, "Jeeze, we'd love to have it all." I said, "Ed, you got it." So I took a box and packed everything up and gave them everything and he took it over there.

Later on I found out – I spoke to Dee, my old office manager, and we were going to have some diamonds appraised. And one of the diamonds was a yellow diamond. I said, "You know Dee, that ring that I got from Judge Froessel that he got from Senator Keating in India. I wonder if that was a diamond." She said, "Bill, it probably was." I said to the guy, "It was a diamond the size of my thumb. What would it be worth?" He said, "Maybe a couple hundred-thousand dollars." I said, "You're kidding. Well, isn't that nice."

So I called up Ed Runbelow and I said, "Ed, what ever happened to the stuff I gave you for the Masonic Lodge at Port Washington?" He said,

"Bill, they never opened the Masonic Lodge. The stuff was put into a closet over there and I never knew what happened to it." And to this day, it's a mystery: what happened to that ring? Where is it? Is it a diamond? Is it not a diamond? But, I figured it out. If Senator Keating, he was a very powerful man in India, if he gave The Judge a stone to have mounted, I don't think he would have given him just a stone. It was probably a diamond. But, what can I tell you? That's how life is: you make mistakes. I hope that ring is somewhere it can be seen, in honor of The Judge, because he was one hell of a man. God bless him. They don't make men like him anymore.

Sands point was a very interesting area. They had a Sands Point Country Club, and I heard Perry Cuomo wanted to join. They wouldn't let him in because they felt he was going to bring theatrical people, undesirable people, I don't know. But, he reached out to Mr. C and he explained to them that Perry Cuomo would be an asset to the club, so they let him in. Sometimes on Sunday morning, on Barkers Point Road you could see two very interesting people talk: Frank Costello and the Mayor Bob Wagner. Whatever they discussed, I'm sure we'll never know. But it was a good place for them to meet and discuss things in private. But, I should have had a picture of them two together. That would have been great.

We did it all. We had a great house there – it was very enjoyable.

Well, that covers us pretty much with Sands Point.

That's me at five years old where I was born in
the Bronx on 152nd Street and Brook Avenue

The only picture I have of my father, my sister
Jeanette, my sister Alice and myself.

Me in the army at Camp Pickett, Virginia

Father Phillip Carey, the Jesuit Priest who was
involved with Father Corrigan in making the film
On the Waterfront starring Marlon Brando.

This is the man who saved my life. James L. Earley,
the Irish Godfather. He was a tough piece of work.

Me by the fountain at 100 Church Street, New York,
when I started the idea of toys for the kids at Christmas.

Catherine Haffele was the head of The Workman's
Compensation Board and was very helpful to me.

These are the other two men who helped raise me.
On the left is Harry Lipsig, attorney, and on the
right is Judge Charles W. Froessel, Supreme Court.

The Spanish Pavilion is one of the projects I took over
at the 1967 World's Fair in Flushing, New York.

Sol Lindner was right along side of
me in a lot of tough spots.

This is a part of the New York Law School in
Downtown Manhattan. This was awarded to me
from Judge Froessel because I did such a good job
on the Masonic Pavilion at The World's Fair.

One of the buildings I owned in
Green Point, New York.

Brother Gerard Boch of Manhattan College. He
was the guy who was threatened and forced to turn
Manhattan College Campus over to a phony union.

Manhattan College Campus.

The house I built in Sands Point, Long
Island. It took 2 ½ years to design.

My family at the time in Sands Point at the Flag Raising
Ceremony. On my right is my daughter Tina, then
me, then my ex-wife Pauline, then my son Bill Junior.

Father Carey giving the invocation at
the Flag Raising Ceremony.

GREAT MARINE HONOR GUARD

The honor guard from the United States Maries
presented the flag that we got from President
Nixon for my son Billy to raise it aloft.

Some of the men at the Flag Raising Ceremony.
Starting from the left is Senator Buckley, Senator
John Cameron, me, Judge Froessel, Judge
Molloy, and Councilman Clint Martin.

The completed flag with the picnic
area built around the base.

My two dear, old friends, Harry Lipsig
and Judge Froessel. I later bought Judge
Froessel's chair when he died.

Old friends sitting at the bar in Sands Point. The
couples starting at the top left are Sol Lindner
and his wife, Judge Vincent Belletta and his
wife, then Doctor Paul Hershey and his wife.

My dear, old friend Jack Coakley, the world-
famous big game hunter, in Africa.

Jack Coakley had "The Big Five" six times over.

Jack Coakley and his wife in their living room in
Sedona, Arizona. This house first belonged to the
architect Frank Lloyd Wright. Their home was on
four acres of property, and we stayed in separate
quarters on the grounds. The two tusks behind them
are called 110 pounders – any hunter will know what
that means. On the coffee table is a black stoned
plaque that says, "Jack, we had a great time. Let's
do it again." This was signed by Frank Sinatra.

Three of the finest men you'll ever meet. Starting from
my right is Herb Terowsky of the Hempstead Outdoor
Stores, then my old buddy Al Cornewal, then Owen
Cottle, the treasurer of the ABEX Corporation.

My dear friends, Owen Cottle (left)
and Al Cornewal (right)

One of my dinner parties in Sands Point. Starting
from the bottom left is Dr. Bill Weary, the treasurer of
St. John's University, Bertha Cornewal, Harry Lipsig,
Pauline, Judge Froessel, Bobby Lipsig, and Al Cornewal.

My old pal, Frank Scobbo, retired Police Commissioner
of Port Washington. We were sent on an expedition
out in the country, sponsored by the U.S. Marines, to
check some of our country's defense systems. It was a
very interesting trip. We wound up at the White House
at the conference table with President George Bush.

My mother, one of the grandest old Irish ladies
you'll ever meet. She died at age 87. She spoke
Gaelic and she hardly ever ate. All she did was
smoke 2 – 3 packs of Camel's Cigarettes a day, drink
coffee and read books. What a treasure she was.

Ed Baragolia was another old, dear friend. This was
taken in Albuquerque, New Mexico. He was making
breakfast and he said that Pauline and I were such a
classy couple that he had to dress for the occasion.
So, he had a tuxedo on in the morning when we
came down for breakfast. He was the one who first
introduced me to Lou Aversa. That was Albert
Anastasia's boss. Lou was the head of the Columbia
Stevedores. We had a lot of good lunches together

On my left is Prince Paul Alfons from the Schloss, Johanissberg Wine Vineyards. On my right is Herr Staub, the wine master. We were on our way downstairs to sit where Napoleon sat, and drank three bottles of his greatest wines. Behind me were two tremendous rooms the size of football fields filled with magnificent wines. We went downstairs to the tasting room, and I sat in the big, velvet chair where Napoleon sat around the year 1815.

This is in the town hall of Frankfurt, Germany.
Upstairs are paintings of King Otto I, King Otto
II, King Otto III and King Otto IV. So, naturally
I took a picture and I became King Otto V.

One of the grandest, old, Greek ladies of our time.
This is Yayia, Pauline's mother. What a gem.

Otto's Pizza in Atlanta, Georgia. I opened
up four restaurants down there.

This was Frank's A Lot. This was a restaurant I
opened at 24 West 44th Street. This is Mr. Lipsig,
his wife Bobby, and my daughter Tina.

The Irish Godfather, smiling. That's James L.
Earley at my desk. I still have this desk.

Group picture of my Judo class. I spent fourteen years at Judo. In the front are my instructors, Sensi Ryohei Kanakogi (left), and his wife Rusty Kanakogi (right).

The top Judo players of the world at my house in Sands Point. On my right is Sensi Ryohei Kanakogi, my Judo instructor. On my left is Sensi Yasuhiro Yamashita, the Japanese Olympic Champion. In the middle is Radomis Kovacevic, the Yugoslavian Olympic Champion.

U.S.B.M REALTY CO., INC.

24 WEST 45TH STREET · NEW YORK, NY 10036

OLYMPIC JUDO TEAM COMES
TO SANDS POINT

As the guest of Mr. and Mrs. William L. Otto.
The Otto House is equipped with a complete
Dojo to play Judo in.

The above photo shows the Olympic Bronze medal
winner from Yugoslavia, Radomic Kovacevic,
kneeling. On his right is the International
3 time Olympic gold medalist from Japan, the
world famous Yasuhiro Yamashita, presently
holding the record of 240 straight matches
without a loss. Considering this means playing
the top men through out the world. That is
quite a record. His accomplishments are
unbelievable.

On Radomic's left is the famous Sensi Ryohei
Kanokogi, a professor of Judo, who presently
teaches at Kings Point Academy. Sensi Ryohei
has appeared in the movies many times including
one with Sean Connery, as well as on other
numerous television commercials. He owns the
Kyushu Judo School in Brooklyn, New York.

The tall man standing in the middle is the
host, Bill Otto, who has played Judo for 14
years and is a holder of the black belt from
the Kodokan in Japan.

They all came here to renew old acquaintances
and relax.

Judo is practiced by over 5 million people
through out the world today, taking its origin
from the Japanese Cultural Heritage going back
to the traditional Martial Arts.

When we discussed the sport with Sensi Yamashita, he calmly explained that he enjoys the violence of the sport. This was confirmed by Sensi Radomic who said it is such a great feeling when you can play someone like Yamashita and hit him and not have to worry about breaking him.

Mr. Otto summed it up by saying that when you play Judo with a man like Yamashita, it's like playing with a Volkswagen, what you can do with it.

A pronghorn antelope that I shot in Mexico. I
hit him from 570 yards and he was delicious.

I got a call from Mike Cozzoli saying, "Let's have
lunch." I knew him for years and this was three
weeks before he died. I visit his grave quite often.

This was taken in Costa Rica with my old friend,
Eric Kirchhofer, who I sponsored into this
country from Switzerland. Eric was a great judo
player and a master chef. He was the chef for
Jacqueline Kennedy at the Colony Restaurant.

Another beautiful, old friend, Herb Terowsky
of the Hempstead Outdoor Stores. This was
taken at his house in Cutchogue, Long Island.
Two old guys enjoying a drink and the fresh air.
Everybody should have a friend like Herb.

Frank Mundus, the shark fisherman out in Montauk, Long Island (left), and Jim Earley, The Irish Godfather (right), on Frank's old, wooden, 32 foot long boat – The Cricket. They made the movie Jaws after Frank's story.

Frank Costello and his wife, Bobbie, at their home in Sands Point, Long Island. A classy couple, my neighbors.

This was in my apartment at 417 West 37th Street. I
had a beautiful view overlooking the East River. On
my left is my girlfriend, Cathi Carley, and next to her
are Rosanne and Joe Bonanno. I met Joe's grandfather
many years ago. He was a tough piece of work, just
like Joe. Good friends, there when you need them.

This clock was given to me by my good friend
Joe Bonanno, when I moved to White Plains

My girlfriend Cathi and my first office manager, Dee Bergmanson, who was with me when I started out in business over forty years. She treated for my birthday at the 21 Club.

Mr. and Mrs. Joe Murania. I've known them for over forty years. Joe was maybe the first and only one to turn down the request of the Italian godfather, Joe Bonanno, to join his group. That's a long story.

This is my family. Starting from the left is my girlfriend Cathi, my grandson Warren, me, my daughter Tina, and my grandson Wesley.

Our Dear Friend, Al Cornewal

Chapter Eleven

"The Good Times"

I was still very active in running the business. I'd be working 12 to 16 hours a day and sometimes on my weekends. We were expanding it all the time – always putting on more men. I think I had 64 of my own men, and had about 189 of Jim Earley's gang downtown. But, I had to give that up a while back because I couldn't take care of everything. So, I just took care of my own business and that expanded very nicely. We bought a few buildings; we got involved with a little Real Estate. Then, I also got involved with the Zaire people. A good friend of mine, Joe Murania, he was the Vice President of Zaire. And before Zaire he was the Vice President of Sperry Hutchinson; I've got to tell you that story first.

What happened was, years ago, Sperry Hutchinson was about green stamps. They don't do it any more, but in those days, when you bought something, you would get green stamps, and you would put the green stamps in the booklet. When you filled the booklet up, you could redeem the booklet, and you could get something for the booklet. You could get a coffee pot, a toaster or something else. And it was a good business; it was a smart business.

Anyway, Sperry Hutchinson had a beautiful apartment in Hawaii, and Joe was after us. He kept saying, "Why don't you go out there, Bill? We got this beautiful apartment and it's just laying there. Why don't you go out there and use it?" So, finally it got to the point where he said, "Bill, I think we're going to be closing up Sperry Hutchinson. I think that you should use that apartment while we've got it." So Pauline and I decided that we were going to make a trip out there to Hawaii, and we did. We went out to Hawaii, and we saw the apartment – it was beautiful. We were up on the 19th floor, and it had a magnificent view. It was a great big apartment, and we enjoyed it.

The next thing that I wanted to do was get a convertible because I figured that a convertible in Hawaii would be nice to drive around with. Well, I went down to the rental place and I said, "I need a nice big convertible for me." He said, "Well, there's only one green convertible on the Island." I said, "Well, that's the one I want." He said. "Well, it's going to be a little difficult to get." And I said, "Well, I'm sure that you could…" and I greased his palm "…do this." Well, to make a long story short, that car was delivered. I went downstairs, and I blew the horn to yell to Pauline. She looked down, and I said, "This is the car we're going to use.

We used that car all over Hawaii and with it had one of the nicest meals we ever had. We took a couple of buckets, and we filled it with ice, and then we put some champagne in there. Then we took cheese, crackers, bread, olives, dips and stuff like that, and then we drove all the way down the end of the Island. The very end of the Island is restricted. It was used to support the army in the event of an attack by the Japanese. You can still see some of the caves where they had the gun emplacements in the cave to ward off any attack. We went as far as we could, and then we drove down and parked on the beach. There was parking for about 600 cars, and there was nobody there. We were the only car on the beach. Well, we sat on the beach, had a picnic, and it was absolutely magnificent. The waves were coming in 12-14 feet high, and they were breaking off the rocks. We were sitting there drinking our champagne. It couldn't have been nicer.

Then we drove all around the Island. It was interesting. We went to Hickam Field where Pearl Harbor was. That's a historic thing but it's very unusual to see that most of the people that own the businesses around Pearl Harbor are Japanese now, and they're the ones that did the bombing. The Arizona lies down below the water and you could stand up there and you could hear the loud speaker – I think it's Gregory Peck telling the story – and it's just inspiring. We had a great time there at that monument.

Another thing that we wanted to do was to play golf, and Pauline and I ended up playing golf with Al Eben, the guy who was the doctor on Hawaii Five-O. The golf course was above Hickam Field, and it was such a strenuous course that they gave you six batteries in the golf cart so it had enough power to get you up and down the hills. Well, that day I couldn't play for beans. I was so bad at playing that I said to Pauline, "Look Pauline, you play golf with the guys. I'll do the driving. I'll be your chauffer." And that's exactly what I did.

Hawaii was nice, but coming back from Hawaii was an interesting experience. We got on a plane, and the plane didn't take off. So, everybody was getting nervous why the plane was not taking off. It seemed that the Queen of England was landing or taking off – I don't know which it was – so, she had restrictions on the fairway. Nobody could do anything on the fairway until she got off. So, we just sat there and sat there and sat there, and the crowd got nasty; they got real belligerent. And it got to the point where one of the guys actually pushed one of the stewardesses, and it got to be a problem. He went around trying to get people sign a petition saying that she didn't do the right thing, and that they were not being taken care of properly and this and that and everything else. We refused to sign the petition. But anyway, after a while, we finally took off and headed back to the United States.

We pulled into San Francisco, and that's another interesting story. We wanted to stay at the Fairmont, and it was difficult to get accommodations in the Fairmont because they had conventions and everything else, and everything was booked up. So, I had a friend of mine, his name was Bob Plimack, he knew someone out there who was in the insurance business. He said he knew connections with the Fairmont, and he'd get us in there. Well, he got us in there all right. He got us into room 1801, which overlooked Alcatraz, and it was a magnificent view, a magnificent room, and it couldn't be any nicer.

The next morning after we checked in, we were downstairs in the Restaurant having breakfast, and a guy came over to us, and he said, "How are your accommodations, Mr. Otto?" I said, "They're great." He said, "I'm Mr. Schweig. I own the Fairmont." I said, "Mr. Schweig, I just want to tell you, you have a great place here." So Mr. Schweig said to me, "Here is my card. If there's anything, anything at all that you want or anything I could do for you, do not hesitate to call me." I said, "You got it."

So now, Mr. Schweig also arranged to have a convertible downstairs for us. So, we got that car, and we took that car; he would tell us where to go. We took that car over to Sonoma and went into the cheese factory and got some cheese. Then, we went to the sourdough bread place on the end, got some sourdough bread, and then went around and about a mile away was the Buena Vista Vineyard. We pulled in there, and they had benches right on the stream. We got ourselves a nice bottle of Zinfandel, and had the sourdough bread and the cheese, and sat there. I want to tell you man, that was living – just breaking off the bread and sitting there and just drinking the wine. It was a beautiful, beautiful day. Remember: if you go to the wine vineyard, take two glasses and a knife from the hotel for the wine, bread and cheese. It will make the meal that much nicer. We had a great time on that trip.

We spent four days at the Fairmont. We left and flew back to New York. We got back home, I got into the house, and I said to Pauline, "You know, the bed and the mattress and the pillow cases and everything else we had in the Fairmont is nicer than what we have. We have this great posturepedic set here, but it's not really as nice." So she said, "Well, what are you going to do?" I said, "Let me see what I'm going to do."

So I called up Mr. Schweig in San Francisco, and I said to him, "You know, you told me that if there was anything I wanted, anything you could do, you would do it." He said, "Of course." I said, "I'm going to put you to the test. In room 1801, we had a very, very nice mattress, pillows and box spring. We had such an enjoyable time sleeping. I'd like you to ship that whole thing to me in Sands Point." He said, "You're kidding me." I said, "No. Didn't you say to me, 'Anything you want?'" He said, "Yes, I did say that. Let me see what I could do."

He called me back a couple of hours later and he said, "Look, I can't get you that set because it's been used; it's against the health laws. But what I can do is, I can call the manufacturer and have the manufacturer ship you a set. Will that satisfy you?" I said, "Absolutely." And that's exactly what he did. He called the manufacturer, and about five days later a truck pulled up and there was the mattress, pillows, box spring and so forth – the same that we had it at the Fairmont.

So now, the guy took out our old (well, it was brand new) posturepedic mattress and pillows and so forth, and he said to me, "Can we have these?" I said, "Of course you can have them; we don't want them." He said, "My God, they're brand new." I said, "That's great; enjoy them." And we got the ones that we wanted, and they got the ones that they wanted, and everybody was happy. So, that was an interesting story, our stay at the Fairmont. I highly recommend anybody going out there to get the sourdough bread, to get the cheese and get the Zinfandel and sit there by the stream and just enjoy life. It's so beautiful out there.

Chapter Twelve

"Back To Business"

Business was going alright. Then I started thinking about expanding into something else, a different venue. A property came up on 24 West 45th Street. It was a nine story building, right next to the Harvard Club. It had been sitting there for a while, so I thought I would take a shot at it, rent it out and see what could be done. I bought it, which was a big step. It cost three and a half million dollars to buy and the rates at that time were fifteen and three quarters for the interest, so it was a tough time to buy. Anyway, I did buy it. I had the contractors come in and we put in ceilings, we put in walls, we put in bathrooms – we did the whole damn thing and it came out beautiful.

We rented it out – well, tried to rent it out. We did alright for a while. Then the market got very, very bad. People started having difficulty paying the rents and so forth, so I started to get into big trouble. I had a Chase Manhattan mortgage. I couldn't make the payment and I didn't know what to do. I was able to get a hold of some fellow at a foreign bank and we negotiated a deal. I gave him $135,000 and he got us a mortgage, which was an unusual situation because you figured I needed about $42,000/ month to cover the mortgage and I only had about $18,000/month coming in. So, why would a bank even think about giving you a mortgage on a building in a situation like that? But, they did. They must have some reason or ulterior motive in mind; whatever the situation was, we took a stab at it. We figured the market would turn around and we would get back in shape again. But, it didn't happen and people were losing money all over the place.

I had one guy come in to me and he said, "Bill, I don't know how many millions of dollars I've lost and I am in big, big trouble." So, I said to him, "Carl, how much do you have left?" He said, "I have about twelve million." I said, "Is that your limousine downstairs?" He said, "Yes." I said, "Take your twelve million and sell the limousine, pay the driver off, sell your place in Kings Point and go down to Florida. You will have about eleven million left over. Enjoy your life and get out." And that's what he did.

Talk about tough times. I can remember when I didn't have the money to pay the taxes on Sands Point. In total I owed $26,000 and it was due Friday. On Wednesday I called my dear friend Herb Terowsky from the Hempstead Outdoor Stores. Everyone should have a friend like this. Herb said, "Bill, how you doing?" I said, "Herb, I'm up to my ass in problems. I'm trying to get money to pay my men, trying to get money from the accounts, and on top of that, I can't even pay my taxes." He said, "Bill you have to pay your taxes." I said, "I know Herb. Where am I going to get the money?" He said, "How much do you owe?" I said everything all together that's due on Friday is $26,000. Herb said, "Don't panic. We'll work something out."

About two hours later, Eddie Francis, the security guard downstairs said, "Bill, there's a big, black car out here. This guy just got out and gave me this briefcase and said 'Don't loose it. Bring it up to Bill.' I'm coming up with it now." Eddie walked in, gave me the briefcase, I said, "Thank you." He left, I opened up the briefcase and had to step back in disbelief. Inside was cash piled up. I counted it, and it came to, you guessed it, $26,000. There was a note inside that said, "Bill, take care of your taxes, it's very important." It was signed by Herb. I called Herb and said, "Herb, you're a sweetheart." He said, "Bill, that's what friends are for. I know you would do the same for me." Herb – If everyone treated us the way we treat them, what a wonderful world this would be.

A lot of people hung in and figured the market would turn around. It didn't. I was getting deeper and deeper into trouble. The only recourse I had was to borrow on my home in Sands Point, where I never had a mortgage. This was my dream house that I worked so hard for, and I had to take a mortgage out on it. I took a 1.9 million dollar mortgage out on it and paid off some of my loans and some of my debts, got some money in the bank. I was trying to get squared away.

> *It's like the guy that's in trouble and was looking to hire a new accountant. He saw four different guys and he asked the fourth guy, "What's 2 + 2?" The accountant said, "What would you like it to be?" He knew in his heart that this was the accountant for him. We all need help at times.*

Chapter Thirteen

Manhattan College

In 1967 I was awarded the contract for the New York Law School because I did such a great job with Judge Froessel at the Masonic Lodge at the World's Fair. He was instrumental in me receiving that award. We had the main building with two other buildings joining on the left and right side. It was a beautiful contract.

One of the men down there was a fellow by the name of Andy Galway. He was a brilliant attorney. He was also on the board of Manhattan College. He called me and he said, "Bill, you're doing a great job down here. I was wondering if you could help us out at Manhattan College." I said, "Well, why? What's the problem?" He proceeded to tell me about this mob organization that got into the campus and threw out the local unions and took over the campus.

"How the hell did they do that?"

"I think Brother Gerard Bach is the best man to tell you the story."

"First chance I get I'll take a run up there and see Brother Bach."

In June I got a call from Brother Gerard Bach. He was in charge of the maintenance of the campus.

"Will you come up and sit down and talk with me?"

"Yes, I will."

I made arrangements to go up there and with him. Well, it turns out that this guy named Benny the Bug, Local Five out on Long Island, came in. Apparently, Benny was on drugs, and he had this black fella with him who carries a 45 and drugs with him. He gives Benny the drugs as he needs them. They're a tough group from Long Island. They came to the campus, met with Brother Gerard and told him they wanted to take over the campus. Brother Gerard said, "You can't take over the campus now. Everything is fine."

Brother Gerard looked at me and said, "What do you think happened Bill? They smacked me in the mouth!" "What!?"

"Yeah, they smacked me right in the mouth and said: 'You listen to me you son of a bitch. If you ever wanna receive communion again you better listen to me. When I tell you we're taking over this campus, we are taking over this fucking campus and we don't want any shit from you and that's it!'

Bill, he scared the hell out of me. And with that other guy with him – forget it. I knew damn well I'd have a big problem, or they'd soon kill me.

"They wound up taking over the campus, Bill, and they've been here for a while now. They threw out Local 32-E."

"How the hell did they do that?"

"They are very strong, tough people Bill. That's my problem."

"Well, you've really got a problem."

So we decided to meet with Tom Lennon who was the Vice-President of the campus. I said to Brother, "Look, get the Union Contract or whatever contract you have with them. Let me take a look at it." I met with Tom Lennon and mentioned Andy Galway, who was his friend, and we started to put the plan in action. I said, "Let me think about it fellas, cause I have to digest this. It's going to be a problem. We're scared to death." I said, "Leave it to me. I'll be in touch with you in a few days."

Well, I met with them a few days later and I said "I'll take over the contract effective September 1st. With that contract I want an increase in the $2,000 a month that you're paying now. I'm putting my life on the line, and I feel that I deserve more."

"Bill, can you get him out of here?"

"I will *arrange* to get him out of here."

"Well, how will you do it?"

"You'll have to leave that to me. Let me see what I can do about straightening this thing out. I'll write up a new contract for you. I'm not gunna do nothing until I got it signed by you and Tom. I want a solid three years. We'll have it set up in August, 1967. It's June now. We should have everything in order in the next couple of months."

"Jesus Bill, it's worth it. That'll be great."

I drew up a new three-year contract to start in August 1967. Now I've got a contract from Manhattan College, what do I do? I called up the Irish Godfather, my buddy Jim Earley, and I told him about it.

"I knew about it, Bill. Local Five is a tough piece of work. Believe it or not, they threw 32 out of the Bronx Local. It's been bad news since."

"Jim, I'll need some help."

"I'll see what I can do."

I got a call from Jim and he said, "Bill, you'll need a union contract with 32-E to get into the campus so we can throw the other guy out, make it legitimate, and get everything back in order."

"That's sounds great Jim. What's the procedure?"

"Okay, here's what I want you to do: on a certain morning at about 9 o'clock, a limousine will pull in front of your building, they'll let you know when. Your driver will be Sol Linder. You'll get in the passenger's side don't look in the back. Larr Lynch will be in the back with two guys from Chicago. The arm rest will go down, and I want you to put an envelope on there with $2,500 cash. The armrest will go back up. Then you'll take off to the Bronx, up on The Grand Concourse to the 32-E Union Hall."

Well, that's exactly what happened. I got a call, met them downstairs, jumped into the limo, went uptown to The Grand Concourse, stopped by 32-E, and they said, "Stay in the car." Larr went upstairs with Sol and the two boys. I never even saw what they looked like. They were up there for about a half hour. They came back down and said, "Have you got your figures straightened out? What you want? What you want to pay these men?" I said, "Yes."

"Come on up and sign a three-year contract."

They called me upstairs and I met Henry Chartier, President of the 32-E Local. He said, "Bill, here's the contract." I said, "Wait a minute now. What do I do with the crew that's up there now?" He said, "You throw them out. Get rid of them." I said, "That's great. What do I do for labor?" He said, "Let me know when you're going to be up there, where you will be, and I'll send you 62 men. Out of that you pick out what you want."

We arranged to meet at the engineering building; we met in one of the classrooms to fill out applications. He sent up 62 men and I picked out Louie who I wanted as the crew boss, and we hired 22 other men. We went around the campus that night, looked everything over, laid out the work, laid out the jobs – keep in mind I'm by myself. It was a tough nut. We were there for hours, and we did everything we had to do.

We notified Local Five, registered mail and so forth, and he was finished. Benny the Bug had to leave the campus, and we wanted him out of there NOW. No nonsense, we wanted him out. 32-E was coming in with the full crew, and the registered local was going to be in on the job. I notified Local Five and said, "U.S. Building Maintenance was taking over the contract and Bill Otto is in charge of it, and that's the way it was going to be. From there on in you're getting no more money, we're firing your complete crew, and you're finished."

At that time I was taking judo lessons. I was going three times a week, sometimes two or three hours a session. And it was good for me; kept my heart strong and my body in shape. I took the frustrations out of what was going on with my business.

The head of the judo school was a fella by the name of Jerry Mackey. He was a very fine human being. I can't praise him enough. He's a decent character, an upstanding man, and he's there when I need him. Jerry and I had become friends because I had been going to school for quite a few years practicing judo. I told Jerry I was going up there and there might be some problems. So he reached under his piano, took the tape off and handed me a 38. He said, "Bill, it's cold. Use it if you have to. Take care of yourself. Make sure you come out alright."

"Jerry, I can't carry a gun. I have to go up there as a business man. I'm not licensed to carry a gun. But, it's a good idea."

"Alright, I'll tell you what. I'll give you two tough men. These guys played judo outside. They are tough, and they are security men. They are both armed and lisc licensed. I'm taking care of them and I want them to stay with you for three days. Make sure that everything goes good, okay?"

I'll take the men." They were my body guards for three days.

A week later I was up in the Vice President's office, the phone rang, and it was the security guard at the gate. He said, "Look, I've got trouble here. These men down here don't want me to call the police or nobody. All they want is for Bill Otto to come out. They want to talk to him." So we went over to the window to look out at the gate, and there were four cars blocking the entrance gate. I said to the security guard, "Don't do nothing foolish, just stay there. Tell them I'll be out there as soon as I can. I've got a few problems to take care of here and then I'm coming right out." He said, "Okay, thank you."

I got on the phone and called Jim Earley. He said, "Describe to me what's going on." I said, "There's four cars out there blocking the entrance way."

"Alright, here's what I want you to do: NOTHING. Don't you go outside. They're going to kill you. You stay in the building, and don't go out until you get a clearance from someone who is going to approach those four cars."

"Okay Jim." He said, "When that clearance comes through, then you're going to call me. Do you understand?" I said, "Yes."

"Now, do nothing. Just watch."

About an hour went by and we were nervous and excited. I was with Lopez, he was the treasurer of Manhattan College, and he was there with me looking out the window. After an hour another four cars come alongside these cars, and guys jump out of these cars with guns in their hands. I'm telling you, it was some sight. They went over to these cars and said, "Get the fuck out of here otherwise we'll shoot you!" Well these guys, they had a job to do, they got paid X amount of bucks to do the job and they didn't want to get killed so they took off. The guy in the lead car waved to me, and to this day, I'm not sure who he was. When he waved to me, and I waved back.

I called Jim and told him what happened. He said, "They're the boys from The Teamsters. They came out to give you a hand." I said, "Thank you, Jim."

I was bringing the payroll up on Wednesday nights. I got their checks and had them cashed because these guys didn't have any bank accounts, so I gave them all cash. Dee was in the office, and she always took care of all this and got the money for all the boys. I always went up to the engineering building and met Louie, gave him the money and he took care of it. But that particular Wednesday I had some problems downtown, and I couldn't get up there. Meanwhile, I had all the cash and payrolls and everything else.

The following day I called up Louie and said, "I'm coming up tonight." He said, "Thank God you didn't come up last night. You had four guys hanging around all night in the engineering building waiting for you. From what I can gather from the discussion, they were gunna kill you, then take you up on the roof, throw you off the roof, and say you slipped because you were examining something – who the hell knows." I said, "Were you there?" He said, "Yeah. Bill, if they did you, who knows what they're gunna do to me. But you didn't show up. They waited till 1:30, and they said 'Fuck it!' and they left." I said, "Isn't that great. Okay Louie, come downtown, the money will be there with Dee. I' going to get a gun."

First thing I did was call my friend Herb Terowsky of the Hempstead Outdoor Stores. I told him, "Herb, I've got to get a gun. What do I need?" He said, "You'll need a pistol permit to carry, Bill. It's tough to get and you'll need three strong signatures on it, otherwise you'll not be recognized. As soon as you get that, you bring it into me, and I'll give you a gun you can carry." I said, "Just like that?" He said, "Yeah. But you have to get those signatures." I said, "Okay, let me see what I can do."

I went to see The Judge, Judge Froessel. He was out in Jamaica. I told him what was going on and what happened, and he said, "Oh my God." He called one of the captains at police headquarters downtown and told him what was going on. He said, "My friend needs three applicants to sign immediately so he could get his pistol permit." The Captain said, "I'm sending a car up with them right away. You'll have them in an hour."

The applications came, The Judge took his out, spent a lot of time on it and then said, "Bill, that's number one. I'm going to call Harry Lipsig and tell him what's going on. I want you to go down and have him sign it." I jumped in the car, went to Harry Lipsig's office and he worked on the application and got it all done. I needed one more so I went to Jim Earley and said, "Jim, you're the Vice President of Helmsley and Spear. That's a pretty strong application. Can you fill out my form for me?" He said, "Of course I can. First, let's go out and have some lunch. We're going to meet up with some friends of mine."

We went down and across the street to a little Italian restaurant on 41st between Madison and 5th. We walked inside and who are we meeting but Mike Genovese and Sammy Salerno. We all sat down, said hello, had a drink, and Mike said to me, "How's it going kid?" They always used to call me "the kid". I said, "Mike, I've got some problems," and I told him what was going on. He said, "Son of a bitch. You see those two boys in the corner over there? Do you want them? I'll give them to you for a week. It won't cost you a fuckin dime. If anyone comes near you, they'll kill him!" I said, "No Mike. I can't do that. I'm gunna carry my own gun. I've got to protect myself as a legitimate business man. I can't go into that kind of a situation." So he said, "Well, what are you doing about getting a gun?" I said, "Judge Froessel and Harry Lipsig signed the application. I'm waiting for one more guy and that's Jim." He said, "Why isn't it done?" I said, "We just got the application now. It's upstairs in Jim's office. He's gunna fill it out as soon as we've finished lunch." He said, "For Christ's sake Jim, get the fuckin application done! Get the kid his gun!" Jim said, "Mike, I'm gunna get the application as soon as I get a fuckin drink and something to eat! Now don't break my balls. It'll be done."

So we had our lunch, talked about a couple of things, went back upstairs, and Jim filled out the application. Now I had three signatures. I took the three, called up Herb Terowsky and told him I was coming out. He said, "Make sure you get three passport pictures taken and bring them with you." Now it's late in the afternoon. I went back out to Herb's place and I said, "Herb, I finished the applications; I made copies and everything else. Do me a favor? I don't want a dark gun; I don't want a black gun; I want something shiny. So if I take the goddamn thing out, they see that it's a gun, and then I could use it."

So now, I've got the applications, I've got the gun, and I'm walking around with a 38 all the time. Things quieted down and we ran the campus and everything was in pretty good shape. Nobody bothered us after that. Benny the Bug was gone, his crew was gone. Now we've got a decent crew in there who doing their jobs. We had a nice rapport with the campus; I was very friendly with Tom Lennon. About ten years later, Brother Gerard Bach died.

Everything was good for about ten years. Then, an ex-cop was hired to run the security department. They hired this guy, who we will call "JM." I think he was somehow involved with The French Connection downtown, and he was involved with all kinds of shit.

This guy would take a hot stove, believe me. He gave the cops a bad reputation. Some of them were decent guys; I knew a lot of them. My great grandfather got killed on the police department up in Harlem. His name was Walsh.

JM was like putting a wolf in with a herd of sheep. We had that contract there for twelve years. Then, JM decided he was going to get me out of there. He made a deal with Arcade, the cleaning contractor. He put the contract up for bid. Meanwhile, I carried a gun around to save their asses; I threw the mob out; all this bullshit that I went through and they're turning around and looking to get me out. That's what you had with JM. I don't give a fuck if he's still alive. He was a scumbag. Garbage. I could tell you some other stories about him, but it would only hurt other people. There is no sense in hurting them because of him.

So now, we had a meeting with Lennon, Moran and JM. Lopez left after all the bullshit to work at Columbia University. Brother Gerard and Andy Galway were dead. Lennon had no balls. So really, I had nobody there. They put the job out to bid, and what do you think happened? I lost the contract. I enclosed the letter that I sent to Tom Lennon so you could read it and understand what my feelings were and what transpired at that time. I got so fucking aggravated that I got up and I went to the president's office – Brother Steven. The secretary said, "Mr. Otto, he's busy."

"I have to see him now," and walked in past her desk, to his office, and said, "Brother Steven!" and what do you think he did? He put his hands up to cover his eyes and he said, "Don't tell me! Don't tell me! I don't want to know about it! Don't tell me!" With that his secretary came in and said, "Mr. Otto, would you please leave?" I said, "Sure, I'll leave. I'll get off this campus. I'll get off it for good." And I left.

Twelve years of all that shit. Meanwhile, JM was still there, Moran was still there, Tom Lennon was still there, but the guy who did the dirty worked and saved all their asses, he was gone. But, that's life. That's the way things go sometimes.

Here's the letter I sent to Manhattan College:

February 2, 1979

Mr. & Mrs. Tom Lennon
400 West 253ʳᵈ Street
Riverdale, Bronx, New York

Dear Tom & Kathy,

I was very surprised to receive your Christmas card this year. After what transpired at Manhattan College, I naturally assumed that this was the end of our friendship.

I can recall Andy Galway telling me, "Bill, stay close to Tom. He is the answer up there. If you stay close to him, everything will be alright." Well, I stayed close to you, Tom. I spent endless months meeting with you at lunch, at dinners, even in your own home, to solve the problems of the college. I can even recall you pushing me out of the snow one evening when it was late at night, after a long discussion, at your home.

I can recall revealing all the facts and figures and percentages showing profits and all our cost schedules so that if anyone should question you, you would have a clear head and know for a fact what my profit was so that you could understand and justify the prices.

I can recall our discussion about the Office of the Physical Plant and how to prepare ourselves in the event that JM and Moran should decide to quit, because you again ordered the contract through me and because they were so opposed to my being there, that we knew they desperately wanted me out.

I can remember you saying, "This will not happen," so we made arrangements and we discussed preparations on how to protect the college in the event that we needed another engineer or security officer and as I told you, it would take a matter of a week in order to reorganize the whole setup and that it would save the college $90,000 to $120,000 per year.

I can recall you admitting to the incompetence of these men and how you desperately wanted to straighten things out and you relied on my help. I can recall all the additional labor I sent to the premises, assured that the contract would be reissued to us, particularly on the basis of your word, which stated that if my price was fair on this bid, that a new three-year contract would be issued to me. I have the list of all the prices that the contractors submitted. Of the seven contractors, my price is in the middle, which can certainly not be any fairer, and surely after spending $3,000 to redo the supply room and contributing $4,000 to your gym, you were aware that my heart was out for Manhattan College and if needed, I would even cut my profit to match the nearest competition, but this opportunity was not granted to me.

I can recall me telling you in January what I heard from a very reliable source, that a deal was made between JM and Arcade to take over the contract and I remember you saying, "Nothing like this will ever happen to Manhattan College," and then for you to call me 14 days before the expiration date and tell me that, not because of price, and not because of our workmanship, but because I did not get along with the Office of the Physical Plant, meaning, JM and Moran, that you decided to give the contract to Arcade. I realized at this point that the man, who studied to be a priest, who had a beautiful family and who was the Vice President of Manhattan College that I held so dear to my heart, was indeed a person who I could not believe or rely upon.

It was fortunate that I had enough sense to tell other Board members in February about this situation. They are aware of what happened. They sit at the Board meetings knowing full well what you have done and they look at you to wonder what you will do next.

I can remember many things, Tom, including the friendship that was shared between the two families. Yes, as Andy said, I stayed close to you and got the biggest screwing I have ever received in my life. I want you to know that as long as the Lennon/JM/Moran combination exists in Manhattan College, I will never bid for the services on the campus.

In the future, if this combination should split, I would most certainly like to become a part of Manhattan College again.

You may have forgotten that I was the one that when Brother Gerard's life was threatened by the Mob Union that controlled the campus, that I came and put my life on the line, that I stepped in and solved your problems. You know, I carry a 38-revolver since that incident and then men who signed the voucher, these are three of the most respected men in our city. They thought enough of the problem to push through the permit for me. We all worked together to solve the problems at Manhattan College.

I talked to some of the alumni and they are thoroughly disgusted.

It is a frightening thing, Tom, what you have become a part of and what you have created. You have let a lot of people down. What has happened here will follow you for the rest of your life.

Regretfully,

William L. Otto

This is the letter that we sent out to prospective customers:

U.S. BUILDING MAINTENANCE CO., INC.

24 WEST 45th STREET • NEW YORK, NY 10036

February 6,1986

Ms. Debrah Charatan-Berger
BACH REALTY INC.
18 East 48th Street
New York, N.Y. 10017

Attn: Ms. Debrah Charatan-Berger

Dear Ms. Charatan:

Our corporation has been in business for the past twenty-six years. In
the course of this period, we have set-up a complete maintenance programs
for some of the following companies:

1) 100 Church Street which is a million square feet.

2) 20 and 30 West Broadway which is 450,000 square feet.

3) The Dept. of Labor Building at 250 Schermerhorn Street, as well as
    their other buildings at 387 Dean Street and 107 Lawrence Street
    for a total of 260,000 square feet.

4) The Spanish Pavilion at the World's Fair. Please take note that we
    were the only Maintenance Contractor allowed in the Pavilion other than
    Allied Maintenance who had the exclusive and 100% control of the Fair,
    and on the second year, we also took on the Masonic Pavilion as well.

5) The New York Law School on Worth Street consisting of three buildings
    next to it.

6) The Manhattan College on 240th Street in Riverdale consisting of eigh-
    teen buildings.

7) The Charles Benenson Properties.

We also maintain areas for commercial accounts such as U.S. Industries, St.
Joe Mineral Corp., Abex Corporation, Norton Simon, etc.

During the course of this period, we have been involved with not only the
cleaning and all its phases, but as needed, we have supplied Architectural
Consultation, Licensed Engineers and have been involved with the construction,
mechanical equipment, plumbing, air conditioning, electrical, etc.

    .../

BACH REALTY INC.

We offer general nightly and special monthly services to upgrade and keep
the standards so that the premises meet with your complete satisfaction.
We provide our clients with the necessary maintenance to meet their needs,
which include: cleaning and waxing of floors, rug shampooing, furniture,
drape and venetian blind care, high dusting and spot washing.

Our staff is fully trained, equipped, uniformed, insured and bonded. Our
prices are fully competitive and the quality of our work is excellent.

We would be happy to furnish you with any additional information you may
require, and would deeply appreciate your consideration of our firm furnishing
you with the necessary maintenance to meet your needs.

I look forward to be of service to you in the near future.

Very truly yours,

William L. Otto
President

/asc

175

Chapter Fourteen

"Who Do We Trust?"

But, money seemed to be disappearing and dwindling away; I couldn't account for it. Annabelle, a girl in the office, came into me one day and said, "Mr. Otto, I know that Nilda (our office manager) is over in London, but I think we have a problem. Money seems to be disappearing from the account." So I said, "Where's it going?" She said, "I really don't know." So, we had this new accountant, and I called him over and said, "Look, I want you to do me a favor. Go into Nilda's desk and take it apart. Take out all the records and bank books and see where we are going." He said, "I can't do it today. I have to meet with my wife." I said, "Forget about your wife. I want you to do it today. Today. TODAY. RIGHT NOW." He said, "Alright. I'll go over and start."

So, he started and at the end of the day he came over to me and he said, "Bill, I hate to tell you, but you have a problem. You are short about $162,000." I said, "Isn't that nice. What the hell were you looking at? Somebody could take $162,000 out of this business – why didn't you see this? Who took it?" He said, "Nilda." I said, "Isn't that great." We had this new account, and Nilda wanted it.

Nilda had just called. I said, "Nilda, you'd better get your ass back in here because we have big trouble here." She said, "Well, don't let anybody touch the books or records until I get there and I'll straighten everything out." I said, "No, it's too late for that, Nilda. We have a lot of money missing and we don't know where it went. The feeling is that you took it. And, you're in big trouble."

I went over to the bank and I spoke to the Vice President and I told her what happened. She said to me, "Well, the girl who was doing all the cashing of Nilda's checks just retired last Monday." I said, "Well, how the hell could she cash checks for Nilda for $25,000." She said, "Well, she had your signature. I understand that you have a stamp pad with your signature and Nilda just had to stamp the check and that's what she did. She would come in with a check for $5,000, for $9,000, for $25,000, whatever it was, and it accumulated." I said, "Isn't that nice?"

Anyway, Nilda came back and I confronted her. She was crying and we fired her. I fired my accountant. We tried to go on from there. I turned the matter over to my new accountant, who was Saul Schneider. He went over all the records and said, "Yes, I can account for $162,000 missing, also. But, there may be more." "What do we do Saul?" "Well, we have to get the Marshall involved in this." "Let's get him."

I told the Marshall what the problem was. I told him to find out where this money was. Two weeks went by and I said, "What the hell is going on?" He said, "Nothing. I can't find out where the money is." "Well, if you can't find out where the money is, how do you expect us to find it?" "If I knew where the money was, we could go after it." I said, "Well, that's great." Anyway, I turned the matter over to the District Attorneys office. At that time there was a wonderful woman working in our office. Her name was Charlotte. She was a beautiful and delightful woman. She was doing some work and then she said to me that Nilda had taken her credit card in London and charged up $7,000 with it.

Then a little old lady came into the office with a cane, and she said that Nilda had taken fifty some odd thousand dollars from her. Then some guy came into the office and said that he had given Nilda some emeralds that she could sell in the Philippines and make a lot of money and bring the money back to him and he would give her a piece of the action. And one story after another came in about Nilda and some way that she had conned someone out of money or something valuable.

I put all the information together and sent it down to the District Attorney's office in Hogan Square and set up a meeting for about ten days later. I went down and Charlotte and the little old lady went down with me. This investigator came out and he said, "What can I do for you?" I said, "Well, we sent you the records down and we want to discuss this case and how to pursue the prosecution of Nilda M." So he said to me, "I've got some bad news. I have lost all your records." I said, "How the hell could you lose all those records, and copies and everything else?" He said, "I don't know. But, I lost them." I said, "I'll tell you what. I have a complete copy back in the office; I am going to make another copy and send it down to you. Then, I want you to call another meeting so you can tell us how to pursue this so we can get some of our money back and so we can figure out what to do with Nilda M."

I went back and made the copies and sent them back to him and he took the copies and called us in for a meeting and said to us, "I don't think that you are going to be able to prosecute. I'll tell you why: this is a woman who has never had an action taken against her, she has two daughters, and her husband works for the Customs Department. Chances are they will just reprimand her, and let her go." I said, "Well, what should we do?" He said, "I don't really know what you can do. I don't think you can get any satisfaction out of this. You might want to try going to the bank to see if you can get anything out of them because they cashed a lot of the checks; see if you can do anything there." Well, we went to the bank, had a meeting, and the bank gave us $46,000. We used that to pay off some of the bills and some of the debts.

Dealing with employees as all bosses know, there are times when they can drive you crazy. Trying to be fair with everyone, sometimes doesn't work out. There are many who look to take advantage. One such incident I'm going to reflect on is a man that cost me a lot of aggravation and money. Here is the story the way it took place:

U.S.B.M REALTY CO., INC.

24 WEST 45TH STREET · NEW YORK, NY 10036

INCIDENT OF APRIL 23, 1986
INVOLVING JUAN A

On Tuesday, April 22, 1986, we were informed that the security guard for our building, 24 West 45th Street, would be unable to work on Wednesday, April 23, 1986. Annabelle, Nilda's secretary, offered the extra work to two U.S. Building Maintenance Co. employees, Juan A and Eddie Francis, asking if they would like to take the extra job for the day.

Juan A spoke-up first, offering to work the extra hours. Eddie Francis also wanted the job and inquired Juan A whether or not he was sure if he would take the job; otherwise, Eddie Francis wanted to fill-in the security guard's position.

On Wednesday, April 23, 1986, Juan A never showed up nor even called. This created a very serious problem since the security desk must be manned to secure the building. It became very necessary for Annabelle, Nilda's secretary to handle her usual work on the second floor and constantly attend to the security desk on the first floor. The effort was so strenuous that she is now out sick and had to have medical attention.

At approximately 2:30 in the afternoon, Wednesday, April 23rd, 1986, Juan A came to the building to pick-up his weekly salary. When Nilda inquired as to where he'd been and why he had not shown-up to cover the security guard position, he replied he had overslept. In response to Nilda's suggestion that he should have at least called, he replied, "Well, I just woke up an hour ago. Anyway, what's the big deal?" His manner was very arrogant and he looked like he was ready to pick a fight. Nilda requested that he leave the premises and come back later for his money since Annabelle was out cashing his payroll check along with the other payroll checks.

He then left our second floor office. Nilda then went to the lobby security desk to cover since Annabelle Cruz was still out of the building cashing in some checks. She found Juan in the lobby leaning against the wall. When Nilda asked him what he was doing there, he gave her a very snutty answer informing her it was none of her business. At this point, Nilda summoned Mr. Otto from the second floor office.

When Mr. Otto came down to the lobby and confronted Juan, there was conservation back and forth as to the problems Juan had created in not appearing, other problems that we have had with the garnishee on Juan's salary and other legal problems he has including inquiries from the Bureau of Child's Support.

At this point, Juan became very abusive and said the following: "I'm tired of this shit around here. You and your fuckin Filipina are screwing everybody just like Maracos and that fuckin bunch. That cunt (pointing to Nilda) never did a fuckin thing for anybody." Mr. Otto walked to the head of the lobby stairs and said to Juan,"You get out of here." Juan said, "Don't you tell me a fuckin thing to do," and he started to confront Mr. Otto physically.

At this point, Juan raised his right arm apparently to strike Mr. Otto who grabbed him by his clothing and pushed him out to the front door. Apparently, Juan purposely fell to the ground and claimed that he injured his back. He started yelling, "Call the police! Call the ambulance!" At this point, Mr. Otto brought him back into the lobby while Nilda called 911 requesting for the police and an ambulance.

The police arrived as well as the ambulance. As the police arrived, Juan appeared for the first time, to start shaking and claiming he was injured. Before the police came, he was perfectly alright.

We were informed that he went to St. Clare's Hospital where he was examined and x-rayed and released the same day because there were no injuries. We have had difficulty with this employee for some time and because of this incident and prior problems, he is being terminated today, April 24, 1986.

Juan A's pay is waiting for him. He will receive whatever else he is entitled to as soon as the accountant can compute it and as soon as he returns our company properties, including uniforms and keys.

Mr. William L. Otto

Nilda P.

We appeared in the Brooklyn Court. We had a black, woman district attorney. There was a six man jury with three blacks and three Puerto Ricans on the jury. That was the total. I walked in all dressed up. We didn't have a chance in hell of winning this case. Bob Starr was my attorney at the time. He said to me, "Bill. We've got a problem here. We're losing this case." I said, "Bob, we should be winning this case." He said, "You can't win it with what you are facing." I said, "What do we do?" He said, "Bill, you need a strong character witness to come before the judge to verify that you are a sincere, honest, business man, and that you did everything right." So I said, "Who do you want?" He said, "Well, who do you have in the area?" "I'm friendly with Mario Biaggi, the Bronx Congressman. He came to the house for lunch. He and I were involved with a situation taking over and rebuilding the Riyadh Airport in Saudi Arabia." He said, "No, Mario's got his own problems right now. He's under investigation with a couple of problems. I don't think he'd be good for you. Who else do you have?" I said, "Well, one of the guys who raised me was Harry Lipsig, the negligence lawyer." He said, "Do you think he'd come down?" I said, "I don't know, it's an unusual situation. He's a busy guy. Do you want me to find out?" So Bob said, "Well, give me his phone number; I'll call him." I said, "Bob, you won't get through to him on the phone. I'll call him and I'll ask him." So I went out to the phone booth and called Mr. Lipsig's office. The secretary said, "Just a minute Bill, I'll get Mr. Lipsig on the phone." He got on the phone and said, "Hiya lad! How are you?" I said, "Mr. Lipsig, I've got a few problems. I hate to bring them to you but I would like to present them to you to see if you could help me." He said, "Tell me what it is. Whatever I could do to help you, you got it."

I told him about the case, and who we had on the jury, the district attorney and how we were losing the case. He said, "You got a problem there. How can I help you?" I said, "Well, my attorney Bob Starr said I needed a strong character witness and we felt that you were the strongest character witness we could have in the area, and you know me. We were wondering if you could come down and be a character witness on my behalf." He said, "Lad, put Mr. Starr on the phone." I stepped out of the phone booth and gave the phone to Bob Starr. They talked for a while, and he got out of the phone booth and closed the door. Bob said, "He's coming here tomorrow morning at 11 o'clock."

That morning I was on the stand, and the black district attorney was really going after me. For whatever reason, the fact that Juan was Puerto Rican and we had three Puerto Ricans and three blacks, I wasn't doing too good. Then, in walks Mr. Lipsig. Everyone sees him. He was a very impressive man; small but impressive. He was dressed impeccably. He had his limousine downstairs that took him over. The judge said to me, "Mr. Otto, will you please step down from the stand. You are excused temporarily." So I stepped down, and Mr. Lipsig approached the bench. The judge said, "Mr. Lipsig, will you accept the chair and be sworn in?" Mr. Lipsig said, "Of course." He walked around over to the chair and was sworn in. As soon as he was sworn in, he leaned out of the chair and looked over at the judge. He said, "Your Honor, you know who I am. I've been practicing law for fifty-five years. During that time, I have never once been a character witness for anybody. I am here today on behalf of that man," and he pointed to me. He said, "I don't know what he said, I don't know anything about the case, but I'll tell you this, whatever that man said is the truth. I've known him for years. That man never lies and that's the type of person he is and that's all I can say. You have to take it from there. Now, can I be excused your honor?" And the judge said, "Yes, Mr. Lipsig, you may be excused." He got down from the chair, walked past me, nodded to me, I nodded to him, and he walked out.

So I didn't know what the hell was going on. Then the judge called the district attorney over, and he called Bob Starr over to the bench. They talked for a while. Bob Starr turned around and came over to me and said, "Get your briefcase." I said, "Why?" He said, "Just get your briefcase and come with me." So I grabbed my briefcase, got up and walked with him outside, and said, "What's going on?" He said, "The Judge just threw the case out. It's finished. You're free." I said, "You've gotta be kidding me." He said, "Nope. And that gives you an idea of the strength of the word of Mr. Harry H. Lipsig. You've got a great, great friend there." And that's the truth. So whatever is in this book, whatever issues you read, please reflect on that statement said in that day in court by Mr. Harry H. Lipsig. What a beautiful man he was.

I was carrying a gun for 31 years. It was only till recently I had to turn it back in because they were picking up all the guns the private citizens were carrying. I'll tell you quite frankly, twice if I didn't have that gun, I wouldn't be here to tell you that story.

The first time was when I took over the Brooklyn Law School downtown. I think the name of the street was Perry Street. I was checking the buildings late at night to see how the men were doing. I got there at about ten o'clock. The street was dead, I pushed the bell and waited for them to open the door for me. A car pulled up and there were a girl and four guys in there all talking in Spanish. The four guys get out of the car, the girl stays in and keeps the car running, and they started heading up the stairs. I yelled out to them, "Hey fellas, the school's closed. No sense in you coming up the stairs, you can't get in there." So they started talking in Spanish and they fanned out. I could see they were a bunch of wise guys looking for trouble. The one guy was telling me, "Hey man, don't be nervous. We just wanna talk to you. We wanna see what's going on up there in the school." I said, "Stop where you are. I don't want you coming up any further. You guys are looking for trouble. There's nobody around and you're going to have trouble." They started talking and laughing back and forth, and they starting coming up. So, I take out the gun. I got my nice, stainless steel 38, and I said to the guy with the big mouth, "Now, listen smart ass. I'll tell you what I'm going to do.

After I count to three, I'll shoot you right between the fuckin eyes. After that, I'll shot each one of these son of bitches that's coming at me, alright? Now that's what you've got. There's no one around and I don't give a fuck." I took the gun out and I aimed it at him and I started to count." He said, "Hold it!" and called his guys back. They started talking and I said, "I'm not fuckin around. You want to die? You die right here." They got back in the car and they took off. That was the first incident I had with the gun.

The second time I was over on the west side. We had another account called Avon Cosmetics. It was a rainy, miserable night. I parked the car over across the street, and I stood there waiting to get inside. A guy walked past, stopped, came back a little bit, and looked at me standing there. I'm a big guy and these guys are fuckin nuts for wanting to start trouble. As he started to reach in his pocket for something, I opened up my jacket and took out my 38. I said, "Hey. You see this? If you bring a fuckin gun out of that pocket I'll shoot you right in the chest so I won't miss you. Now, keep your hand in your pocket and get the hell outta here." He said, "Man, don't get excited." I said, "Excited? Man I don't like you scumbag. Get the fuck outta here or I'll kill you." With that he knew I wasn't playing games and he walked up the street and was gone. Who the hell knew what he was taking out of his pocket, but I wasn't going to take a chance. Those two times the 38 was worth it. It saved my ass and I was thankful all the time when I had it.

Chapter Fifteen

The Last of the Dinosaurs

I had a mortgage at Sands Point. I was having trouble making payments because I didn't have enough rent money coming in. I had this other building at 3 East 44th Street that had empty space. I was losing about $12,000/month on 45th Street. Then, on top of that, I had a mortgage on my house in Sands Point which is $18,750/month. And, if you don't think that grabs you for a mortgage, try it. All in all I was going down into the hole for about $37,000/month and I couldn't get out.

I called up the bank and said, "I can't get out. What do I do?" The banker said, "Let me come out there." His name was Pazel Jackson. He came out, looked at the place and said that it was a magnificent home and this, that and everything else. He said, "I am going to see what I can do about getting you some help and a low rate mortgage. Let's see if I can get you a stay for payments until you get on your feet. You have my word that I am going to do everything I can to help you." Now, I only found out later that when an Executive Vice President gives his word it is almost as good as a written contract. Time went by and we couldn't make the payments. The bills were piling up and it got to the point where I said, "Pazel, look, I owe you almost $340,000, where the hell am I going to get that kind of money?" He came into the office and we had lunch; he had a sandwich and a coffee. He said, "Bill, how can I help you?" I said, "Pazel, you gave me your word that you were going to get me a low mortgage rate, and a low interest rate, and to do whatever you could to get me something so that I could get out of this hole. But, you really didn't do anything." He agreed, "I really didn't do anything. Bill, I am sorry. What can I do now?"

I said, "What can you do now?" I said, "I am going to give you the house. Take over the house. I owe you one million nine plus the $340,000. I want you to forget about the $340,000 and the house is yours." And, that is exactly what happened. He ate that money. See the attached letter – I named my book after him. He was one hell of a man. He's alive today out in Los Angeles.

William L. Otto

U.S.B.M REALTY CO.,INC.

24 WEST 45ᵀᴴ STREET ·NEW YORK, NEW YORK

April 13, 1992

Mr. Pazel G. Jackson
Senior Vice President
Chemical Bank
277 Park Avenue
New York, NY 10172

Dear Pazel:

Well, it's all over. This past Friday, April the 10ᵗʰ at 10:00 A.M., Mr. Michael Cozzoli, one of my neighbors from Sands Point, and I were met by two very fine young men from your bank, Mr. Timothy J. Lynch and Mr. Al Monday.

They were extremely courteous and confident, and under your directions everything went well. The Otto house keys were handed over to them and we inspected the house together. It's not an easy task to move from this big house that was designed and built for my specifications and where we lived for 20 years, to relocate to a small two bedroom apartment.

Life doesn't always turn out the way we want it to.

I want to thank you for all your patience and understanding in this terrible ordeal I have gone through. However, I must say that because of your help, it was accomplished and I was still able to maintain some sense of dignity.

Pazel, we are <u>the last of the dinosaurs</u>; there aren't too much like us anymore.

Thank you again and God bless you.

Very truly yours,

William L. Otto

GOD BLESS YOU PAZEL, WHEREVER YOU ARE.

Chapter Sixteen

"Garden City"

So now here's a guy who was on bread lines as a kid, ate the crumbs out of the bread box, worked his ass off all those years, and wound up with a magnificent home in Sands Point. Now, I am forced to turn it back over to the bank and vacate the premises. We put ads in the paper, and Pauline started selling things. All total she raised about $82,000. I never saw a dime of it. We had a lot of furniture; we had some great stuff. A Korean restaurant man came in and bought the dining room set, which consisted of a magnificent piece of travertine, 9 feet long, 4 feet wide, and 2 inches thick. It weighed about 870 pounds. We had to reinforce the floor with the steel beam underneath in the basement to support it. Around it we had a match set of 1933 English leather chairs. Up above you had the chandelier given to me by the Irish Godfather. That chandelier went every place with us, and it wound up in my ex-wife's home in Greenbriar New Jersey. You are talking about a house in Sands Point that took 2 ½ years to plan and design – a house with a Judo room, and a pool room, and a barbeque area for bad weather in the basement on the ground level. It also housed the wine cellar where I kept 170 cases of good wine. The main floor consisted of a fire place with imported stones from Delaware that weighed 47 tons. It had a 5 foot by 3 foot open fire place through the dining room into the living room. It had a bar on the corner that took an Italian craftsman 3 weeks to make. And behind it was the porthole from the liberty ship given to me by Jim Earley, the Irish Godfather. So you could sit at the bar, look through the porthole, and see the Twin Towers in Manhattan. You had a magnificent view looking out into the New York skyline, and part of the

East River, about 175 feet away. I can go on for a week telling you about this house; it was a masterpiece. Consider this masterpiece. How would you feel about walking away from it? But that's life. And we keep on going. It's like Donald Trump said, "How do you go through life? You get up in the morning and you put one foot out and then the other and you start the day."

We took whatever we could take with us and moved to a two-bedroom apartment in Garden City, right behind the Garden City Hotel. It was called the Windham Apartments. We had a nice apartment on the third floor overlooking the pond. It was very cozy and we stayed there for a while. We had some nice neighbors, some that you read about but I am not going to go into any names.

There was a pond in front of the apartment. We wanted to put some fish in the pond. We went to the local aquarium and I said to my grandsons Wesley and Warren, "You guys pick out the fish that you want. Whatever fish that you pick out, you have to name, and then we'll put them into the water." So they each picked out a fish and named it, and we took movies of the fish going into the water. Pauline and I put a fish in also. We had a nice time. We would sit out on our porch overlooking the pond, and have breakfast. It was delightful.

We had a pool and a gym there. The boys would come over and we would take them down to the pool. There was a local bakery where we would go for rolls on a Sunday morning, and if my grandsons stayed over they would take turns coming with me to get rolls. We had good life there in Garden City.

There was a golf course on the south shore where Pauline and I would golf. We would bring fishing poles and we would fish in the canal sometimes after we played golf. It was very relaxing. One time there was a little boy there. He just stood there watching me fish. I asked him, "Would you like to try this pole?" He tried it and boy he got such a big kick out of it. I said to him, "Son, that pole is yours," and I gave him the tackle box too. He seemed really thrilled with that. In fact, I think he will remember that for the rest of his life. I took a picture of him when I gave him the pole. He was a nice little boy and that was a great moment to share something with somebody who really appreciated it.

Pauline had decided that she wanted a Mercedes Benz. So, I told the dealers in three different places to take there time and pick out a good car for my wife. It took them three months, but they finally picked a good car for her. It was black on black. It originally cost $82,000 but, it had 41,000 miles on it so we go it for $47,000.

Pauline got very sick at one point and we didn't know what it was. She kept throwing up. We called the doctor and he put her in the hospital. She was in St. Francis hospital and they kept checking her and couldn't find out what was wrong.

We had taken a trip to Mexico and the two kids and I got Montezuma's Revenge, and we flushed out everything, but Pauline didn't. When I told that story to Dr. Bill Peters, an internist in Port Washington, he called the hospital and told them to examine her for Typhoid fever. They isolated her, tested her, and found out that she did have it. She was in the hospital for three weeks, and they cured it.

I contacted the President of Mexico and told him what happened. He was very apologetic, sent me a beautiful letter, and invited the whole family back to Mexico as his guests. I told him, "No thanks. Once is enough."

Mexico, D.F. June 17, 1975

Mr. William L. Otto
342 Madison Avenue
New York, NY 10017
USA

Dear Mr. Otto,

On behalf of Sr. Lic. Miguel Alemán, former President of Mexico and President of the Mexican National Tourist Council, we wish to apologize for the bad experience you went through in your recent visit to our country.

We are taking the necessary steps so that problems such as those are not repeated. We are getting in touch and sending copies of your letter to the proper authorities in order to solve the above mentioned.

We regret this unfortunate incident, and only hope that you will come to Mexico again, for which we will do everything possible to make your next visit an enjoyable one.

Respectfully yours,

Enrique Monroy O.
Director of Foreign Affairs

We thought about what we could do with our apartment. I met with the owner of the Windham Apartments, Anastasia. There were about 73 people, like us, who were renting there. We had a big meeting and discussed it, and I approached the owner and said, "60% of the tenants want to buy. You bought this place at a 55% reduction. Give us 20% off the asking price." (At the time he was asking about $440,000 for the two-bedroom apartment). But, he wouldn't do it. He wouldn't budge. He said, "Bill, if they can't afford it, I don't want them. I want a Rolls Royce crowd – that's what I am looking for." The figures for the units got out of hand, because they were allowing you one car there and if you wanted an additional car it was another $20,000 a year; the maintenance charge and the upkeep just got out of hand. We decided to look around for someplace else.

Chapter Seventeen

"Greenbriar"

We went to closing in October of 1996. We moved into there and started to fix it up with the furniture we had. We converted the dining room into a den, had shrubs put in, had the patio put in, had the garage painted, had a place put up in the attic, and we put up Jim Earley's chandelier. This chandelier came from our home in Syosset, to Sands Point, to Garden City and then I brought it to our home in New Jersey. That was my gift from the Irish Godfather.

Anyway, we started fixing this place up and it turned out that Greenbriar happened to be a lovely, lovely development. We had a great golf course in our backyard, a nice swimming pool, and a patio out back with the shrubs we put in for barbeques. We had everything nice, except our immediate neighbors.

We wound up with a lot of problems with our neighbors. I'll tell you how it started. The guy on my left side, his name was Sy, we hardly ever spoke. One day he said to me, "We're going fishing. Would you like to go out for?" I said, "Yeah, I would love to."

Meanwhile, just a week before that, some of us in Greenbriar had been talking about putting in screened in porches in the backyard so that we could sit out there and not be bothered by the bugs and mosquitoes. The one couple on the other side of them had a serious problem. The wife was dying of cancer. Her husband kept coming to me saying, "Jesus, Bill, did you get approval for that screened porch? "Yes, I did get approval." "Great." So then we started getting some prices. I got prices for him and prices for the guy on the other side.

So, now I am out fishing with this neighbor, Sy. I came back, and the neighbor across the street, Simon, said to me, "Bill, do you know what's going on?" I said, "Excuse me, Simon. What do you mean, 'What's going on?'" He said, "Well, while you were out fishing with that guy, his wife went around getting a petition signed against you, so that you couldn't put a screened porch in the backyard." I said, "You're kidding, Simon." He said, "No, Bill. I am telling you the truth. They asked me to sign, and I refused to. I just want you to be aware of what's going on because you are good people."

I went back inside and I told Pauline. She said, "Well, I can't believe that." So, I said, "Well, let's call them up and ask them."

I called Sy and Flo next door and I said, "I would like to come over and talk to you two." They said it was fine so we walked over and sat down at the kitchen table. I said to them, "I just heard a very interesting story. I heard that while I was out fishing with your husband, you were going around and getting a petition signed against me for the screened in porch." She said, "I was." I said, "But why, Flo?" She said, "Because if you put a screened in porch out there, it is going to block my view of the golf course."

I said, "But, Flo, you were talking about doing it too; and so was Al next door. In fact, we were all talking about doing it. This way, if we each build a screened in porch, it will be equal to all of us; it wouldn't be blocking anybody's view. Your neighbor next door, Gerry, is very concerned about his wife, who is dying of cancer, and he has asked me about five times already whether we have gotten permission. He would like one so his wife could sit outside and not be bothered by bugs and mosquitoes. He feels it would be a blessing to her. I told him we would do our best to get it. Flo, what are you going to do about them?"

She said, "Well, that's their problem. I am not concerned about it." I said, "Flo, what are you talking about, their problem? She is dying of cancer. We are trying to make life a little easier for her. We all agreed and all approved that we would get this screened in porch. Now you are telling me that it is her problem? Is that the neighborly attitude that you have?" She said, "That's the way we feel about it." I said to Pauline, "Let's get out of here. These people are shit." And I said to them, "Both of you can go to hell. And, if my house burns down, both of you stand there and watch it burn down. If your house burns down, I am going to make myself a drink and I am going to watch it burn down, too. From here on out I don't want to know you people. You are bad news." And with that, we got up and walked out of the house.

I asked some of the other neighbors on the block if this was true. They said, yes, that they had been approached to sign a petition as well, but none of them said they had signed it. Then, about three weeks went by, and the neighbor on the other side of me, Al, came back from some vacation trip. I went over to his house and I said, "Al, I said, you'll never guess what happened." I told him about Sy and Flo's petition, the 118 people who signed it, and how the Board of U.S. homes declared it illegal.

I said, "Imagine all those people signing that petition." He put his head down. I said, "What's the matter?" He said, "I signed the petition, too, Bill." I said, "What? You were getting prices with me. You were getting estimates to do the job. Why would you sign the petition against something that we both wanted?" He said, "I don't know, I just felt it was a good idea to sign it because we would be blocking the view." I said, "How is my putting up a screened in porch going to block your view? My house is on the right side of yours. The golf course is on the left." He said, "Well, I signed the petition. But, I hope that's not going to affect our friendship, and the fact that we are neighbors." I said, "Are you kidding me? You go and sign a petition against me while we are trying to get something done? What kind of shit are you? Any man who does what you did, going behind my back like that – What kind of neighbors do we have here? Al, go fuck yourself. I don't want to know you anymore." I walked out and went back to my house.

I told Pauline what happened. She said, "Well, Bill, these are the neighbors we have. We're going to have to try to live with them and get along with them." I said, "I don't want to know them. They are not my type of people. I want nothing to do with them." So from there on in we weren't close, or friendly with them; we had problems.

A little while later while we were in Florida, apparently, one of my neighbors measured our patio. Somehow it was 32 square feet over the requirement. Somebody made an issue with U.S. Homes that our patio was too big. They wouldn't tell me who, but I am sure it was Al. We had a big problem with it.

There were two women on the Board of the Architectural Committee with me. One of the women was an ex-law professor by the name of Sari Zitter. She was a classy woman. She came over to me and said, "Bill, I've got a serious problem. Your next door neighbor, Al, confronted me at the general meeting. He stuck his finger in my face, and he wanted to know what I was going to do about 'Bill Otto and the patio.' I told him that just because I'm on the Architectural Committee doesn't mean I can tell Bill Otto what to do with his patio. He then stuck his finger in my face, a couple of inches from my eye, and said, 'I want to know what you are going to do about it. If you don't do something about it, I am going to come after you.' He threatened me, Bill." I said, "That's terrible." So, I brought it up at the general meeting of the Architectural Committee.

I felt it was very necessary to bring this up at the meeting. I mentioned it to the chairman, and then another woman, who was the treasurer of the committee, said, "He approached me and threatened me." I said, "He threatened you, too?" I said to our chairman, "You are going to have to do something about this. We can't have our women being threatened like this. It is not a normal situation; we have to straighten this guy out." He said, "I'm not going to do anything. That's not my job, or my responsibility. My responsibility is the Architectural Committee. It is not to get involved with the neighbors disputes." I said, "I am on the Architectural Committee. I am part of the committee. These women are part of the committee. You don't have to defend me. But, surely, you are going to have to defend these women. They are entitled to it. They deserve to be defended." He said, "I am not defending anybody." I said, "If you are not going to defend them, then why don't you step down as chairman and put somebody in this chair who is going to protect the committee." He said, "I am not stepping down as chairman and I am not going to defend these women. That's the way it stands." And surprisingly enough, these women did not make an issue of it, and the issue died. The meeting was over in a little while, and we all left. I came back and told Pauline what happened, and she said to me, "Bill, don't get involved with Al; he's a bad apple." I said, "I'm not going to do anything Pauline; I'm going to stay out of it and try my best to stay away from him."

Well, about four days went by, and I went outside to throw out the garbage, and I saw Al getting on his bicycle to take off and go for his morning jaunt. I said, "Al, come here, I want to talk to you please." So he came over and said, "What's up?" I said, "What's this business going around about you making an issue about my patio and about the fact that it's too big? And what about you going around threatening these women that if they don't do something against me that you are going to make an issue of it?" He said, "I'm not threatening any women." I said, "Why are you lying to me now? Both of these women told me that you confronted them and threatened them. Why would you?" He said, "I'm not lying. I didn't tell them that." I said, "You're a liar. What is it with you? Are you looking for some action? Are you looking for a fight – looking for trouble? If you want some action, come on, between the two houses, I'll give you all the action you want."

And with that, he said to his wife Barbara who was standing by the garage door, "Did you hear that Barbara? He threatened me." She said, "I heard that Al; I heard him threatening you." I said, "I didn't threaten you. You're sick." I walked away, but I turned around and felt that I had to straighten this guy out. As I turned around my neighbor from across the street yelled out, "Hello guys, how are you?" We both looked at him, and then I went back into the house.

Well, the next day, I got a call from the local police department. They said, "Your neighbor Al came in here and filed a complaint against you. He listed you as a terrorist." I said, "Terrorist? Did you look at this guy's eyes and see that there is something mentally wrong with him? The man is off the wall." They all looked at each other, the three of them, but they didn't say anything. They said, "Look Mr. Otto, we want you to do us a favor. We want you to stay completely away from this man and have nothing to do with him." I said, "That's fine by me. And could you please convey the same message to him that he's to stay completely away from me? I'll have nothing to do with him, and we'll leave it at that."

It didn't end at that because the action was filed, and I had to go before the board. We had meetings; I had to hire an attorney. It cost me $12,000 in legal fees. I had a reporter come over from the Star Ledger. The article appeared in the newspaper, and Pauline and I had our picture taken on the patio.

That was the final picture on our patio. We wound up having to take two feet off the patio. To this day, it is still there and it still looks good. We should have taken off the two feet in the beginning. Unfortunately, we didn't realize that it was such an important issue – thirty-two square feet, which is about six feet by five feet. But, that's the way it goes with the neighbors

This issue with Al carried over everyplace. When we went into the dining room, he stayed away from me; I stayed away from him. If we went into the Golf Pro Shop and he was there, I waited till he left, then I went in. Or if I was there, I would tell him to please wait outside till I came out, and we stayed away from each other.

There was one incident on the golf course. He was like an instigator, this guy. He looked for trouble. He knew that I played with a foursome every Saturday morning. So, this Saturday morning, we had one man short. We were coming around for the second round of the tenth hole, and he jumped in to join us. He sat with Jim MacLaughin who was by himself; I was with Joe. So I said to Max, the starter, "What's going on here?" Max put his eyes up in the air and pointed to the cart, and who was sitting there with Jim but Al. I said, "This guy can't play with us. We're not supposed to be near each other. The police said that we should stay at least 50 feet apart from each other, and I can't stay 50 feet apart if we go up on the Tees. You've got to get this guy off." So, Max said, "You better go back into the Pro Shop and talk with the pro."

I went back into the Pro shop and told the pro what happened. He said, "Well Bill, I can't outwardly refuse him to play. He wants to play, and he joined in. How about if you play ahead? That way you could keep moving forward and you won't have to see him." I said, "I'll buy that." So we played up in front of him. He played the tenth hole, and he quit.

These were the type of things that we went through with our neighbors. It was very interesting, but by and large, the neighbors were very good. We had nice neighbors. We had the Italian-American Club which was fine. We used to go to the dances; the food was great. The comradeship was great. They had singers and dancing and eating, and we always had good tables together. It was a wonderful time we had in Greenbriar.

We played golf on Wednesday, Friday and Saturday, and on Saturday Pauline would play with the girls. We started playing Volleyball on Monday nights. All the men would get together, and we'd put the net up in the pool. If it was warm, we'd play on the outside; if it was cool, we'd play in the inside. They had water polo, dances and movies. They even had trips to Europe. We did a lot of great things together, and we enjoyed Greenbriar.

Chapter Eighteen

"Riyadh Airport"

I was going into the office on Monday, Tuesday and Thursday. In fact, sometimes on Thursdays, Pauline would come in with me. She'd drive the car in, we'd get things done like paper work, and then head home. Things were running smoothly in the building. We didn't have any serious problems. The money was coming in; we were able to pay the rent, pay the bills, and we had enough money left over for ourselves. We lived very comfortably and very well.

I was going down to the pool, having a swim, and I met a fella by the name of Henry Pirotti. Strong, upstanding man, the type of guy you want to know. We started talking about the old days and the boys and how times have changed and everything else. He started telling me about Albert Anastasia who used to come to his house for Sunday dinner. I said, "You're kidding! His boss was Lou Aversi." He said, "I never knew Lou Aversi." I said, "Lou Aversi was the head of The Columbian Stevedores. Lou and I used to have dinner with Ed Baragolia. He was the driving cop for Congressman Mario Biaggi." Mario was at my house a couple of times for lunch. We were involved with a couple of things and trying to build the airport in Saudi Arabia.

A fellow, Oscar Telesko, and I had a meeting at LaGuardia at the private club. Mario Biaggi was there. Governor Carey sent down this general for a meeting with us. They wanted me to go to Saudi Arabia and set up the Riyadh Airport. The reason they wanted me was because

I wasn't Jewish, and King Faisal ibn Abdul Aziz Al Saud of Saudi Arabia said he didn't want a Jewish person handling it for him. In fact, when we had our first meeting at the hotel on 61st and Park, Oscar Telesko took me in. And there were security people who watched you and checked you to make sure you didn't have any weapons. Inside there was no furniture. They had a big rug on the floor and food was in the middle of the rug. Everyone had to reach out with their right hand. You can't use your left hand otherwise they'll cut it off, but with your right hand you grabbed the food and you ate.

Anyway, prior to that, they called me into a meeting with King Faisal, a big, heavy guy with a mustache. He said to me, "You have a good reputation with the cleaning business. Would you be interested in building an airport in Riyadh?" "Well, I don't know. It's a very complex situation over there.

How do we handle it all?"

"My people will tell you how it's all going to be handled. They'll lay out the ground work for you. You come highly recommended to us by Oscar Telesko. We are very fond of him, and he says you're the man to handle it."

Anyway, the whole situation was that they were going to give me 5,000 workers to build the airport. I said, "How will I handle these people? They're getting them from the Philippians and the island."

"We are going to give you 200 people to keep them in line."

"How are 200 men going to keep 5,000 guys in line?"

"Well, they have special gloves that have brass on the knuckles, the men listen and do whatever you want."

"That sounds interesting. But tell me, what's in it for me?"

"Well, we'll give you a check for $250,000 to start off with."

"That's pretty good. Now what?"

Well, you go over there and you start to set up the operation.

"If I have to leave my operation and business over here, I have to put someone in charge of everything. When I get over there, how do I handle the passport?" "Well, your passport is handled by your agent over there."

No good. If you give me an international passport, I'm interested with the deal. If I can't get an international passport where I can get in and out and walk away if I want, I'm not interested then."

Well, we can't get it for you."

Then I'm not interested in the deal.

Biagi was a very nice and competent man, and so was Oscar and the General from Governor Carey's office, but I wasn't going to get involved with that kind of a thing where I'd get over there and I'd never get out.

Anyway, we had a couple of nice drinks and then we left. Now, getting back to Henry Pirotti, we're talking there and discussing different things, and I told him that Lou Aversi was a hell of a guy and he was the boss of Anastasia. He really didn't have anything to do with Murder Inc. He just handled the Stevedores. So I said, "I know him through my good friend Ed Baragolia. He was the driver when Biaggi made that move against the narcotics guy up in The Bronx." So he said, "Jesus Bill, you know a lot of guys." I said, "I do." He said, "I wanna tell you, we got a hell of a guy here in the complex." I said, "Who is that?" He said, "Joe Bonanno." I said, "Wait a minute. Joe Bonanno? I knew the old man." He said, "You knew Mr. Joe Bananas?" I said, "Yeah! I've got pictures with him!" He said, "Holy Christ, Joe would love to have those pictures! He would love to meet you." I said, "Good, set it up. We'll have a meeting."

So, that night we went back to the pool and we sat around and talk. Joe said to me, "Do you really have pictures of my grandfather?" I said, "Yeah." He said, "Could I see them?" I said, "Not only could you see them, you could have them!" I took the pictures out of the file, brought them out, and I said, "You got em." He hugged me, and when he hugged me, it was like we had a bond between us, and it stayed that way. We're still that way. In fact, in my apartment here in White Plains, I have a magnificent grandfather clock and inside it has the name Joe Bonanno. That was my present from him for my apartment. He's a hell of a guy, Joe. If you see the television show *The Sopranos*, I mean, they should have a guy like him playing the lead part. He's a natural!

His grandfather was a hell of a guy. He had two sons, Bill and Joe, and Bill was the guy who was involved in writing *The Sopranos*, and Joe went away for 18. He never got along with the other son, Joe. You never see anything publicized about him. It was always kept quite – I never knew why. But Joe Bananas was a hell of a guy. He dressed impeccably, he looked great, handled himself well, the only thing he did was he had a rough accent. He talked like he just came off the boat. And that's the way he was. He was extremely intelligent, very competent, very sharp guy.

There was a restaurant called La Champs on 41st Street – it's closed now. I would go there with Jim Earley, the Irish Godfather. Jim owned a piece of the action; Frank Costello owned a piece of it. Rocky Graziano was there all the time. He'd be sitting at the bar talking. In fact, one day I'm there on the other side of the bar were Frank Costello, Jim Earley and Sammy Salerno (that's the guy who brought in Joe Bonanno). From the other side of the bar a guy yells out, "Hey, what's going on there? A meeting?" And Costello yells, "Come on over, Frank!" And Frank Erickson came over. He owns a lot of Long Island properties. We had a good time, we had some drinks. They were great guys. Let me tell you, if you shook hands with those guys, you had a deal. You didn't need lawyers or accountants in them days. Those were different days, and you'll never have them again. Times have changed.

Chapter Nineteen

"Down to Florida"

In the wintertime, around October, November, we started to prepare and go down to Florida. We'd drive down to Florida, and we'd stop maybe six, seven or eight stops on the way down, all different places. We would usually stop at the Hampton Inns because they were always clean and neat, and the prices were right, and we had breakfast there in the morning which made it convenient so you didn't have to shop around for a place to have breakfast.

One of the key places we used to stop off at was the Hampton Inn in Charleston, South Carolina, right across from the visitor's bureau. Around the corner was a place called The Fish. We met the owner and his wife and became friendly with them and always had enjoyable dinners with them. We used to talk about different things in business. He was a very dynamic young man. He had tremendous potential. He wound up taking over that one restaurant. It was an empty store, and he built it up. He also built the building next to it. Then, he took over the movie theatre next to that, and he had a great idea for it. He turned it into a little restaurant so that people could sit down, have a dinner and drinks, and then, the movie would go on. It was very comfortable with round tables and nice chairs. It was a smart idea.

Then, he took the balcony area upstairs and converted it into a disco area. That was another smart idea. He had a lot of great ideas. He bought out the corner store which was an old building that housed the former owner of the railroad. He started to renovate that, and I haven't seen it since it's been done over but I'm sure that he did a great job because he was a very talented, very ambitious and very competent young man. It was a pleasure knowing him. He could run a large corporation or be the mayor.

So, we would make our trips all the way South. On the way down, we'd stop off and see Eric and Mary Lou in Palm City. Then, we'd head on down to St. Augustine and spend a day there. By that time we were ready to head into our beautiful condominium in Palm Aire. It was 1,740 square feet and had a lovely balcony overlooking the pond and the fifth hole on the Oaks. This was the golf course that Tiger Woods played when they had the Nike Tournament, a lovely golf course.

We always had great times in Florida. We would get up in the morning, grab juice and some vitamin pills and go out for a walk. We'd walk along the canal and get our exercise. We'd walk about a mile and a half to two miles, and then we would come back, take a shower, put our bathing suits on and have our breakfast out on the porch. Then, we'd go down to the pool, and we'd lie by the pool until twelve or twelve-thirty. We'd come upstairs, have a little lunch and then meet the Jim and Fran Hourigan. We'd go out and would play golf at all different courses. After golf, we would either go out to dinner or to a movie and then go home and watch a little TV. We used to go to the library to get these foreign films, and we'd put them on. We had a great time; it was a great life down there. And we did this for many years. For at least three or four of the winter months we got away, and things were quite good up north at the office. We had the office staff running everything; they took care of it all.

Then, we'd come back and have our good life in Greenbriar. So we had the best of both worlds. We missed the winter, enjoyed Florida in summer, and we'd come back to Greenbriar and spend our time in Greenbriar with the new group there.

While we were in Florida, we would have brunch almost every Sunday at the 17th Street Causeway. It started at twelve o'clock, and we would be there until about two-thirty. We would either have two people or we would have twelve people, depending on who was going to join us. Then, we would walk around in a big circle to look at the boats and then we'd head back to our cars.

After brunch, Pauline and I would go to an antique place or go shopping or we would look at some art work. There was always something to do. We would sit around on an afternoon and read the Sunday newspapers and maybe watch a foreign film, and then next Monday would start the same ritual again. We'd go for our walk, get our swim in, play our golf, go out to have dinner, and there was nothing wrong with the life. I can remember one time at the seventeenth hole on the Oaks, Jim Hourigan said to me "Bill, it doesn't get any better than this." I said, "Jim, you're right; this is beautiful. We're living a good life." And we did, we lived a good life.

Every time we came to Florida, we would visit the Rogers in Miami. Pauline would take off with Alma Rogers for a day, and Jack and I would sit in the back yard and have a few drinks and fish in his pond. We would talk and the girls would be out shopping. Pauline would come back loaded with nice clothes because Alma knew good places to take her where she got some good buys. She would fill up her wardrobe; she was always happy.

Jack, Alma's husband, was a wonderful man. I miss Jack. Jack was a Captain in the Battle of the Bulge with General Patton. When he was in the army, he approached this one house, and they assumed that everyone was gone in the house. He went up the stairs and there was a German at the top looking right down at him with an 8 millimeter rifle. He shot Jack through the stomach. It went right through him. He fell down and the German figured he was dead. In fact, as he came down the stairs, he stepped on him, and went past him. Jack couldn't move. But, being a Captain, I guess, the other men scouted around the area looking all over for him, and they found him. They brought him back to the medics, who performed surgery and did what they could for him. Only recently, last year, Jack was taken into the Veteran's Hospital and they removed his stomach and Jack died.

I can remember when Alma said to us, "Let's go down to the Keys." I said to Jack, "You want to go down?" He said, "Yeah." So we called up and made reservations down at the Keys. Jack liked his Martinis. I rented a big Lincoln and made up some Martinis. Jack sat in the back and drank his Martinis as we drove on down to the Keys. Alma is beautiful woman; she is a tall, Cuban gal. Her father was Francisco Perez San Guan, the Mayor under Batista. She had to flee Cuba at that time because things were very bad. But she is a hell of a gal and we had some great times together with them. Jack was a dear friend, and a classy guy. He was an actor, by trade, and he used to do Shakespearian theatre. He looked like a Shakespearian actor; he had that classy way about him; he would talk and quote something from Shakespeare, or say something profound in his own, flamboyant way. He always had three Martinis – and I think they kept him going. Jack was 86 when he died. He did volunteer work in hospitals; tried to help out anyway he could. He put his time in with everybody.

Alma appreciated it and I know to this day, Alma has said to me several times, "Jack was a pain-in-the-ass, but I would love to have him back now, sharing a drink, and having him around me." But, unfortunately, those times are gone. We have to move on to other things.

I did a lot of fishing in the back pond in Florida. I tried all different types of bait, and different techniques. One night, I even got some fresh shrimp. I put them on the line and I cast out the line in the back of the pond. Then, I would walk the pond, so that the line came through the lake, all the way to the other end. Well, I hooked on to something big, and the line went down. I said, "What the hell is this?" It was a heavy, heavy weight. It was as if you had an old shoe. But, I knew there was something live on it, because I could see the pole bending. I tried to reel it in, as best as I could. I got in, close to shore, and then the line snapped. I said to myself, "Damn it! I would have loved to have seen what it was." Well, two days later I am up on the porch, looking down. As I am looking down, I said to Pauline, "Look at the size of that turtle that is laying on the side of the pond." She said, "That is a big turtle." I couldn't believe the size of it. Well, that day went on and later in the day I said to Pauline, "That turtle is still there, Pauline. It hasn't moved." So she said, "That's strange, isn't it." I said, "Yeah. Let's go down and take a look at it." So, we went down to take a look at it. Low and behold, it had the hook, my hook, in its mouth, and I had killed it. I said, "Holy Christ. Pauline, I am going to run up and get the camera. I want you to take a picture of the size of this turtle that I have killed because this is terrible." Pauline took the picture, showing the size of the turtle. I took a plastic bag and I put it into the garbage. But, I felt bad about it.

Another time I was down there, looking at the pond. We used to have these carp. They were about four feet long, and sometimes ten, twelve inches around. They were put in by the Florida people because they eat the greens around the ponds, and keep the ponds clean. One time I was sitting on the porch and I saw a fellow sitting down there. He was casting his pole out. Boom! He pulled in a large mouth Bass. Boom! Another large mouth Bass. He was throwing them back in; he's not keeping them. But, he is catching the fish. I yell out to him, "Don't go away. I am coming down. I want to see what you are using." He said, "All right, c'mon down." I went down and he showed me what he had. What had was a little, tiny weight, maybe an eight of an ounce sinker, and that was about eight to ten feet down; then he had a plastic worm and in the plastic worm he had put in a rattle. When he pulled the line back, and kept pulling and jerking the line, the rattle would make a noise and attract the fish. I said, "You've got to be kidding. I never heard of anything like this." He said, "Well, you see it's working." I said, "Damn right, it's working. Where the hell can I get these little rattles?" He said, "Well, you can go over to K-Mart, or one of those place and they have them. The Home Depot has them. Sports Authority has them. They are very inexpensive. You stick them in the way I did." I said, "Well, that's a hell of an idea." We became friendly with him.

He was telling us that he was the manager of a restaurant on Federal Highway, up above Deerfield Park. He said that we should come up there one day and have lunch, which we did. I would up using his technique, and I did catch some fish. I tried it in different ponds and it was a good idea. We also went to his restaurant and the restaurant was crowded and packed outside. I walked in and asked to see him and he came out and he said, "Did you make reservations?" I said, "Well, I couldn't even get to the front table, it was so jammed." He said, "When your name Otto is called, just come up to the front." I said, "Okay." A few minutes later, "Otto" was called out. We came up to the front; he took us around and gave us a nice table. We sat down and had a great time. On top of that, he picked up the tab for the dinner! That was very nice on his part.

We had a good talk with him, but unfortunately, he told us that he was leaving the restaurant to go work for a company called Lucent. Lucent, at that time, was starting to lose money. We had bought Lucent at $52.00 and it went down to a dollar. He said that Lucent was putting together a real estate department and he was going to be involved in the real estate department down in Miami and he felt it was an opportunity rather than stay in the restaurant. We kind of looked at him and said, "Jesus, Lucent is no a solvent company anymore; it's going down the tubes. Are you sure you know what you are doing?" He said, "No, it's going to be good. It is going to turn right around." I said, "I hope so. It would be great if that did turn around. It would be good for everybody. But, you know, I haven't seen him. He went to work for Lucent, he's not in the restaurant any more. And, you know what's happened to Lucent. That's the end of that story.

Meanwhile, I still fish in the pond in the back. Jim Hourigan and I have tried fishing on what they call "drifters." They are boats about 50 feet long and only have seats on one side. What you do is take Atlantic Blvd. down to the end, down by the water. It is a half a day trip out; whether it be four hours in the morning or four hours in the afternoon. You get your fishing boat, and they give you the pole and they give you the bait. Then they go out in the ocean and they shut the motor off and your drift. You put your lines out – and boy they go way down. Sometimes 100 feet down. You don't know what you are going to catch. You could catch anything. You see all kinds of fish and all kinds of shapes and sizes and everything else being brought in. They have pool for the biggest what they call "edible" fish. We all put in $2.00 and whoever wins that, wins the pool. You never know what you are going to catch, and it is always such an enjoyable day. It is a nice ride out in the boat – it's good to get out in the ocean. I went there a couple of times with Jim Hourigan and I also went there with my friend next door. Then we would go to a nice place after that for lunch and get a nice corned beef sandwich and head home. It made a pleasant day. Fishing was always good in Florida. I tried a number of different places. I like fishing.

I remember when my grandsons, Wesley and Warren came down. Warren is not much on fishing; but Wesley loved fishing. We would go fishing for the day and at the end of the night, Wesley would say, "Papau, let's go over by the canal, by the damn." I would say, "It's starting to get dark." He would say, "No, let's fish for a little while longer." So I would say, "Okay, let's go over there and fish." We went over there to fish. We are up on the rocks. You are up about twelve feet high and for some reason, something happened, and my legs just gave out. I fell down. I turned over three or four times and Wesley was scared. He said, "Papau, Papau are you alright." I was all bloodied and banged up. My head and so forth. He said, "Gosh, Papau, if you fell in the water, how could I get you out?" I said, "I know, son, I am alright. Come on; let's go back to the house." We took our poles and so forth and got back to the house and they were shocked that I had some blood on me, but we washed it all off and got all cleaned up and everything else. Wesley was alright. He kept hugging me and asking, "You all right, Papau?" I would reply, "Yes, I am all right son, I am alright." Warren said, "Boy, at least if I had been there, I could have helped you." But, Warren was back in the house with Yayia. They were watching television, or something. I don't know exactly what they were doing, but they were back at the house.

I had great times with Wesley and Warren. We used to take them up to a place in the park. I can't think of the name of the park; I'll get the name of it. You go out on a line, and the line takes you out about a quarter of a mile for water skiing. First, they had this little type of thing that you'd put your knees on, and that would take you around, and you would ski on that. Then you could stand up on it, move around on it, and if you liked that better, you could try water skiing or you could try standing up on that thing and going around. The two boys had a ball with that; they didn't want to leave.

The, we would go get some nice lunch, and we'd take them for ribs. It was a black couple who started this place in Boca Raton. It was a little tiny place, maybe about 200 square feet. The ribs were beautiful, and everybody loved them. Then they expanded, and they got a little bit more, and they saved their money. They would close on Sunday, and they said that's how they gave back to God. They were very religious people. Well, they grew and grew and expanded and expanded, The restaurant today holds I guess 200 people, and it's jammed all the time; you either have to make a reservation or get there early. It's Tom's Back Ribs, and it's great. It's in Boca Raton, and I highly recommend it to anybody; you will enjoy it.

And then we would take the kids to Boomers, and they would have a hell of a time in Boomers. You would give the $75 each, and they'd go right through that. They had all kinds of games and different things to try, and they had a rock climbing thing and boats to go on. They could try practicing baseball, and it was a very enjoyable day. Oh, and they had miniature golf. The two boys would play and be competitive with each other. The age difference between them showed. Wesley had a tough time trying to keep up with Warren, who was a little older, and handled it better. The waterfall was there by the golf, and we had a nice time. And then we would come back and have a nice dinner someplace, go back to the house and watch some nice TV or a nice program, or go out swimming, and there was always something to do. We had a great time together; we enjoyed it each other. They are great boys, our grandsons.

We were friendly with our neighbors. And as years went by, we lost a lot of them because of age. As one after the other would pass on, it broke your heart to see them go because they were good people, and you can't replace them. They are just like rare treasures that you just don't find anymore. And when they go, it's like taking an antique dish or an antique piece of porcelain and breaking it. It's gone; you can't get it back. And that's how we felt about a lot of the old timers. Most of the names I don't remember but their faces I won't forget. I remember them being a part of our lives.

Most of the time we would be with the Hourigan's, Jim and Fran. They were delightful people. You couldn't find nicer people. Sometimes we would take a ride up to have dinner at the Flamboyant Hummingbird (that was Eric's restaurant). It was up in Palm City, and we'd go up there and have a nice dinner, talk and have a couple glasses of wine. There were humming birds flying all over the place – yes, live ones.

Pauline and I played golf by ourselves a lot of times. There was a brand new gym with relatives, company or the kids coming in, and they were busy with them so it meant that we would play together, and we would try different golf courses. At the end of the day, we would decide where we wanted to go. We either went to the Macaroni Grill or to the Red Lobster or a French place. Sometimes after we had dinner, we would go to the theatre right next to the restaurant and see a movie. That was our day. We went for a walk, went for a swim, had lunch, played golf, had dinner, and then went to movie. What could be nicer than that? Then we would come home and watch a little TV if we wanted to.

The apartment was always delightful. It was a corner apartment. We had a big terrace in the front, and we had four windows in the bedroom so that there was always a breeze coming right through. We very seldom used the air conditioner; it was always cool, breezy and very pleasant. It was a very delightful apartment. Pauline did a great job decorating it. We were very happy in that apartment; we had a lot of good years there. We had it for eighteen years and it was always enjoyable.

We had a big round table in the dining room that was 72 inches around and about an inch and a half thick. It had green glass with beautiful brass and glass work underneath. The story behind this table is that Pauline ordered it from California. It cost $3,400 at that time. The moving men came with the big truck; however they couldn't get it in the elevator. So they had to rig a hoist up on the forth floor with a pulley going down to the street. They hoisted it up by the outside stairwell, then swung it over on the landing, opened it up, and brought it in to our apartment. This took them hours. When they brought it into the apartment and started to set it up, Pauline was shocked. This table was supposed to be rectangular.

When she told the men that this was not the table she ordered, they said, "Lady, we just brought this in from California. We had to hoist it up to get it into your apartment. I have the bill here, and it shows it at $7,200. I have no intention of taking it back. It's too big of a problem. If you want this table, you can have it." So that's how we got our $7,200 dining room table. And it is a beauty.

Chapter Twenty

"Highlights and Events"

My dear friend, Mike Cozzoli owned all of Cozzoli Pizza Parlors throughout the United States and even into China. He told me he was opening up a restaurant in the Lenox Mall in Georgia, and later on he was also going to open up three restaurants in the North Lake Mall in Georgia. At that time I was doing very well, had a lot of extra money, so I said, "Mike, I'll take all four restaurants," and I did. What a headache that turned out to be. I wound up, due to absentee management, loosing a great deal of money. It caused a ton of aggravation and endless problems due to the fact that the man I had managing everything was a thief. This bum had the nerve to take me to court to say that I owed him money. At that time he was getting a good salary which was $350 a week. Now, you tell me how this honest man was able to wind up with three homes, two restaurants and a bakery, all in different names, on $350 a week! Like you say, you win some and you loose some. He was a winner, I was a loser.

My daughter Tina got engaged on November 9th, 1983. Then two weeks after that, she smacked her beautiful car into a tree and wound up being in St. Francis hospital for six weeks with a pin through her leg.

The Sons Dilemma:

I'm putting this section in purposely because it is the truth. It reflects on the problem that seems to be nationwide: fathers having trouble with their sons. The beginning of this problem, believe it or not (I'm sure you mother's out there don't want to hear) most times is caused by the wife siding with the son against the husband. If a wife respects and sticks tight with her husband, forgets the children's outbursts, the chances are it will work out. But when the child sees it has support of one parent or the other, that's when the problems begin. The dictionary defines "family" as a group under one head.

As a hopeful solution, I asked my son to join our firm. That was in December of 1983. It didn't work out. I had to let Billy go in February 1984.

I can remember February 1984 when Yayia, Pauline's mother who was staying in the maid's room next to my den, was having an argument with Pauline. I heard Pauline hit her. I went inside, threw her out and onto the floor. She left and got the police, they came, and they wanted me to leave the house. I told them, "No way." They said they thought it would be best. I said to the police, "Look, there are two of you. You've both got guns, and I could care less. I am not leaving this house. If you want to shoot me or want to fight, I don't care. But I am not leaving." I did not leave. I took Yayia back to her other daughters house.

In March, Billy was out of work, so I gave him his job back. In April I bought a building at 102 Norman Avenue which had at a later date become the settlement in our divorce.

June 9th, 1984, Tina got married. We were the first ones to use the Garden City Hotel's new glass enclosed ballroom. I spent $64,000 on the wedding. It was a great party.

In August of 1984 Pauline went down to Florida with her girlfriend Laurena. She wanted to get a place down there. At that time I was trying to scrape up enough money to buy my middle partner's out on the property on 44th Street. Pauline said, "I'll buy it." I said, "Pauline, what have you got, a couple thousand dollars stashed away?" She said, "No, I've got $52,000 I could use." So I said, "Go ahead and buy it." Pauline stayed on and closed on the condo, and she went ahead and furnished it.

In March 1985 I opened up a restaurant called Franks-A-Lot on 44th Street between 5th and 6th Avenue. The idea was tremendous. It would have been a great winner. The only problem was I was having problems with my wife, having problems with my son, trying to run three different businesses, working day and night. I asked my daughter if she wanted the restaurant and she said no, I asked my son and he said no, so I kept it for about a year and I closed it. In between that time I sold the pizza parlors in Georgia.

Once again, in March of 1986, Billy left the company.

In April of 1986 you have the story of Juan A who filed an assault charge against me.

April of 1986 I also sold the building I owned downtown at 103 Lexington Avenue.

In August 1986 a little sweetheart was born, Warren Jr., my first grandson.

In June 1987, Pauline said to me, "Billy's not doing so well. Can I help him out?" I took him to the Japanese restaurant across the street and we had lunch. I said, "Billy, we still have the maintenance business. You can have it if you want. If you work hard with it I'll help you find a small building up in the 60's. You can buy a building that needs work if you work your ass off. You need to work at least 6 days a week, 7 if necessary, get the contractors together, get your electricians and plumbers together, get your whole crew together and know who you got and who you can depend on. I'll put the building in your name and in Tina's name. You work your ass off the first year, get the building in shape, rent it out, and now you got some income to pay off the loan. Next year, you buy another building, do the same thing. You've already got your crew; you know who you can count on and who you can work with. Third year you do the same. Fourth year you do the same. Fifth year you do the same. Now you go and do a big project – fifteen to twenty million dollars. You go into the bank to borrow the money. They say, 'Whatever you got is collateral.' You say,

'I own 5 buildings.' You get the money and from there on you become a wealthy man."

Billy looked at me and said, "Dad, I appreciate what you want to do, but I don't want it. I don't want to work as hard as you did. I'll do my own thing." So, what do you say to a kid like that? You turn around, walk back to your office and make yourself a drink. And when you tell your wife what happened, her answer is, "You didn't give him a chance. You're always hard on him." Like I said, we were having marital troubles.

June 20th, 1987 was a tragic date for me. One of my oldest and dearest friends, Al Cornewal, died. I can't tell you how I miss that man. He was a gem.

I sold the maintenance business in July of 1987 – got out.

From June to September of 1987, Pauline and I were having nothing but trouble. She was taking off a lot on the weekends. I didn't know where the hell she was going.

Chapter Twenty-One

"The Facts"

Summer 1998:

At the swimming pool, Margie, my daughter-in-law, asked me if she could talk to me. My son was upstairs with his mother; everybody was relaxed. Margie and I went and had a cup of coffee. She said, "Dad, I have a problem. We can't make it. He doesn't get up until 10:30 a.m., gets dressed, goes out and hardly brings any money home. I am supporting us both." I said, "Margie, let me see what I can do." I said to Pauline after we went back, "I want to talk to you. The kids are having trouble financially. Why don't I bring him in and let him check the buildings, keep an eye on things and run it? This will give me some free time and I will put him on the payroll for $800/week. That should help them out." Pauline thought that was a good idea. My Son accepted. As it turned out, this became a big headache for me.

It was around this time that Margie asked for a divorce and My Son had to find his own living quarters.

U.S.B.M REALTY CO., INC.

3 EAST 44 STREET, NEW YORK, NY 10017

AUGUST 24, 2001

WILLIAM J. OTTO

1. Responsibility as the 3 EAST 44th Street & 102 NORMAN AVE. BUILDING MANAGER.

2. DUTIES are to see that all problems are solved sensibly as possible.

3. Maintain a level attitude of fairness and respectability in dealing with all tenants and contractors. This level is a must in office problems and for your superiors.

4. Serious problems are to be listed and brought to the attention of the President.

5. Weekly hours are 9AM – 12NOON and during that time the company phone is available for use in outside business.

6. Business emergencies such as land appearances, meeting with contractors, leasing space and building problems are your responsibility to allow time for.

7. Starting September 1, 2001 your gross salary will be $900.00 per week.

8. The mobile phone the company bought you for emergency, use the monthly allowance of $48.36,

we would allow you 300 minutes. **Anything beyond that will be paid by**

9. **The company will continue to pay your medical insurance and dental bills with DR. CECCACCI**

10. **The company will also, as long as you can afford it, put into your AIM account $250.00 a month towards your retirement. As of this day you have $22,000.00 in the account.**

11. **The company has always been aware of the employees' appearance and attitude. We expect the example to be continued.**

_____   _____

Building Manager   President

I told Billy's friend, Rob, "If Billy gets into any trouble and he needs some money, whether it is $5,000 or $10,000 or $15,000, I'll give you the money to lend to him. That way Billy will pay you back, and he won't know the money came from me."

Pauline asked me to do something to help him out. He wasn't working. I told him to go down to Joel Stanislaw, who had a large cleaning firm and work for him. Joel accepted him on my recommendation. A month went by and Joel said, "He comes in late and I don't know where he goes all day. He has brought no money in. I can't even make him a night supervisor because he doesn't want to stay late. I hope you understand, but I have to let him go. I can't use him. I'm sorry." I said, "I understand. Thank you."

I sent him to the Hempstead Outdoor Store to my good friend Herb Terowsky. Herb put him on. He lasted two weeks. Herb didn't want to tell me why he was letting him go. He suggested I talk to Bob, the foreman. I spoke to Bob and he said, "It doesn't seem like he's interested in the business. I could have got him on other jobs, but I could read the handwriting on the wall, and I really didn't want to be embarrassed anymore."

Three months went by and Pauline was after me to try and help Billy. I still had the maintenance business and the real estate. I called Billy and said, "I would like to meet you at Yamaguchi's on 45th Street." We met at the Japanese restaurant for lunch and I told him that he really was not going anyplace with his life and I would like to offer him some suggestions to help him. I wanted him to come back and take over the maintenance company. It had all the equipment and all the men and he could run it completely. That meant all day and all night. I made a lot of money out of this business and I figured he could too.

I am giving you this background because with Billy not working, I was concerned with Pauline giving money to him.

In October Pauline swore to me that she would not give him any more money unless we discussed it. I told her of the arrangement I made with Rob to help him if he needed it so that he wouldn't be desperate.

Now Pauline and I were making plans to go to Florida. We were leaving on December 10th. We made hotel reservations at the Hampton Inns for twelve days on our way down to Florida.

12/8/01

On Friday, December 8th 2001, Pauline was inside packing. I got up and walked out to get the mail. Normally, I don't touch the mail – Pauline likes to get it. Now, I can understand why. I opened up all the mail and came across the Franklin Tax Free Fund, which I knew we had and knew it was headed Pauline Otto. Well, now it was headed Pauline Otto/William J. Otto. This was for $140,000. I called Pauline and said, "What is this?" She grabbed it out of my hand and said, "That's none of your business." I said, "Pauline, this investment was put away for the kids to split in the future. If you did this for Billy, what did you do for Tina?" She said, "That's my money and it's none of your business."

Needless to say, that day was a disaster. At 3 a.m. I couldn't sleep. I went over to the file cabinet and opened it. Pauline had about 8 – 10" of stocks and bonds in a row. The first one that I picked out was Putnam Fund – that's $80,000 – and the caption on that was Pauline Otto/ William J. Otto. Pauline came over and said, "What are you doing?" I said, "What am I doing? I can't believe what you have created by separating the children. This is a terrible thing you are doing, Pauline. I want you to take his name off these things." I didn't know what else she had but we just drew up a new will a few months before, in early October. It was a joint distribution. All of my personal stuff was to go to Billy and all of Pauline's personal stuff was to go to Tina.

I got dressed and left. I had a coffee and bagel and went to Thompson Park. I sat by the lake to watch the sun come up to try to figure out what to do. At about one o'clock in the afternoon I went back to the house and

I said, "Pauline, we have made all of our hotel reservations, the woman is cleaning and opening the condo, and the car is packed. Let's leave and go down to Florida tomorrow – see if we can solve some of these problems."

The trip down was very uncomfortable. I kept thinking about God only knows, and here I am sitting next to a person that I have been married to for 45 years, and I don't even know her.

In Florida it was very uncomfortable also. I asked her again to please take Billy's name off anything she had him listed on that takes away from the joint distribution of the will. She said, "I won't change it. That's the way it's going to be and you can't change it."

Christmas and New Year's went by without a card or a present between us. I had a difficult time trying to sleep and I would be out in the den at three or four in the morning by myself just sitting and trying to figure out what to do. One morning I said to Pauline, "You know, I am having a lot of difficulty with this problem. Why don't you cancel his name out and we can go on from there." She said, "No. That's the way it stays and there's nothing you can do about it."

1/15/02

I had to be back in court in New York. It was scheduled for January 21st, 2002. This was for the case on the building that was caused by my son. I told Pauline I was able to get a flight out on January 15th so that I could be back in New York and get the papers prepared. I had my friend Jim Hourigan pick me up on Tuesday the 15th at 6:30 a.m. As I was going to the door, I put the light on, and Pauline woke. I said, "Pauline, we have been married to each other for 45 years and I have been taking care of you all that time. Now, once again, I am asking you to take Billy's name off of whatever you have his name on so that it can be fair to the kids. When you look at yourself in the mirror this morning and put on your makeup, make sure you say to yourself, 'I have hurt Bill a great deal. I am ruining our life, hurting Billy, hurting Tina and the grandchildren.' This is what you want? Because this is what you have. How do you destroy your family and marriage of 45 years?" And with that, I walked out the door.

Back in New York, I found out that the court date was scheduled for Martin Luther King Jr. Day, so it was cancelled and they made it for the next day, the 22nd. Robert Abe, whose wife just had a baby, was not well and he did not want to appear in court so he rescheduled it for the 30th. Meanwhile, I was supposed to fly back down to Florida on Saturday the 26th. I said, "As long as I have to be in court on the 30th, I might as well stay up here," and I cancelled the flight. We went to court on the 30th and the case was not resolved. It was scheduled again for February 13th. Meanwhile, I spoke to Pauline on Sunday, January 22nd, for at least an hour and explained to her what I was doing and I asked her again if she would please remove his name from all the accounts, and again she refused.

Tina had asked me that being that Billy was on the AIM account for $250/month for his pension, if I could put her on it too. I figured, why not? I could put all the kids on it: Billy, Tina, Warren and Wesley. I called AIM on Friday, February 1st to make all the changes and they said they would. They said that the WJO custodial account had been changed and now it was in WJO's name only, which gave Billy access to over $20,000. I said to the AIM representative, "While I have you on the phone, please check the balance for the joint account I have with my wife. It should be $73,000." He said, "It has diminished to $58,000. But, the account is no longer in existence as your wife withdrew it all last week."

I went to the bank on Monday, February 4th and I spoke to Iris Gerber and she said that the $58,000 had been deposited into the joint account we had in New Jersey and then withdrawn by Pauline. At the time there was over $10,000 in the account, which meant that she withdrew approximately $70,000 and left $17.00 in the account. I said, "We have 2 CD's on file. Are they still active?" She said, "Yes." I said, "I would like to close the account and take the money." I was getting nervous, so I closed them.

I was looking for the key to the file cabinet. And I knew that Pauline used to hide things in the shoe boxes in her closet. I knocked over one of the shoe boxes and out fell $12,000 in 100 bills. I took $6,000 for myself and left $6,000 in the box.

2/4/02

I went to work on February 4th and parked my car in the garage. That night I went to use my credit card to pay the bill and the attendant said, "Mr. Otto, this card is no longer valid." It was my Visa card. I said, "Here is my Master Card." He said, "This card is no longer valid, either." I said, "I have been using these cards for 25 years." He said, "Well, they're no good now." I paid cash and left. When I went on the New Jersey Turnpike, I went through the E-Z pass lane, and it should say "E-Z Pass – Go" but mine said, "Call Sub Station" which meant she cancelled my credit cards and my E-Z pass. I had everything under her name. I had the complimentary card.

On February 4th, after I found out that she took the money out of the AIM account, and that she changed the custodial account from me to WJO himself, and that she had cancelled my credit cards, I called the law firm of Paone & Zaleski to discuss my problem and schedule a meeting. On February 7th I had a consultation with them.

On Tuesday February 5th I noticed that I wasn't getting my mail, so I called the post office. They said, "Your wife stopped the delivery to the house and is having it all delivered to Florida." I said, "Cancel that. I want it all to be delivered to 69 Leeds Lane." They said, "Okay."

On Wednesday February 6th, I came home from work. There was no mail. I felt that was odd. I entered my laundry room and the alarm didn't go off. I went over to my desk where I had $400 in cash and that was missing. Now I started to get nervous. We had two keys in a special spot, so I got them and opened up the file cabinets. I opened it and found $6,000 missing and all of Pauline's jewelry, worth about $150,000, missing. I immediately called security. They called the police. They checked the house and asked if anything else was missing. I looked and saw that all of Pauline's stocks, bond and certificates were gone. She also took all personal records and some business records of mine. The police officer said, "Please check everywhere." I said, "We have a serious problem. A Browning automatic with two loaded clips is missing." He said, "What does it look like to you, Mr. Otto?" I said, "It looks like someone knew how to get into the house, knew where the cash was, where the jewelry was, and where the gun was. It would have to be my wife, Pauline, and my son, Billy, but my wife is in Florida." The fingerprint people were there until two in the morning.

The first detective, Jason Cohen, was called in by Greenbriar Whittingham Security Guard, Steve Meschkowski. Then, the patrolman called Detective Pete Piro, who came and asked all the questions. He sent for the fingerprint expert, Sergeant Bryan Taylor. Pete Piro said, "Can I have your wife's phone number in Florida?" I gave him the phone number. He said, "I will try to make contact with her. Meanwhile, I suggest you change all the locks on the doors, garage, the alarm system and keypad. Notify Security and do the same thing with your office. With the cash and jewelry missing, that's one problem. With the automatic missing, that's a serious problem. Is the automatic listed?" I said, "No. I received it from my dying friend, Mike Cozzoli and just stuck it up there."

When I came home on January 15th, I had ample time to go through these stocks and bonds of ours and I was quite surprised. I imagine that was why she came up – she didn't want me to see the information that was in them. But, I went through them carefully and found out that she had P.O. Boxes in Port Washington, Roslyn, and Flushing on Long Island, and even in Jamesburg in New Jersey. I also found out with reference to my son, that she had the AIM account transferred into his name. She had him listed on the Franklin and Putnam Tax Free Bonds. She bought him Bell Phone stock and then, interestingly enough, on December 5th, right before we went to Florida, she bought him $15,000 worth of GMAC bonds. There were also cash withdrawals and money orders from the bank of about $9,000 and then a "Pauline Otto" cashed check signed by William

J. Otto for $10,000. So, all in all I got the feeling the reason my son didn't have to work was because my wife was giving him money.

After going over everything, I found out that she had bonds worth about $235,000 and stocks worth about $104,000.

Total: $339,000

She had been buying these investments on her own, without my knowledge, as far back as 1980, and I do not know how much else she has accumulated and given our son. I trusted her implicitly. She has the Mercedes, two houses, $150-200,000 worth of jewelry, and all the clothes she could ever want. I gave her $9,000 a month to take care of the bills, and that was my reward.

The policeman said, "We don't know where she is living. We found out mail is being sent to her sister's apartment in Flushing at 147-37 Roosevelt Avenue."

2/7/02

On February 7th, 2002, after the break-in at 69 Leeds Lane, and as per police instructions, Maximum Security Locksmith came and changed the front door locks and the garage door locks. Then I went for my consultations with Paone and Zaleski, and retained them. On that same day, Tina was in the NYC office having the locks changed there, also as per police instructions.

Tina went out to see her mother twice at the home of Dora Lubera, her aunt and Pauline's sister, with whom she believed her mother was staying. Friday night, February 8th, she realized nobody was home. Then after work on Saturday, February 9th, she suggested we pass by there on our way home from work. I was with her because I was going to spend the weekend with her and my grandsons. Tina entered the building and went to their apartment on the second floor and heard them inside. She knocked on the door. Dora opened up the door and saw Tina and slammed the door in her face. She said, "You're not coming in." Tina was upset and said, "I want to come in and see my mother and talk to you both to resolve this problem." They would not let her in. She got so upset she was crying and kicked the door. Dora threatened to call the police. Tina came downstairs crying and we left and went to her house.

Tina said to me, "Dad, what did I do to Mom and Aunt Dora? I had Aunt Dora over for Christmas and she kept telling me I was like a daughter to her, and now she won't even let me into her house to talk to my mother." I said, "I don't know, Tina. Let me ask you the same question: what did I do to Mom to have her act like this?"

Tina called her brother, even though he has called her "scum", in an effort to find out where her mother is so that I can sit down with her and try to see what it is she wants and settle this problem in a fair and civilized manner. She has only gotten a machine and no return call.

3/7/02

On March 7th, 2002, a meeting was set up to prepare for an Order to Show Cause. That meeting included myself, R. Zaleski, and the speaker phones with J. Paone and Herb Terowsky. The purpose of this meeting was to obtain an order of protection so that in lieu of the fact that Pauline Otto was listed as the owner of the business and the home, I needed to try to get a restraining order to protect both so that she would not try to take over.

The meeting lasted three hours. The reason the meeting lasted so long was because I was informed by my attorney that the state of New Jersey would not issue a restraining order against the properties and the house unless a forceful act was committed, such as a stabbing, a shooting, a beating that required hospitalization etc. In view of my wife's size and my size, it was unlikely that this would happen. The alternative was to get a docket number; otherwise it would take seven weeks before the court would hear you. In view of the urgency of this matter, we could not wait. Pauline had withdrawn funds from the bank account; she had P.O. Boxes hidden away; she had broken into the house and cancelled my credit cards without telling me. The general feeling was that we did not know what she was going to do next. In order to protect myself, I had to agree to file for a divorce so that we could get a docket number and I could immediately get on the calendar.

3/12/02

On March 12, 2002, the papers were filed by my attorney with the Family Court to temporarily restrain and complain for divorce.

3/13/02

On March 13, 2002, I received Docket Number FM-12-1930-02C from the court.

A meeting was set up verbally for the attorneys and ourselves. This was after many telephone conversations from our dear friend, Herb Terowsky, to sit down and have some sort of settlement. It was scheduled for Monday March 18th. Then we were going to go into court on March 27th to have it legalized.

3/20/02

Bypassing her attorney and before another judge she got a sheriff's authorization to get a complaint against me and was granted a restraining order. Then Pauline went to the local police station and accused me of beating her, choking her and bullying her. Dora Lubera, her sister, said I was threatening her and said that I told her I was going to drag her out of the house and beat her. They mentioned how I had loaded guns throughout the house and that I was 6'5" and 295 lbs. with a black belt in judo. They said this to forewarn the police to expect trouble when they came to the house. Her intention was to get me removed from the premises. She was crying at the police station, as was her sister. They were sympathetic and told her to go up to the family court house and get a domestic violence complaint and restraining order against me, which is what she did.

At 11 p.m. I was in my pajamas and bathrobe and I was just getting ready to go to bed when a heavy knock came at my door and I was greeted by four policemen. They said they had a restraining order saying I had to leave there in fifteen minutes. My wife and her sister were parked a block away and they wanted me out. I called my neighbor, Gene Spitz, who is an attorney, and he came and read the papers. He said that I have to leave and invited me to stay at him home. I got some clothes together and went over and stayed at his house for two nights.

After that I stayed at the Holiday Inn until we appeared in court on March 27th and 28th. The results of the court hearing were that I kept the business and Pauline got the house.

She wanted me to be fired and her son back in the business. The court overruled that and said that I would continue to run the business and that she and her son should stay out of the business. In sympathy of Pauline, the Judge said that she had the house and I have two weeks to find another place to live.

During those two weeks, it was necessary for me to work seven days, which gave me a total of seven days to find a place. I also have to pack my personal belongings.

I vacated the premises on April 11th and stayed at the Holiday Inn. Pauline moved into 69 Leeds Lane as of April 12th, 2002. During that two week period, especially the last week, I was going crazy trying to adjust my life and put things in order. My neighbor said they saw me walking the streets at four in the morning in my pajamas. It wasn't an easy task trying to pack up my personal belongings and trying to find a place to store them. And then where would I live? Where would I go?

I was able to get a moving company; arranged them the only day I had, which was a Saturday, to have my personal items moved into a rented bin. My daughter Tina was kind enough to bring her two sons over. She kept them out of school to help me pack up my personal belongings. It was a terrible, hectic experience. I would not wish it on anybody.

I had to work seven days a week, four days going back and forth from the city, trying to fix some of the problems that were mainly caused by my son. He probably meant well, but in trying to satisfy the tenants, he caused quite a few problems, and it was necessary for me to try and solve them. I was exhausted. Coming home at night after working all day, driving home on the turnpike, coming into an empty house, trying to prepare something to eat, trying to sleep, which I couldn't – that's why I was seen walking the streets at four in the morning.

I went back to the Holiday Inn and spoke to the manager, and told him I would need a relocation rate for about 35 days. They set up a reduced rate package and I moved into Room 611. Fortunately, they had a swimming pool. I used it every morning, and sometimes at night, and I was able to take out some of my frustrations by swimming.

I spent each morning going to work, coming home at night. I invited some of my neighbors to join me for dinner, and their company took some of the pressure off of me.

I was looking for some place to rent for several months and was not successful. I was in the George T.V. Store in the Concordia Shopping Center and I asked George if he had an answering machine tape and he said that he did.

There was a tall man standing next to me, whose name I later found out was George Kelly, and he said to me, "How do you like living here?" I said, "I like it, but unfortunately, I may have to relocate." He said, "Why?" I said, "My wife and I are getting a divorce after 45 years and the court gave her the house in Greenbriar/Whittingham and told me to get out. I have been trying to get into Rossmoor, but I can't get through the gate. I don't know anyone in there." He said, "That's bullshit. Let's go outside," and he told me that he was the head of the Veterans of Foreign Wars and asked me if I was a veteran. I told him about being a tank commander and a guinea pig for the atomic bomb. He said, "That's enough. I live in Rossmoor. Follow me in."

231

William L. Otto

I did that and followed him through the North Guard Gate and to his house. We stopped along the way and picked up the Rossmoor monthly paper. There were two listings to rent. I called the one house and it was rented. I called the second one and spoke to the Blanchard's. They asked if I was in Rossmoor. I said, "Yes," and told them where I was.

While I was there, I made arrangements to rent a house in the Rossmoor Village, a senior citizens community. I was able to rent a house from Shirley and Al Blanchard at 513 Old Nassau Road. They were a beautiful old couple. She was 86. He was 82. They wanted to go up to Maine to meet with their children and grandchildren, and they left on May 15th and would not return until October 15th.

What was I doing? I was sleeping in someone else's bed, using someone else's bathroom and eating with someone else's dishes. I was alone at night, eating alone in the restaurant, going through movies by myself, and hoping I wouldn't bang my head against the wall for self pity.

After 45 years of being with the same woman, and no others, I was alone. I taught her how to swim, how to fish, how to play golf, how to shoot skeet and trap, and how to judge wine.

This woman decided she wanted to be alone with her son and decided to throw me out at 73 years of age. What do you do? You don't eat properly. You don't sleep properly. You're like a different person living a different life.

You're in a state of disbelief – it must have been a bad dream. You find that you are not smiling – why should you? You are not happy. It's a terrible turn-around, especially for someone at my age. I find myself going through the daily routine – this new, unfamiliar routine – in a trancelike, unbelieving state. After 45 years with the same mate, living our life, and now it's over. Was it a lie? I kept hoping she would come to her senses and our life would resume. Meanwhile, I went forward and tried to smile.

As far as work is concerned, I had been driving back and forth to the city four times a week (on Tuesdays, Wednesdays, Fridays and Saturdays).

232

On Wednesdays the secretary, Dorothy, was there. On Saturdays, my daughter Tina was there. I wound up sleeping in the office a few days a week to save me from making that trip back and forth, and that was very helpful..

A great number of the Greenbriar neighbors invited me over their homes for dinner, and I had gone out with them, as well. None of them could understand what had happened and neither could I. It was like a bad dream. I have discussed many times that Pauline may need mental help, but she refuses to go to a psychiatrist, marriage counselor, or talk to a priest.

Dr. John Verdoni of the Monroe Township recommended that I see the psychiatrist, Dr. Sam Schneider. On my visit with him, we discussed my situation and he suggested, "Do you mind if I call Pauline." I said, "Try." And, he did. Pauline answered the phone and Dr. Schneider told her that he was sitting with me and would like her to come to the next meeting for an open consultation to hear her side of the story. She refused and told him that she was not interested. Dr. Schneider said, "It's apparent you have lived a very good life for 45 years. You have been all over the world. You have two homes; you have an abundant amount of jewelry and clothes; and driving your Mercedes and playing golf is not all that bad. Now, Pauline, tell me what it is that Bill did that was so horrible that warranted your doing what you did?" She answered on the other end of the phone and his response was, "Oh, you don't want to discuss it. That's very interesting. Well then, I thank you for your time." After he hung up, he said, "Bill, you shouldn't be here. Pauline should be here. She's the one who needs help.

I explained to Dr. Schneider that Pauline has a widowed sister, Dora, who lives in Flushing. Dora has a divorced girlfriend who lives next door. Pauline has been going over there on the weekends to be with them. She also sees her son, who has moved into a new, bigger apartment in the city someplace – I don't know where. Apparently that is enough to keep her happy.

All of our old friends had called, whether from Florida, Mexico, Cape Cod – they all knew the story. She refused to answer their calls, because, quite frankly, when they ask her, "Why?" what can she say that makes sense?

With the new people in the development came new friends. I had been told by one of the men that I played golf with that Pauline has called him to come over and hang up some pictures, which he did and she told her story. She told him that I was abusive to her for 45 years and did not give her any money. Well, she can tell that story to the new friends because they are not sure what the truth is, but the old friends know better and that's why she doesn't answer their calls.

I have tried everything within reason to try to understand what Pauline is about and how we can get this family back together again. I have sent her flowers, and she has refused them. I have called her on the phone and she gets nasty. I have tried to have our friends talk to her and that hasn't worked. I have sent her and my son letters expressing my love and wish to get our family back together. They have been torn up, thrown out, or unopened.

6/18/02

Dear Pauline:

Michelle at the garage just asked me, "What happened?" I said, "I don't know." I still don't know what happened. How could we end up like this after 45 years?

If I did something so bad, why didn't you at least talk to me and see if we could have straightened it out?

Think back about our life:

Going to New Hampshire with the kids and the Cornewal's each year.

Our recent trips to California and the wine country.

Our recent trip to Washington, D.C. and the Holocaust Museum, etc.

What happened that made you sneak back to New Jersey? For what?

Was it necessary for you to throw me out of my home at 11:00 p.m. at night – with <u>NO</u> place to go?

Now you are going around telling everyone that I beat you!!!

Everyone remembers us always holding hands and being together. What happened? Why?

Now with the few years we have left, we are apart, alone and empty. What happens if we need someone to help us at night? To rub our back, to cut my hair, to look out for one another?

I used to make you breakfast, polish your golf shoes and clubs and keep your Mercedes polished. Now what?

Pauline – what could I have done that was so terrible for you to end all we had together?

Do you think it is going to get better? No. It will get worse.

Now we are going to have money problems too. The tenants:

> *6th Floor – Can't pay his rent*
> *5th Floor – Dr. Marie has moved out*
> *4th Floor – We are losing $134,000 over the ten year lease*
> *3rd Floor – Won't pay A/C start up and shut down costs or any building repairs.*
> *Restaurant – Case is still adjourned to July 16th*
> *Basement – Loving Hands wants to move.*

102 Norman:

> *3rd Floor – Tenant has moved*
> *2nd Floor – Gustavo asked if we could hold off depositing his check*
> *Maimondies Medical Center – Still owes us money!*

Our legal bills will eat us up and I still have to get a place to live and spend more money.

I can assure you – we are NOT in good shape!!

So, now, what do we do? You are giving the orders –

Do you see any way we can get back together and forget all this and put our lives in order?

I am willing to try – what about you?

Pauline – look at the films of the family and all the albums. That's a lot of memories and a lot of good times.

The family is so small and we don't know what the future holds for us. Either of us could get sick and need each other to take care of them.

The world is such a mess and we don't have forever – time is going by –

Now we should be doing things together and sharing each other, hugging each other.

I miss our life and what we had. Surely I couldn't have done anything that WAS SO BAD that could cause us to END like this.

Just think about it.

Pauline, no one will ever love you as much as I do.

Could we meet, maybe at Thompson Park? I'll get two coffees and we'll talk …

I'm willing to forget. It's up to you.

We have to meet now – before it's too late.

Your loving husband,

Bill

6/26/02

Dear Billy:

I am going over all the real estate calls you made to get the 5ᵗʰ floor

tenant, Dr.Marie, and I am very impressed. You really did a thorough job. I am finding it now – because I am calling the same real estate people to get another tenant and it is a lot of work.

You have some great qualities, son. It's such a shame that we never had a chance to sit down and talk calmly with each other and really get to know each other.

Some day you'll realize that everything I ever did was to help you and for your own good. I never wanted for us to end up like this. I hope you have a son and grow up with him and then you'll understand what it means for a father to love his only son.

I love you son and I miss you. I don't know if I'll ever see you again or even talk to you, but always remember all I ever wanted was the best for you.

If someday you want to meet and talk to me, please open your heart and call.

I wish God would get our family back together again.

Love,
Dad

9/26/02

Dear Pauline,

This will probably be the <u>last</u> time I will write to you – so please read it carefully!

What we have <u>BOTH</u> done is made a terrible mistake.

We have two great children and two great grandkids and what we have done is SPLIT up everyone. The small family we had is gone!

We had a good financial base. We had enough money with it all together and now we have to split that up – so we both don't have enough now!

We had a great life style with Florida and golf and skeet shooting and traveling and the Italian-American dances and all the friends we shared as a couple.

We traveled all over the world. We enjoyed the wine country and shopping for antiques. Our life was a dream. We were the ideal couple.

Our friends and neighbors cannot understand <u>WHY</u> we have destroyed all this.

We wanted Tina and Billy to run the business so we could enjoy the few remaining years we have left.

That has fallen apart. Billy has left the business; he should be running it. Why?

I'm sorry Billy feels I didn't support him enough. Ask John Lubera or Steve – did their father do what I did for Billy?

Billy seems to be the key issue here and yet if he loves <u>you</u> so much, he should have said, "Mom, Dad has taken care of you for 45 years, and <u>now</u> when you're getting older you need him more than EVER. Go back to him. I'll meet with Dad and we'll work it out." And get <u>OUR</u> family back together again, the way it should be.

The world is full of so many serious problems and life is so short – why are we tearing each other apart? Why?

Pauline, you and I, with the help from our kids, can put it <u>ALL</u> back together again.

It will be a big job. We will have to swallow our pride and give in to <u>EACH</u> other – but it can be DONE! I'm willing to try, are you? Can we sit down and try to lie out a program to get us all back together again.

Nothing is easy. It will make us stronger as a family – if we all work at it.

We had a great life. Don't let it <u>END</u> like this. It's such a waste of 45 years. We have a great family. Let's get it back together again.

This is a decision you will have to live with for the rest of your life.

Let's put the smile back on our faces and laughter back into our home.

I've asked you before to sit down with professional help. You have refused – why? We need it. This is too serious to end it like this.

Don't spend the rest of your life tearing your guts out over a mistake that could be <u>avoided</u>.

Think about this letter – read it again – if you don't want to make the effort to put the family back, may God have mercy on you – you'll need it.

I'm ready – are you?
Call me.

> *Your Loving Husband,*
> *Bill*

11/23/02

Dear Mom,

I am enclosing all those "things" that I "stole" from your house. What you fail to see is the sentimentality behind the things that were my mothers – I wanted some momentos from you, from the home that you shared with dad – they were sentimental keepsakes more than anything else. If I wanted to "rape" you I would have taken things of value, not a picture of you and I, as well as other little things that reminded me of you.

I called you on Tuesday to make an effort to communicate to my mother; but you were not interested. You were more interested in your "things". So, here, take them.

You have shown me what your priorities are and have tainted my memory of you and the significance of the "momentos". I don't want them anymore – keep them.

I hope they bring you happiness.

I feel sorry for you. You have forsaken the relationship of a mother and daughter, which should be priceless, for a few insignificant keepsakes.

Happy Thanksgiving.

Tina

The attached letters are self-explanatory. They show my sincerity; they show my effort.

I even went as far as making novena to St. Jude at St. Patrick's Cathedral. To do this you have to make nine copies of the sheet with the prayer and bring them with you every Tuesday when you light the candle at St. Patrick's Cathedral, by St. Jude.

I discussed this with my dear friend, Catherine Hafele. She said, "If you want to pray to St. Jude, go to St. Catherine of Senia Chapel on 68th Street off Second Avenue," which I did.

An interesting thing happened there. While I was praying at the St. Jude alter, there was a woman next to me. She said, "I hope that your prayers are answered." I said, "I doubt it very much. It has gotten completely out of control and I see no way to solve the problem." She said, "God works in very strange ways." She asked me if I was always a church-goer. I said, "No." She said, "Well, you're back in church now, aren't you?" I found that to be very interesting.

She said that she was a member of the Greek Orthodox Church on 74th Street. I said that I was Greek Orthodox. She was very surprised and we spoke for a while. She suggested that I visit Father Robert Stephanopoulos. I said, "Thank you, Lucia. I am going to do that."

I contacted Father Stephanopoulos and he said, "Bill, why don't you send me a copy of the "fact" sheet you have so that I can review it before we meet." I thought that was a good idea, and I did just that. I sent all the information to his office and then we met on Friday, October 11th, to discuss the case.

10/9/02

Dear Father Stephanopoulas,

We were married in the Greek Orthodox Church in Flushing by the Father who had the eye patch, Father Voliadis.
We attended the Greek Church in Greenlawn, St. Paraskevi.
I was on the Parish Board for 9 years and President of the Mr. & Mrs. Club for 4 years.
We moved away to Sands Point and it became difficult to make the long trip to church.
We then moved to Garden City and attended St. Paul's there.
My wife has decided, after 45 years of marriage, that she now wants to live alone.
I have worked day and night, sometimes 7 days a week, to give everything to her and the children, and this is my reward. My wife's name is Pauline, our daughter is Tina and our son is William.

It was a great family and now she has destroyed it. Why? No one can truly answer that.

I have been to Dr. Sam Schneider, in Princeton, New Jersey, 1-609-924-3980, and now Dr. Mary Sillup, 1-732-536-8520. Both doctors have tried to get Pauline to come in and talk to them. She has refused!!

When our old friends call her, she will not answer them. Why? Because what reason can she give? That I was "abusive" to her and did not give her money? They all know that's a lie.

We lived in a big estate on Sands Point, Long Island, then to the Wyndham Apartments in Garden City, and finally to Greenbriar, New Jersey, so we could play golf and semi-retire.

Semi means I still work. I have worked since I was 7 years old and believe me, I'm tired.

I wanted my son, William, to take over for me, but he has quit on me 3 times.

Now he has moved to a bigger apartment, I DON'T KNOW WHERE, and his phone number is unlisted now.

The last time I spoke to him, he said, "Don't call me again or I'll call the POLICE!" Nice!

So, what do I do? I have written her long letters, which she ignores. I have sent her flowers, which she refused and sent back.

She is supported by her sister, who is a widow and now has company every weekend, and by her son, who is hanging on, I'm sure for a financial award.

Otherwise, as a good, caring son, he would tell her, "Mom, Dad has supported you for 45 years old and now that you're 72 years old, you'll need him more than ever. Go back with him. Let's get the family back together again." That's what he should say.

If Pauline gets sick, who is going to be there to take care of her? Her sister, in Flushing, Long Island? Or her son, our son, in Manhattan?

Pauline has destroyed everything I have worked for all these years – why?

I have tried everything. Maybe you can help. I hope so. Thank you for your time and consideration.

William L. Otto

Father Stephanopoulos said that he would try to contact Pauline. He left three messages. She has never answered him. I asked him to try and leave the message in Greek. He said he would. He called me five days later and said that he left three messages in Greek and she still ignored him. She completely ignored all of his messages. I think, "What reason can she give?" That is the problem. She has no justifiable reason for destroying our family.

12/07/02

Dear Pauline,

We won't be seeing much of each other in the future, but I want to clear the air on a misunderstanding that you have.

The only reason I filed for the divorce was to get the Docket number so I could go to court and defend myself from you and Billy taking over the 44th Street building.

You can read the fact papers on page 10 Re: March 7th.

It clearly tells how Herb Terowsky was on the phone with me and we were trying for 3 hours to come up with another approach to the problem.

My mistake was I went to marriage lawyers, and all they want for their clients is to get the divorce.

I found this out talking to the Bank Corporate Lawyer, who now said it wasn't necessary to do it that way – I'm sorry Pauline.

I would never have left you or divorced you.

Pauline, ask your new attorney about it and he'll explain it to you.

It seems all my lawyers wanted was to file the divorce. They never helped in getting us both together.

Lawyers are a special breed, as we are finding out. We wasted over $100,000 for nothing.

I miss Billy. I hope he is all right. If I can help, let me know.

God bless you and keep you well.

Your loving husband,

U.S.B.M REALTY CO., INC.

3 EAST 44ᵀᴴ STREET · NEW YORK, NEW YORK

May 8, 2002

Honorable John W. Bissel, Chief Judge
50 Walnut Street
Newark, NJ 07101

Dear Honorable John W. Bissel,

YOU HAVE GOT TO DO SOMETHING!

The divorce rate in this country is going out of sight. Unless someone takes an active position to change this system legally, or there is an order of the church, we will soon be going back to the dark ages.

For example, I was recently in a separation situation where it required me to protect myself from the underhanded actions taken by my wife against me. I was trying to protect the business and the retirement income. In the course of doing this, I was forced to look for the top matrimonial attorney I could find.

I hired the law firm of Paone and Zeleski. They informed me that in the state of New Jersey, in order to get an Order of Protection, it was necessary to have the opposing party having committed either a criminal act or either shooting me, stabbing me or brutalizing me to the extent that I require hospitalization.

Otherwise, I would not get a docket number and without a docket number it could take five or six weeks before the court would hear the case. In five or six weeks, I could have been completely wiped out. Everything was in my wife's name.

Needless to say, their advice was that in order to obtain a docket number, it would require me to file for an action of divorce.

I signed for the action of divorce and received a docket number the next day. So, I was well on my way to protect myself. But, what had it done to a marriage of 45 years?

The action of filing for divorce completely terrorized my wife and forced her into an action of defense. That action allowed the attorneys to prepare their best opposition of defense against each other.

Now, when people get into the Court, the attorneys brief them as to what to say. Husband and wife begin to tear each other apart for the act of defense. Again, the attorneys present this.In your position of authority, you have got to look into this problem strongly; if you don't, the sacred bond of marriage, the responsibility of raising children from a family and the act of children and parents going together to church on Sunday will be threatened. Furthermore, the respect of children to parents and parents to children – all of this will be going into oblivion.

Now, you can take this letter and throw it in the garbage, or you can talk about it and see what I am telling you is fact. The divorce rate is the highest it has ever been in the country. Children are suffering, the church is suffering, society is suffering; needless to say, the parents are suffering.

So, what can we do? I'll tell you what you can do. Put an intermediary group of paralegal aides to sit down with the husbands and wives without the attorneys and have them mediate the act of putting families together.

How can you fluff this off and say that they should go to marriage counselors, psychiatrists, or local priests? People are just not doing it. They are winding up in court. People are suffering, the children are suffering and the country is suffering.

You have the responsibility to digest and consider what I am telling you. I am a perfect example of what has transpired in our court system. It is supposed to be the best system in the world, but it stinks. It desperately needs correction and improvement and the human element there, and not what we have now.

You have the facts. If you want to call me, I will be glad to sit down and discuss it. I am seventy-two years of age, and I have been through things that I have probably forgotten that you haven't learned yet.

Consider what I am telling you. If you don't act upon this, God help us.

Thank you for your consideration.

William L. Otto

U.S.B.M REALTY CO.,INC.

3 EAST 44TH STREET · NEW YORK, NEW YORK

December 31, 2003

His Holiness Pope John Paul II
Vatican City States
Europe

Your eminence,

I have addressed the letters to Cardinal Eagan at St. Patrick's Cathedral and much to my regret, there seems to be no interest.

The act of divorce is spreading like a disease through out the country. We have the highest divorce rate in the world. Something has to be done.

The old cliché that says in the marriage ceremony: "To love, honor and obey till the death do us part," is becoming a joke. I can envision that some day in the future it will be stricken from the marriage ceremony.

I know that you are very busy and are not feeling well, so would you please be so kind and assign this to one of your strong and capable men of the church who will follow through to see what can be done to stop this from spreading through out the world?

I also sent the letter to the Chief Judge Honorable John W. Bissell, who just like Cardinal Eagan, ignored my problem. If something is not done, it will not only affect the Catholic Church, but all the churches as well.

The United States was built on families from all over the world, that's what made this

country great, and it allowed us to be able
to help other countries.

I hope that someone on your staff will take
the time to inform me on any program that is
in the works to solve this problem.

Sincerely yours,

William L. Otto

How are we going to get out of this mess? Who can we go to? Who can we talk to? How do we get an answer? You see, I have the privilege of being 80 years old now. It gives me the right to question what's going on. It gives me the right to sometimes knock somebody, or not knock them, for not doing their job or not handling things properly. What are they going to say? "Bill, be careful. Watch what you say"? I don't give a shit. I'm talking straight off the cuff, the way it is. We need somebody with guts. We need somebody out there with strength to put this country back together. We've got to oppose so much graft and so much corruption and so much bullshit going on that I don't know how you can even do it. I don't know where we're going from here. It's a very scary future we have.

I've lived my life. I told my girlfriend, "Good Lord willing I'll be here till I'm 92, sweetheart. I'm a tough old son of a bitch and if they want to knock me down, they're going to have to work at it."

But I'll tell you one thing – if anybody says different they're lying – thank God for liquor. Liquor has helped me get through a lot of serious problems. Difficult hurdles. There were times when I didn't know who to talk to, where to go, or what to do. Walking through the streets at four in the morning in your pajamas is not the answer. I've gone through it all. So where do you go from here? You have a drink. A drink relaxes you and takes the pressure off you. Makes you see things a little bit nicer than you did before. And you keep hoping that somehow it's going to get better.

My girlfriend keeps saying to me, "Bill, you've got to stop looking at little babies and little kids because you have such an emotional feeling for them." I say to her, "I can't help it! I love little kids! I look at their faces and they are so honest and they are so sincere. They don't know about corruption or devious things about life. All they know is that if you smile at them, they smile at you back, if you love them, they'll treat you good." I have such a feeling for little children. I guess because as I was growing up I never had the time to spend with my kids. I was working day and night, 14 - 16 hours a day, sometimes six days a week, sometimes seven. It was necessary. I built an empire. A small empire, but it was there. From breadlines as a child, to a big estate in Sands Point. These are two accomplishments which I'm glad and I'm proud of. All mainly because of my friends, all the people I've known, the things I've gone through. I'm sorry I'm getting sentimental. Sometimes you've got to. I've been shot, I've been beaten up, I've been stabbed, gone through 3 atomic bombs and on top of that, divorced. I've been through all kinds of shit, and still to this day, whenever I hear *The Star Spangled Banner*, my throat lumps up and I get a tear in my eye. We need more emotion in this world of ours today. It seems to be disappearing. Let's hope that something happens that turns this country around to what it was meant to be: family, honesty, integrity, and trust. We're supposed to be able to shake hands and know we have a deal without needing accountants and lawyers and all the bullshit that goes with it. Where do we go from here?

Chapter Twenty-Two

"Keep Going"

Well, you've read most of the letters in the previous chapter explaining what I was going through. The life I was leading, it's no bargain. You wonder where the hell you went wrong. Sometimes you don't know the answer. When I was moving out, putting my stuff in storage, trying to find out where my clothes were, staying at the Holiday Inn for a month, then moving into the senior citizens place called Rossmor for six months, and then after that I moved into Concordia, another place for senior citizens. Meanwhile, I'm going back and forth to work. I was having a difficult time. Most of these men who have gone through this understand what I'm talking about. Nobody else, unless you've gone through it yourself, can possibly understand what I've gone through. It's a little bit different for most of the women. They maintain the quarters. They go into court, they cry a little bit and they get their money. The man has to keep working, making the money, taking care of the bills, taking care of the problems. Meanwhile he's still faced with all these headaches. It's an unfair situation but that's what life is. Nobody ever said it was going to be fair. If you thought it was going to be fair, forget it.

My daughter and I looked around for apartments and condos in the city because I was working in the city. We tried all different places: Uptown, Downtown, Eastside, Westside. I was staying in the office a lot of times, sleeping there. It was set up very nice, my office. We had a shower and a bathroom and a bar and a kitchen and everything else that was necessary. That was at 44th Street so it was handy to go to all the different places. Each night I was walking over to St. Pat's Cathedral, saying a little prayer by Veronica's Veil on the left side. By the way, all you divorced or single men out there looking to make acquaintances, that's a hell of a way to meet women. I can't tell you how many people I've met in St. Pat's Cathedral.

A lot of times I'd be in the office at night, working, and my daughter would call me up. One night she said to me, "Dad, what are you doing?" I said, "I don't know sweetheart. I've got a lot of paper work; I'm trying to get some of this nonsense off my desk. I've got court cases and lawyers and bullshit and everything else." She said, "Why don't you get the hell out." I said, "You know, Tina. I was invited to a wine tasting right off Lexington Avenue on 56th Street – nice restaurant right there. I was thinking about going, but I don't know anybody there." She said, "Dad, why don't you go. Promise me. Close up the desk and get the hell out of the office." I said, "Tina, you're right." I closed up the office, jumped into a cab and went to the wine tasting. Inside there were women all over the place. I saw an attractive woman sitting down, tasting the wine, and I walked over to her, tapped her on the shoulder and said, "What do you think?" She said, "Bill, how are you?"

"Jeeze, I haven't seen you in a long time!" It's an old friend of mine, no sense in mentioning names. "What do you think of the wine?" She said, "Bill, on a scale of 1-10, I don't think we have anything above a 5."

"Honey, you're in the business."

"I know, that's why I'm here testing it."

"Let me go try a few." I walked around and this blonde girl came up to me, very attractive, and she said to me, "What do you think of the wine?"

"Well, I've got it from the horse's mouth that on a scale from 1-10, we don't have anything above a 5."

"I don't find it that good either."

"Well, we'll try a few more and see what it turns out to be." She said, "You know, I'd like to learn about more about wine and it'difficult."

"No it isn't! You see that girl over there? That good looking woman in that black outfit? She works for a wine company."

"Boy, I bet she knows a lot about wine."

"She does. In fact, if you want to meet her, come on over. I'll introduce you to her." So I brought her over, introduced them, and I left them alone, and I drifted around. I met a couple of women, had a few drinks, and the night passed on.

I've got to tell you one story. There was this one woman, a stunning woman, in a brown, leather outfit. I don't care if she reads this and she says, "That son of a bitch, he shouldn't have wrote this," because I'm going to tell you. She was very nice to me, getting me my drinks. We sat down, had our appetizers and we had a nice time. And I said to her, "Are you married?" She said, "Yes." I said, "Well, are you divorced?" She said, "No." I said, "So, where's your husband?" She said, "He's home watching the kids." I said, "Hold it a minute. You take off, you come to New York (she lived in New Jersey) and he's home watching the kids?" She said, "That's right." Well, I don't know how it strikes you, but it struck me as, this was not the type of woman I wanted to know. So we had a few more drinks, I put her in a cab, and I said, "Sweetheart, I'll talk to you next week," and I threw her card away. There's the husband home with the kids, and she's out drinking wine, meeting guys. Nice, huh? I could do without her. And if you're around sweetheart, I could care less.

So now, I went back to the bar, and there was this good looking blonde there, and I said to her, "How you doing Lisa?"

"Oh, I'm fine Bill. I'm drinking some more wine." And we started talking, and we talked and we drank, and naturally you let your hair down and you become a human being. That's why I said to you before: drinking has been a blessing to me. I can recall Lauren Bacall, Humphrey Bogart's wife, saying, "I never trusted a man that didn't drink." Anyway, she said to me, "You know Bill, you're quite a guy. I like you."

"Thank you very much." I figured maybe she was coming onto me, but I really wasn't interested because she was too young.

"I want you to meet my mother." I said, "What."

"Yes, I want you to meet my mother. My mother is prettier than I am."

"That's hard to believe."

"I'm telling you Bill. She is prettier than I am."

Well, if she's prettier than you are, I want to meet her."

"Bill, I'm going to set it up. We'll get together and have a dinner."

"You do that. Set dinner up, it's on me. I'm going to take you girls out."

Well, a couple of weeks went by, and I got a call from Lisa. She set up the dinner for us in this restaurant over on 45th Street and Lexington

Avenue. Lisa and I met over there and it was a mad house. I said to the Mâitre D', "What the hell is going on here?"

"They are having a business party."

"Are we going to be able to get a table here for dinner? I've got another guest coming."

"No, I'm sorry Mr. Otto. We can't accommodate anybody. It's just for this particular party." I "Where the hell am I gunna take these two girls? I've got to take them to a nice restaurant for a nice dinner."

"Go up to the Pan Am building. It's right up the block."

"Okay, that's what I'll do." Lisa and I had a drink and we waited until her mother came. And sure enough, Lisa said, "There's Mom!" And there was Cathi, and she was, as Lisa said, a beautiful woman. We met, I had the daughter on my right, the mother on my left, and we went up to the Pan Am building. We had a hell of a dinner. We walked back after dinner. Cathi said, "Where's your car?"

"I don't have a car."

"Well, where are you staying?"

"I've got an apartment up on 37th Street."

"I'll drop you off." She dropped me off at the door, kissed me good night, and that was the start of our relationship that has continued for nine years. It's been a stormy relationship, but she keeps me going! You can't be a couch potato around here. We've been through a lot of things together, good and bad.

Cathi would visit at my apartment on the East River on 37th Street. We always had parties and dinners together. She had an apartment up in White Plains. We would alternate weekends. Tommy, the doorman at White Plains told me of an apartment for sale on the same floor as Cathi's.

"Let's go up and take a look at it." Kelly answers the door. Her name is Kelly Walsh. Walsh was my mother's maiden name so we had an association right off the bat.

"I understand you're going to put your apartment on the market."

"Yes." I said, "Kelly, can I see your apartment?"

"Sure." I looked around the apartment. There were a few things I wanted to change, but certainly workable. Meanwhile, the apartment I had on the East River, I was paying $2,700 a month, and then it went to $2,800 a month. And from what I understand it was going to go up again.

So I said, "The hell with that, I've got to look around for something." So I said to Kelly, "Kelly, what are you going to ask for this apartment?"

"Well, I'm going to put it on the market tomorrow."

"Don't put it on the market. I'll take it."

And that's how I got that apartment. So now, Cathi had one apartment and I had the apartment next door. It gave us a chance to have a little reprieve, because sometimes you get on each others nerves and it's a good idea to get lost in some place else and sit there and do a little paper work, or watch a little TV, or just relax. I think all families should have that. But we've got it.

Anyway, so now I've got Kelly's apartment. I moved everything out of 37th Street and East River, and I've been here ever since. Tony, the superintendent made a few changes, put up a stereo system, cabinets and a little bar for me. I'm writing this book from this place. Sitting at the desk where the Irish Godfather sat, one of the few pictures of him with a smile on his face. Harry Lipsig sat here. Judge Froessel, Court of Appeals, sat here. In fact, I bought his chair from the court house. All kinds of good guys, wise guys, all types. This desk could write a story itself. My daughter said to write all these stories down, and I'm trying to do it.

Cathi likes to travel, so we've done a lot of traveling. We've been to a lot of places together. We've got the place in Florida, and a lot of friends. My old buddy has a place in Albuquerque, New Mexico. We've been up to Cape Cod, New Hampshire and Canada. We've been all over the place. We had a great time in Costa Rica with my friend Eric Kirchhofer. He lived in a place that's way out on the island. It's three hours out from the small airport, not the major airport. When you get out there, the roads are terrible, there's no police, you're lucky if you find a restaurant. You have to push the button so the gate opens to his house, and there's a big dog inside. He kept a machete in the car, a gun inside, bars on the window – that's Costa Rica in this area. I understand there are some beautiful areas in Costa Rica, which we never saw. We went down to the beach to walk a half a mile and the water is absolutely beautiful the beach was absolutely beautiful – nobody there! He built a magnificent house up on the cliff. This was the chef I told you about, who took care of Jacqueline Kennedy at The Colony. He's a master chef. We spent nine days there. Nine days in the house. You can't find a restaurant, but you've got a master chef and he's got a big double freezer, so it's not so bad! He said, "What do you feel like having?" We told him whatever we felt like having and this guy would go into the kitchen and start putting things together. We would have a few drinks, sit out on the terrace, look out on the ocean, and go for a dip in the pool. Can't complain. It was a crazy situation, though, in the morning. The monkeys woke us up. Screaming and hollering and jumping all over the place! They would start at about five o'clock in the morning. I thought they were coming in! It scared the hell out of me! I thought, "What are we going to do? How are we gunna fight the monkeys?" But they stay outside. They just make a lot of noise, and jump all around, and Eric is used to it. It doesn't bother him.

I said to Cathi, "Let's go up to New Hampshire. There's a place I've been going to for years called The Woodbound Inn." The Woodbound Inn is up in Jaffrey, New Hampshire. It's a very famous, historic place. I didn't realize that the place was sold by the family that owned it, Ed and Peggy Brummer. Wonderful people. I called the Brummer's up, spoke to them. I said, "We're coming up there and we'll take you out to dinner." Now, Ed at the time was 93. We went to his house, beautiful house. They moved out of that big place up on the hill and into a smaller place. We had a martini, got in the car, took off and went to this fancy restaurant in town. Well, apparently they hadn't seen Ed in quite some time. Everybody in the town kept coming over to them saying hello – thought he was the mayor. He knew everybody for years. He had another martini. God bless him, that's two martinis at 93. He said, "Excuse me folks, I'm going outside by the Men's Room." He took off and we all talked and carried on and nobody said anything. Then I got up and walked outside by the Men's Room to see what was happening and there he was, asleep. He picked a nice, big, soft chair, and he took a little nap. God bless him. Nobody woke him; he slept for a while. After coffee, we woke him up and took him home. We went back to the Wood Bound Inn and nobody was there, the place was closed. Meanwhile, we had our suitcases and everything up on the third floor having registered earlier that day. Cathi said, "Bill, what do we do?" I said, "I don't know."

"We'll have to break a window to get inside."

"We're not breaking any windows. Let's see what we can do." So I walked around and I found a phone number for emergencies. The fellow that bought the place, drove over and opened up. Now, we're sleeping in this great big place, up on the third floor, with nobody else there. So Cathi said, "Do me a favor. Put a chair in front of our door." So I said, "Okay, sweetheart." So I did. We came down the next morning, people were there. We had some breakfast, played a little golf there, walked around, saw some antique shops. We went to a restaurant, Cathi said, "I'm treating tonight." I said, "Okay fine." We sat down and she was facing out, I'm facing her, so my back is to the people. All of a sudden I hear *Happy Birthday to You* and everybody started hollering and making noise. Well, the whole staff came over – must have been sixteen people. I said to Cathi, "It must be someone's birthday." She said, "Yeah it's yours." I said, "It ain't my birthday!" She said, "Shut up! It's your birthday!" Well, Cathi told them it was my birthday and they all came over and brought me a cake.

Years ago I used to go to Keene, New Hampshire. I'd go outside of Keene and I'd take a road up on highway number five, head north, and there was an antique shop called Potter's – fella by the name of Bill Potter. Bill had arms on him like a normal man's calves – powerful man. He was a sparring partner for Joe Lewis. I don't know how it goes back that him and I became friends, but we were friends for many years.

So I pulled up the car on the lawn and he saw me and he said, "Holy shit Bill! Come on in! I've got some new guns to try!" I said, "Okay." So we closed the store, went in the back, took out a bottle of bourbon, had a few drinks, and took out whatever guns he had and we tried them out. Well, we always had a good time together. Straight guys. No bull shit. Anyway, so we heard a horn outside. Bill said to me, "Bill, that's that kid who comes from a very rich family. Look at the car he's driving." I said, "Yeah, I see it. What do we do?" He said, "Well, he's probably got something he wants to sell." So I said, "Tell you what. If it looks like it's anything worth while, I'll stand behind him, and you stand in front of him. If I scratch my nose, I'm interested in it. If I put my hands up, that's the figure we're talking about. He said, "I got you." So, we went out in the front and the kid's there in the big, Cadillac convertible and he said, "I've got a couple of guns I want to sell. Mr. Potter, I know you like to buy guns." He said, "Well let me see what you've got." So, the first gun he brought out was a matched British piece with a bayonet – 1830. Bill said, "That's a nice piece, I like that. What else you got?" He said, "I've got a rare, old matchlock from Japan – 1640." He said, "How do you know it's from 1640?" He said, "Well, that's what I heard." He said, "Well, let me take a look at it." Bill took a look at it and said, "Okay kid, what do you want?" Meanwhile, I scratched my nose because I'm interested in both of these guns. So now he said to the kid, "Alright, what do you want for both of them? We're very busy here today." The kid said, "I want $1,000." He said, "What!? Are you kidding me? $1,000? Forget about it." The kid said, "Okay, give me $500." He said, "$500!? Are you talking crazy numbers or what?" Meanwhile, I'm in back of the kid and I put my hand up for two. Bill said, "Tell you what, kid. I'll give you $200 for both guns and that's it. Otherwise, we gotta get busy with doing things in the back." The kid said, "Are you fuckin nuts!? These guns are worth a fortune! Goodbye!" and he jumped in the car and took off. Bill said, "What do you think?" I said, "Those were beautiful pieces. They were worth what he was talking about, but who the hell knows." Bill said, "That kid probably has a ton of other stuff he wants to sell. He'll be back, just you watch." And sure enough, twenty minutes later we hear a horn and it was the kid again. He said, "Make it $300." Bill said, "I said $200. That's my price. I don't need them." The kid said, "Fine, take the two of them. Give me $200." So now we've got both guns and the kid drove off. Bill said, "You bought two nice guns." I gave him the $200 and we put them in my car and left them there. Then we went back outside, had a few drinks, and fired some more pistols in his big backyard. We had a hell of a time. It was a good day.

I'll tell you one more story about Bill Potter. Someone had told me at one time that they needed black powder. Whatever they needed it for, I didn't ask, but they needed black powder. I said, "You're talking about gun powder?" He said, "Yeah." I said, "How much do you want of it?" He said, "I want five pounds." I said, "You want five pounds of gunpowder? Well, if I come across it, you got it." Now, I had mentioned this to Bill and he called me up one day and said, "Bill, when are you coming up again?" I said, "Why?" He said, "I've got five pounds of gun powder in a little keg." I said, "You've gotta be kidding me." He said, "Nope." So I went up there, picked it up, had it in the trunk of my car, came back to New York and for whatever reason I had to be over in the area where Khrushchev, the Russian President, came in and was speaking at The United Nations. Now, I had to meet some people over in that area. I got the gun powder in my car, I parked the car and a cop came over to me and said, "You can't park the car there." I said, "Why not?" He said, "We've got Khrushchev at the United Nations, and we're concerned about terrorists and so forth and I don't want you to park the car there." I said, "Okay, fine. I'll move it." I moved the car and I said to myself, "Jesus Christ. Here I am sitting with five pounds of dynamite – black powder – in the trunk of my car. If they would have opened the trunk and saw that, they would have thought I was a terrorist or some other god damned thing. So I was lucky I got the hell out of there. So anyway, I delivered the powder and that was it.

Bill Potter was a hell of a guy. I'm sure he's passed on by now because he was older than I was. But he was in terrific shape. Powerful man. Good drinker. That's the story on New Hampshire.

Getting back to Cathi – she decided she wanted to make a big trip. "Where do you want to go?" She said, "I want to go to China." "Holy Christ, China, are you sure?" She said, "Yes." Anyway, women will always have their way, so we went to China. But that trip to China – that was a headache. We went from Beijing all the way down to the bottom. Cathi got very sick. I thought she was going to die in this hotel. We had this woman come in and she performed Reiki, which is a spiritual type thing where they put their hands over you, and the gods are going to come down from up above and take the badness out of your system and cure you. Well, for about 6 hours she laid there – I thought she was going to die. And then she finally turned around and came out. And the Reiki, it pulled the poison out of her or whatever the hell was in her system.

We've been making little trips. We went up to Woodstock. My friend has a place, Dee, my old office manager. We went up to my old friend's place up in Cape Cod. Now that's an interesting story in Cape Cod. My old buddy up there, Joe Murania, him and I were up there playing golf in November, having a hell of a time. I left, came back down here, and a couple of weeks later I got a call from his wife, Joan. She said, "Bill, you'll never guess what happened." "What happened?" She said, "Joe's dead." "What are you kidding?" She said, "No. He ran his car into a tree, wrapped the whole front of the car around the tree. Then they had to pry him out and he was on his coumadin to keep his blood thin – blood was all over the place. They took him to the hospital and they couldn't fix him there so they had to fly him to Boston to see a specialist. As soon as his got off the helicopter in Boston, he died." I said, "Holy Christ, Joan. I can't believe it." Joe died. What a blow that was to the family.

Now you take a person, and like what I said earlier in the book, "Behind every face there's a story." You want to hear some of the stories behind this particular guy? This is Joe. I'm going to give you some background on this man. You'll find it interesting, as I have always found Joe interesting.

Joe's uncles – a lot of them are in the books on the stories on the mobsters like John Gotti. Joe was born in Sicily. There's a place called Santa Margherita Di Belice. It means St. Margaret the Beautiful. It's near Corleone where they made that movie, *The Godfather.* Joe's back and forth to Sicily all the time – he's got some relatives over there. Joe told me the story when his grandfather took him to see the big godfather – that was Joe Bonnano. Mr. Bonnano hung out at the Green Garden Diner on Troutman Street in the Bushwick Section of Brooklyn. Sometimes he was there. He was in different places. Naturally he didn't stay at one place all the time. Anyway, the old godfather wanted Joe Murania to join the boys. The godfather said to him, "You have *alousconga.*" That's good Sicilian blood. Joe didn't want to get involved with the boys. He wanted to go into business, and he was very successful at a later date. His uncle was Patty Mangiaricina. That means eat grapes. He was a little bit disappointed, but he was glad in a way that Joe didn't want to get involved with the boys. They said hello, they always talked back and forth, and he went on his way. Thank God Joe never got involved with that.

Anyway, so now Joe was the controller of Sperry Hutchinson, he was the Vice President of Woolworth, Vice President of the Zaire Corporation – all big, top jobs. Joe and I knew each other for 48 years. Our kids went to school together. We lived out in Syosset together. We used to take the train together in the morning and go and have our coffee. Anyway, his wife Joan told me he died and he was going to be buried at the Air Force Base up in Cape Cod. I said to Joan, "Should I send flowers ? What should I do?" "No, Bill. Send a contribution to an organization that he supports." I said, "Like what?"

"Well, he was with The Knights of Columbus – The Christ of the King Parish up in Cape Cod." I sent them a check, and they called me back and said, "We're going to take the check and we're going to put a section in the golf magazine saying: 'In Memory of Joe Murania, on behalf of Bill Otto.'" I said, "Hold it. Don't put that in the golf magazine. Joe and I played golf together, but why waste the money on the magazine? Look around up in that area. You must have a family up there having a tough time making ends meet. Give them the check, will you?" He said, "Okay Mr. Otto..." I said, "Call me Bill." He said, "Alright Bill. We would be glad to do that." Well, they gave the check to – I don't know who it was and I could care less – as long as it was someone who needed the money.

You know, when they give you the cards when someone dies? I said to Joan, "Could you please send me one of those cards from the funeral parlor?" She sent me the card and on the card was: "In Loving Memory of Joseph C. Murania." Then there was a poem called *Afterglow*. I'd like you to read it because it was inspiring.

Afterglow

I'd like the memory of me
to be a happy one.
I'd like to leave an afterglow
of smiles when life is done.
I'd like to leave an echo
whispering softly down the way,
of happy times and laughing
times and bright and sunny days.

I'd like the tears of those who
grieve, to dry before the sun,
Of happy memories that I leave.
When life is done.

There's just one person that you meet in your life, and the story that's behind them. Joe and I have been through a lot of things, I can't begin to tell you. A lot of stories, but it's not necessary to go into them. He's a good man, lived a good life, took care of his family, his wife, and kids. He became a successful business man, and is well loved by everybody. I got a beautiful letter later on from The Knights of Columbus thanking me. They liked the idea of giving the money to a poor local family.

I just turned 85 a couple of weeks ago, July 5th, born in 1929. Cathi's son called me up and said, "I'd like to take you and Mom out to lunch." I said, "Gee that would be nice." He said, "How about Saturday?" I said, "Okay, fine." He said, "Okay, I'll talk to you then." So I was dressed up in casual clothes, because I never figured we'd go some place fancy. Well, it was about 10 o'clock, 10:30 in the morning, and I said, "Cathi, how do I look?" She said, "You look fine. You might want to put a long sleeved shirt on; it'll look a little nicer." I said, "Alright, maybe I'll change." Then I got a call from John, and he said to me, "Hey Bill, I'm coming from New Jersey. We just went to the fair and I'm all dressed up. We're going to a nice restaurant. Put a sport's jacket on so you look a little nicer." I said, "Alright, I'll put a sport jacket on." "I'll pick you up at a quarter after one." "Okay fine, I'll meet you downstairs." So now I changed my whole outfit, and Cathi and I went downstairs and there's John and his wife. "Where are we going for lunch?" He said, "There's a nice place over there by Scarsdale." So we go over there, park the car and there's no cars in the parking lot. I figured, "What the hell is going on here?" Anyway, we went inside, and my daughter yelled out, "SURPRISE! SURPRISE! HAPPY BIRTHDAY!" I said, "Holy shit." There's my daughter jumping up in the air, my grandsons – Jesus, I looked around at all the people that were there – Ali's mother and father were there, Frankie Scobbo, the old police commissioner and his nephew. Owen Cottle, Jesus, he and I go back 50 years. He's there with his wife, Betty. Dee, my former office manager and Vinnie Vanella and his gal, Joan, all my wonderful friends showed up for me. I couldn't believe it. It brought tears to my eyes. I started to cry – had to hold it back. What a blow out. We had a private room in a nice restaurant and we had a beautiful time. Everyone got up and made a little speech. Frankie Scobbo got up and he said, "I'll tell you a story about Bill and the kind of guy he is. Let me tell you what he did." And this is the story:

We were in the bar having a drink – we were over at an affair in Port Washington – and Frank was a little bit down. So I said to Frank, "What the hell's the matter Frank?" He said, "I've got a big fuckin job. I've got a tremendously big parking lot to do." I said, "What's the problem?" He said,

"I can't get any black top." I said, "What do you mean you can't get any blacktop?" He said, 'They're on strike. The blacktop people are on strike." I said, "Holy shit. Do you really want the job?" He said, "Jesus Bill, it's a really big job." I said, "Alright, let me see what I can do." So I went over to the phone and I called my old buddy Angelo Charielli. Angelo's father was the old, union organizer of the blacktop industry. I said, "Angelo, I need some help with a friend of mine." He said, "What's the problem, Bill?" I told him what the problem was and he said, "Bill, put him on the phone." I said, "Frank, I want you to talk to Angelo Charielli." So they talked, I went to the bar, was having a drink, and Frank came out of the telephone booth all smiles and said, "You son of a bitch! They're gunna give me the blacktop!" I said, "Are they gunna deliver it and everything?" He said, "Bill, they said at 6:30 in the morning the trucks will be there on the job. Everything's gunna be alright. How the hell did you do that?" I said, "Well, that's what friends are for, Frank. Friends are there to help each other. If the world were to take that attitude, we would have a beautiful world." He said, "Bill, I can't thank you enough." I said, "Don't worry about it. As long as it's all taken care of and as long as you're in good shape."

Well, Frank told everyone at the restaurant, "I got on the job at 6:30 in the morning. Angelo showed up, right behind him a big limousine showed up, two guys got out, kissed him on the cheek, and shook hands with him. Then come two trucks with stones and the guys started laying stones. Then another car comes over. A couple more guys come over to hug Angelo. They were driving with blacktop and they start spreading blacktop all over the place." Then he said, "I couldn't believe it Bill. I couldn't believe what he did and how he did it! Then, the last truck came and the guys smoothed out the blacktop. They finished the whole goddamn thing in *one day!* You don't know what that means. That was like a miracle." He pointed to me and said, "That guy at the end of the table there." I said, "I was glad to do it, Frank." And that's the story with the old Police Commissioner, Frank Scobbo. He's still there! God bless him! I want him to stay around! He's got to keep me company. And Angelo, God bless him. I haven't seen Angelo in years. I hope to God he's still around. If he reads the book he'll tell you the story. He may laugh and smoke another cigarette. He won't say nothing. But when you needed him, he was there.

Then, Owen Cottle got up and he said, "I've know Bill for over 45 years. We've been to many different lunches, dinners and business meetings together We've always gotten along well and Bill was always there for me. He's a hell of a friend."

And then Dee got up and said, "I can remember every time Bill got angry or aggravated about something, his jaw would pop out on the left side. He came in one day; jaw all popped out, all excited and pissed off. He had some trouble with some union guy"

What really happened, we were servicing the Avon Cosmetic building on the Upper West Side. They told me they wanted the windows done. The window cleaners started the job and they were approached by some goons who told them they could not work on this building without a special union contract. Now what do you do? That contract was not available. But I had an idea. I called the head of the windows cleaners union, told him I wanted to talk to him privately, have some lunch and take care of it. We met in a restaurant on 5th Avenue between 35th and 36th Street. I was right around the corner from the old union hall. He was asking for too much money for a payoff. So I told him, I wish I could use his name, but I won't. I said, "I'll tell you what I'm gunna do. I'm gunna reach over the table and punch you right in the nose. I'm gunna break your nose and the blood's gunna be all over the place. The waiter and everybody's gunna come over wanting to know what the hell is going on. I'm gunna make such a stink in here; maybe I'll hit you a few more times. Then the cops will come and good! That's what I want! I want to put it in the papers that the head of the window cleaning union gets punched in the mouth for shaking down a contractor and asking for too much money. Now what are you gunna do?" Meanwhile, I reached over and grabbed his tie. He said, "Relax Bill! Relax! We'll work it out!" I said, "Give me your hand. Do we have an agreement that we get a contract, or not?" He said, "I'll get you a contract, Bill." We shook hands and that was it.

Dee said, "But, there Bill was pissing and moaning, so I made him a drink and he relaxed." Dee knows that a couple of days later the contract came in signed.

I'm glad my daughter didn't start telling stories, because she could have told a thousand of them. But that's why I'm writing the book, because she asked me to do it. That's how you go through life, with people that you meet, stories that you tell, friends that you have, people that you trust. It's good to *have* those kind of people. We're running awful short on them in this world today. We're running awful short on people we can trust and rely on. I don't know what's going to happen in the future for the kids. They've got a tough nut ahead of them. I think about the kids that are not raised strong – not street wise – how they're going to cope with some of these problems coming along, I don't know. Let's hope that they somehow survive, because they've got a lot of opposition coming up against them. If they think it's going to be a bed of roses, God bless them. They are in for a rude awakening. This country's got a lot of problem, lot of trouble. How we're going to solve them?

My daughter and Cathi had gotten together before the party and made a whole collage of all the old pictures, different times, different friends. And that was up on the table with a bunch of presents there. I've got to tell you, I don't like presents. At my stage in life, I've got so much of everything; I'm looking to give everything away. You go through life, you gather until you get older, then you want to give everything away because what are you going to do with it? It's almost like that story I read about Mrs. McDonald. Mrs. McDonald had just given $75 million away to charities. Mrs. McDonald was in the funeral procession for her husband's funeral and they talked to her after the burial, and they said, "Mrs. McDonald that was a wonderful thing you did giving $75 million to charity. That's an awful lot of money." So she said, "Behind the Hurst – did you see a Brinks truck carrying money? You're not gunna take it with you. What are you gunna do with it? The idea is to give it away to the world to do some good. And that's what I did." Mrs. McDonald, my hats off to you. That was a nice gesture, nice thing you did.

Anyway, after the party, John drove us home, we got home and relaxed and it was nice. And that's what happens on your 80th birthday. I still feel strong, still feel good. I'm going to stay that way. Like I told Cathi, "I'll be here till I'm 92. After that I'm not guaranteeing anything. But 92, I'll be here. I figure I can make that." My mother was here till she was 87. She used to smoke three packs of Camel's Cigarettes and day and she drank coffee all day. She never ate, never exercised. She never had any good, cheerful moments in her life. She had a lot of aggravation, lot of bull shit.

She was married to a monster. She had a family that was a pain in the ass. But, that's the way it goes.

There's one more thing that aggravates me sometimes: you see a movie, and it's so full of bull shit. I mean, I saw that movie *The Departed* where Scorsese got the award for what!? That fairy story!? Frank Costello was a classy guy. He may have been a killer, but we all have killer instincts in us. But he was a classy human being. He had his nails done, had his hair done, dressed impeccably, he talked a little rough because of his voice, but he was a classy guy. That guy Jack Nicholson that played the part, he made him look like such a bum! I got sick! I told my girl Cathi, "Let me get the fuck outta here! This is sickening!" I'm surprised some of the boys didn't go up to Jack and Scorsese and say, "Where the hell do you come off making Costello look like such a bum!" I can't believe it. They might as well say that Ronald Reagan was a pimp! Sure, it will sell. But if they use a man's name, it should have some facts to support it. I'm surprised the boys didn't make a move on this. They should of. They should have paid a little respect for this guy. He deserved it. I can't believe what they did in that goddamn picture it was such a bunch of phony bull shit. Well, that's what life's about these days.

I mean, did Jack Nicholson need the money so bad that he had to make a picture like that? And make Costello look like such a bum? I can't believe what goes on in our society today. What turns people on? What makes people do the things they do? Nicholson should go over to Costello's grave, bow his head and say, "I'm sorry Frank. I should have never done what I did." But he didn't, and it's over, and Scorsese gets the award.

When you ran into a serious problem, and you needed a guy with balls, and you called on Frank, he was there. He helped you, solved the problem, took care of you, did it nice and easy, no nonsense. And this is what we need today. We need these type of men today, but we don't have them. I mean, they're going after the mob, putting this guy away, putting that guy away. Meanwhile you've got these fuckin politicians stealing million dollars here and there, getting away with it. What puzzles me is that the banks lose money and have to borrow from the tax payers, then where do they get the money to give out these large bonuses? This is ridiculous. All this going on in Washington. And we're voting them in! How our system will ever be corrected, I don't know. I'll probably never see it in my age. I wish we'd see it in some age.

Just taking out this beautiful oriental box I just got and I'm going to put the knife in that I was stabbed with – wrap it up nice. My grandson said, "Papau, can I have the knife you were stabbed with?" I said, "Sure you can son." I'm glad it's going somewhere. It's been in the drawer for all these years. He can have it. He'll remember me by it. Anyway, I'm going to wrap it up nice for him – his birthday's coming up. It's hard to get together with the grandchildren. Time goes by so fast and they're growing up. He's going to be 26 now and I can't believe it. Where did the years go? Where did the time go? Time is flying by so fast, and the older you get the faster it goes. So just be prepared out there.

Well Tina, there's the story you wanted. I hope it's enough information for you to remember me by. I gave you a good part of my life: all of my friends, all the things I've been through, all the things I've been blessed with, all the problems I've had. Tina, you'll find some of the wording is a little bit rough, but that's the way I've always talked. You know I talk straight from the shoulder all the time. It's like Sinatra said, "I took the blows, and I did it my way." That's what you have to do in life. You can't predict the future, Tina. You don't know what the future holds. It's very difficult to lay out what you want in the future, like what everybody does with their families, and what they've planned, and it don't turn out that way. So you have to adjust your life and try to get by.

So, I've tried to put down some of the stories. They're not all there. Some of the things I can't even reveal. Some of the things I have are secrets and stories that have to go with me to my grave. Nobody will ever know, but we all have that. We all have things we have to keep to ourselves.

So sweetheart, this is your story. I'm sure your boys will get a kick out of it. I love you, love the boys, Cathi and all my dear friends.

Goodnight sweetheart.

- Dad

To All My Dear Friends

Over the years I have been blessed by knowing some outstanding people. Friends that I wish I could be with, even though they are gone. I miss them that much. They were all such beautiful people. All different types, from business people, personal friends, judges lawyers, mobsters, godfathers and priests. I have listed them on the following sheets. You will read about them somewhere in this book. Every one of them has a story. Some of the stories are complete, I can't tell you the endings.

Father Carey, the Jesuit, involved with the movie *On the Waterfront,* was very, helpful in steering me to the Irish Godfather, Jim Earley. Jim saved my life. I had a little skirmish at Union Hall 32J. I was pissed off at what they tried to do. I broke up some furniture and threw type writers around. They were a little mad at me. The word got out that I was going to be knocked off in two weeks. That's when Jim stepped into the picture and pulled everybody off me.

Judge Froessel was there when I needed him, for good advice, and a lot of support.

Harry Lipsig always had an open door for me to talk to him. He and I talked many a night. He used to call me Lad, and Jim called me The Kid.

Frank Costello was there when I had a problem and solved it.

Sol Linder was there when I had a union problem, and solved it.

A lot of old, dear friends. I just want to dedicate his book to them, because I think of them, and miss them. Wherever they are, they know that I miss them.

I've put together a poem that I think says it nice and easy. I signed it Papau. Papau is Greek for grandpa. That's what my grandsons call me,

Papau. I listed down all my friends who have died, and when they have died. This is a book about me, but without these people I wouldn't be here. These people made my life. These people got me through life. They were there when I needed them. God bless them all.

Friends

Friends are a special breed of people –
That you think about often
And wish you could see
And be with more.

Unfortunately with everyone
So busy these days, it
Seems harder to do.

This doesn't mean you
Think of them less –
It only means you miss them more!

- Papau

This Is A List Of My Dear Friends Who Have Died

Friends	Date of Death
William J. Keating	5-20-1963
John J. Metelski	7-13-1965
Talbot T. Hayden	5-26-1968
Martin Hershey	9-19-1972
George Stefanidis	11-23-1972
Stan Wieczorek	1-13-1973
Frank Costello	2-18-1973
Sol Lindner	12-8-1974
Harry Lindner	1-29-1978
James L. Earley	5-13-1980
William F. Quirk	12-19-1980
Judge Charles W. Froessel	5-2-1982
Albert W. Cornewal	6-20-1987
Michael Franco	3-22-1988
Father Philip A. Carey	5-30-1989
Jeanette V. Otto	9-14-1991
Joe Stanislaw	12-24-1992
Harry H. Lipsig	8-11-1995
Judge Kenneth D. Molloy	3-9-1999
Jack Rogers	2-15-2001

Lou Rosenblum	3-27-2001
Mike P. Cozzoli	9-4-2001
Jim Hourigan	11-2-2002
Robert E. Campbell	3-5-2003
Sal Baragolia	11-18-2003
Joe Murania	10-14-2008
Jim Rodetis	4-12-2009
Rusty Kanokogi	11-21-2009
Ed Baragolia	8-2-2012
Catherine Hafele	7-6-2013

<u>The Last of the Dinosaurs</u> chronicles Otto's dealings with these colorful, but very real, figures in business and social circles, and includes that kind of "tough guy" stories that most people think are confined to the movies. Otto's tales include friendships with Olympic champions, office brawls with union leaders, life-saving interventions from mob bosses and showdowns with the city's most powerful figures.

Despite Otto's resilience and hard work, he is eventually confronted with financial ruin, betrayal, and heartbreak at the hands of those he loved and trusted the most. Still he tries with all his might to persevere and find happiness and peace with what remains, and to this day is indefatigable.

<u>The Last of the Dinosaurs</u> contains vivid stories, life lessons, business wisdom and revelations about the life of a man and a city. The book contains unusual photographs that will never be seen again.

"VIVIVO ET ARMIS"